Civilizing the Economy

When a handful of people thrive while whole industries implode and millions suffer, it is clear that something is wrong with our economy. The wealth of the few is disconnected from the misery of the many. In *Civilizing the Economy*, Marvin T. Brown traces the origin of this economics of dissociation to early capitalism, showing how this is illustrated in Adam Smith's denial of the central role of slavery in wealth creation. In place of the Smithian economics of property, Brown proposes that we turn to the original meaning of economics as household management. He presents a new framework for the global economy that reframes its purpose as the making of provisions instead of the accumulation of property. This bold new vision establishes the civic sphere as the platform for organizing an inclusive economy and as the focus of a move toward a more just and sustainable world.

MARVIN T. BROWN teaches business and organizational ethics in the Philosophy Department at the University of San Francisco and in the Organizational Systems program at Saybrook University in San Francisco. His previous books include *Working Ethics* (1990), *The Ethical Process* (2003), and *Corporate Integrity* (Cambridge University Press, 2005).

Civilizing the Economy

A New Economics of Provision

MARVIN T. BROWN

CAMBRIDGE
UNIVERSITY PRESS

CAMBRIDGE UNIVERSITY PRESS
Cambridge, New York, Melbourne, Madrid, Cape Town, Singapore,
São Paulo, Delhi, Dubai, Tokyo

Cambridge University Press
The Edinburgh Building, Cambridge CB2 8RU, UK

Published in the United States of America by Cambridge University Press,
New York

www.cambridge.org
Information on this title: www.cambridge.org/9780521152464

First published 2010

Printed in the United Kingdom at the University Press, Cambridge

A catalogue record for this publication is available from the British Library

ISBN 978-0-521-76732-3 Hardback
ISBN 978-0-521-15246-4 Paperback

Cambridge University Press has no responsibility for the persistence or
accuracy of URLs for external or third-party internet websites referred to in
this publication, and does not guarantee that any content on such websites is,
or will remain, accurate or appropriate.

Contents

Figures

Tables

Preface

This is not a book I had been waiting to write. At least I didn't think so. Now that it is finished, I can see that it belongs to a particular personal story that began with my participation in the civil rights march from Selma to Montgomery, Alabama, in 1965, surfaced again years later with my work in the ethics and diversity training programs at Levi Strauss and Company, and now continues with a tale of slavery and economics. That is my story. It is not, however, the primary story of this book. The book sets up a contest between two economic frameworks: One is based on property relations and focuses on the accumulation of property; the other is based on civic relations and focuses on the making of provisions. The first one treats the planet and people as commodities and values them by the price they can fetch in the market. The second one treats the planet and human communities as living providers and protects them for this and future generations. In this book, the second framework wins. If it doesn't win, we all lose.

This contest is not between capitalism and socialism or between government control and private control. It is a contest between an uncivilized and a civilized economy. In a civilized economy, economic transactions are based on civic norms and people in these transactions are treated as citizens. An uncivilized economy, on the other hand, ignores the civic rights of persons and measures only what can be priced. It is based on property relations rather than civic relations. This is not a new contest. Since the eighteenth century, we have been slowly replacing property ownership with civic membership as the basis for our life together. This book brings this evolution of civic consciousness to the workplace and to the economy.

And what is the connection between the book's primary story about a contest between two economic frameworks, and my story about a white male writer and teacher involved in the history and legacy of slavery? It turns out that slavery was an integral part of the creation of wealth in early capitalism, and yet the economic framework we have inherited from such works as Adam Smith's *The Wealth of Nations* never acknowledges this pivotal part of its beginnings. Why the disconnect? I don't know. I do know Smith saw slaves as property rather than as laborers. They were bought and sold. Smith, however, remains silent about all of this in his account of wealth creation. We live with the legacy of this silence, focusing on the accumulation of property without much regard for those who provide it.

The crux of the matter is whether we exclude or include the real providers of wealth in our economic models. It is also about how we interpret land, labor, and money. Are they properties or providers? It is about how we interpret property. Is it a private or a government institution? It is about how we divide up the economy. Should we think of different economic sectors or of different systems of provision? It is about who should organize the economy. Should it be property owners or all citizens? It is a highly charged contest. Obviously, this book will not settle it. Not at all. I hope the book brings the contest to the classroom, to the boardroom, to the workplace, and to city councils, where it can be refined, corrected, and expanded.

In some ways the contest is more about ethics than about economics. If ethics were about how we should live together, then economics would be a dimension of ethics. In any case, I would like to see this book included in conversations about justice and sustainability, about corporate responsibility, about poverty, about human rights, about viable communities, and about the process of making good decisions. There are literally millions of people involved in these conversations in a multitude of projects and programs in an untold number of daily activities and practices. They are working to provide, to protect, and to fulfill the purposes of their communities, and in such practices one finds the management of making provisions or economics.

This brings me to a central assumption of my work: Words make a difference. Not always, of course, but in some cases they make all the difference in the world. If we were to share our understanding of how we use the word "wife," for example, we would probably have a fairly good idea of whether we operate in an economics of property, which defines wives as property, or an economics of provision, which honors what wives and husbands provide for each other. In a sense, the contest between an economics of property and an economics of provision is a contest over words and more specifically the meaning of words. From this angle, the book belongs to the practice of loving wisdom – to philosophy.

For some of us, philosophy begins with Socrates. He said that the unexamined life is not worth living. That seems to be true. He also said that he saw himself as a midwife. A midwife? What about the "economic man" or "rational behavior based on self-interest"? How could a man see himself as a midwife? Easy. Wisdom is not gender specific. Socrates loved wisdom, not because he possessed it – it was not self-love – but because he sought to bring it out in conversations with others. Above all else, Socrates was a dialogical philosopher. If we are to have a wise economy, we will need to engage in similar processes of dialogue – asking questions, examining answers, going deeper – so we can examine our life together and make it truly worth living. As you will see, the heart of an economics of provision is the idea of civic conversations, where citizens engage in deliberations that shape their common future. Maybe that is what economic midwives do.

Countless conversations with other people have helped birth this book. Many of the ideas and even words have been borrowed. Because the book draws on knowledge from multiple disciplines, I have had to rely on others. Sometimes I was lucky to find a book or article that answered a question I had just asked. At other times, colleagues suggested I do more reading or look at some literature if I was to venture into a particular field. I think the result is a book that sets an agenda for future thinking more than it provides conclusions to the arguments in which it engages. So there are many colleagues and friends to thank for their contributions. Many have given me important encouragement to finish the work, including Michael Boylan, Georges Enderle, Mike Hoffman, Jim O'Toole, W. Barrett Pearce, Martha Schloss, Brian Schrag, and, most significantly for my life as a writer, my family – Erdmut, Mark, and Kirsten. Others have offered helpful responses to early versions of different chapters or the completed manuscript, especially Steve Piersanti and Mark Brown, as well as Mark Becker, Stan Buller, Dennis Jaffe, Jeff Lustig, Tucker Malarkey, J. D. Moyer, John Moyer, Burkhard Mueller, Julie Nelson, George Scharffenberger, Murray Silverman, Nancy Southern, and Ron Sundstrom. I appreciate the insightful and critical reviews by the anonymous reviewers, and the support and cooperation of Paula Parish, at Cambridge University Press. I am grateful for the work of Rich Clogher, who vastly improved the text through his professional editing. I alone am responsible, of course, for the result of their contributions to this book.

As you will see, an economics of provision begins with the recognition of the actual providers of wealth. It breaks the silence about who really provides for us – the members of our households, the workers who suffer from the misery of exploitation and exclusion, and our planet whose life is now threatened by our consumer culture. Many people have provided for those of us who read and write books, and they have not always been recognized. If we are to civilize the economy, all providers must become visible and their contributions adequately recognized. I would like to dedicate this book to all providers.

I Introduction: creating a just and sustainable economy

Would you vote for a just and sustainable economy? If a just economy provided for everyone's basic needs and a sustainable economy provided for this generation without compromising the capacity of future generations to provide for their needs, would you vote for that? I think most of us would. So why is our economy so far away from what we desire and, in some cases, moving in a contrary direction? It is because of a mistake – one that will continue to frustrate our efforts to create a just and sustainable economy until we correct it.

Many of us are aware of the mistake, at least on some level. In 1998, Ray Anderson, the CEO of Interface Inc., told an audience that the first industrial revolution was a mistake, in spite of all the good that had come from it.[1] The mistake was that our focus on economic growth had blinded us to the destruction of the natural environment. Instead of "captains of industry," Anderson argued, future generations would see corporate leaders as "plunderers of the earth." People in the early days of the environmental movement or more recent advocates of sustainability have made similar arguments. We are on the brink of bringing chaos to the planet like it has seldom seen before. Al Gore, among others, has worked tirelessly to get us to recognize this "inconvenient truth."[2]

What is the mistake? In a nutshell, it is to base our economy on property and property relations. In fact, it was the cause of our blindness to the planet's life. Even before the beginning of the industrial revolution, economics had been framed as the production and trading of properties among property owners. This meant that whatever could

---

[1] Ray C. Anderson, "A Spear in the Chest," lecture at North Carolina State University, February 26, 1998, No. 1.

[2] *An Inconvenient Truth: A Global Warning*, Paramount Classics and Participant Productions, 2006.

not be treated as property was not recognized as having economic value. The dignity of persons, the attachments of families and communities, as well as the planet as a living system were and are invisible to this economics of property. If we are to protect these living systems from destruction, we must create a new economic framework. The aim of this book is to outline a plan for correcting this mistake. Central to the plan is to create a new story of how we provide for one another: a civic economics of provision.

The current economic story has its origin in the eighteenth century during the Scottish Enlightenment, at the beginning of the first global Atlantic trade between Europe, Africa, and the American colonies. During this period new theories of property and property relations were developed to explain and to justify the Atlantic economy, which involved the enslavement of more than eleven million Africans to supply the labor for the growing economies of the Americas. Slaves, at the time, were treated as property. They received no more sympathy and consideration than cattle or horses. This is a hard truth, but it is the dark stain that continues to influence how many of us think about economics today. The refusal to integrate this history into our views of Anglo-American economic development prevents us from telling the truth about the current destruction of the environment or to acknowledge – really acknowledge – the misery of workers today who provide us our goods. But facing this history is the only way out of the economics of property and into an economics of provision that could save the future for our children and grandchildren.

The economics of property, as it has come down to us over the past three centuries, disconnects the burden borne by the real providers of wealth – Adam Smith's silence about the role of slaves in creating wealth is a perfect illustration – and leaves society with a belief in the benevolence of the market's "invisible hand." (The Appendix contains a more detailed examination of the economics of slavery and free enterprise.) In the following chapters, we will contrast this dissociative economics to the idea of a civic economics of provision. The framework of an economics of provision integrates the three basic practices of any human community: providing for one another, protecting one another, and creating meaning together.

This view of economics has both classical and modern adherents. In Aristotle, we see the origins of the idea that the economy belongs to the civic sphere. More recently, Julie A. Nelson writes in her book *Economics for Humans* that the purpose of the economy "is about the provisioning of goods and services to meet our material needs ... the way we manage our time and money so we can obtain groceries and shelter and thus 'keep body and soul together.'"[3] Daniel W. Bromley, in his philosophical work on subjective pragmatism, also writes that economics should be about "how societies organize themselves for their provisioning."[4] Although neither author uses the notion of provisioning as a major theme, they open the door to such an approach. The real economy, it seems to me, should be evaluated and improved in terms of whether or not people actually are able to make provisions for their families and communities.

Some economists may feel that I am trespassing on their territory, but I am really trying to change our understanding of the territory. The language of trespassing, after all, belongs to an economics of property, which I hope to replace with an economics of provision. Furthermore, we should remember that Adam Smith was a moral philosopher, not an economist. How we envision the economy, in other words, is not so much an economic question as a philosophical question, and, more specifically, an ethical question. Ethics, after all, is about how we should live together. The answer we give to this ethical question will finally determine our understanding of economics.

This book provides a new framework for the global economy that is based on the original meaning of economics – household management. Household management was about making provisions, not accumulating

---

[3] Julie A. Nelson, *Economics for Humans* (Chicago, IL: The University of Chicago Press, 2006), p. 1.

[4] Daniel W. Bromley, *Sufficient Reason: Volitional Pragmatism and the Meaning of Economic Institutions* (Princeton, NJ and Oxford: Princeton University Press, 2006), p. 180.

We don't need commodities; we need provisions.

We don't need a large retirement account; we need security.

We don't need an automobile; we need access.

We don't need to own a house; we need privacy and security.

We don't need a big expense account; we need contacts.

FIGURE 1.1 What do we really need?

property. Some groups and organizations are already thinking this way. The commercial carpet company Interface Inc., for example, thinks in terms of providing a service that covers floors rather than being a business that sells carpets as a product.[5] Interface found that commercial clients do not want to own a carpet, but they do want their floor to be covered nicely. By providing what buildings need, Interface has been able to make its business much more sustainable than it was before. They manage the whole process of making, maintaining, and recycling the floor coverings they offer. Figure 1.1 gives more examples of how a switch from an economics of property to an economics of provision would change our way of thinking – from thinking about products and commodities to thinking about provisions and services.

In our modern economy, of course, making provisions occurs through various systems, such as the transportation system or the health-care system. These systems can be seen as "systems of provision" that could be organized to make provisions for all. How they are organized, of course, is a major question. Many people see only two organizing options: capitalism or socialism. This book offers a third option: a civic option. As citizens, guided by such civic norms as reciprocity, we can engage in civic conversations to turn economic systems toward sustainability and justice. If we are smart citizens, we will not discard things that can work, such as markets and property rights, but we will also not allow them to control our fate.

In a sense, moving from an economics of property to an economics of provision continues the ongoing shift from ownership as the basis

---

[5] www.interfaceglobal.com/Sustainability/Our-Journey/Interface-Model.aspx

for citizenship to citizenship being the basis for ownership. In the eighteenth century, ownership was really the basis of full citizenship and the right to vote was contingent on property rights. In some states, citizens without property did not get the right to vote until 1850. Women did not achieve full citizenship until the twentieth century. The economy, however, has continued to remain under the control of property owners. It is time – in fact, is it past time – to replace property rights with civic rights as the basis for our life together.

The new framework outlined in the following chapters does not eliminate property rights. Instead, it places them in the context of making provisions. An economics of provision does not eliminate the market, but it sees civic relations rather than market relations as a basis for a global community. Non-market norms and institutions – things such as stability, trust, and the rule of law – already provide a foundation for market transactions. Labor unions, government legislation to protect workers and the environment, and financial regulations have also constrained the reach of an economics of property. Nonprofits and voluntary organizations are doing amazing things to help people's lives. In his recent book *Blessed Unrest*, Paul Hawken presents the work of many of these groups, which he called "the largest movement in the world." This movement, he believes, now includes between one and two million organizations.[6] These non-governmental organizations are growing all over the world as people of all ages try to protect themselves and the planet from the current trends of an economics of property. In an economics of provision, all these non-market programs and protections will be strengthened so that all persons will be treated as citizens existing in relationships of basic moral equality and reciprocity.

An economics of provision is not so much a new economy as a new framework that gives us a perspective from which we can see what really happens in economic transactions. It is also a framework that is informed by and supports such current ideas about economic

---

[6] Paul Hawken, *Blessed Unrest: How the Largest Movement in the World Came into Being, and Why No One Saw It Coming* (New York: Viking, 2007), p. 2.

development as Amartya Sen's notion of measuring human development in terms of the capacity of people to get what they have reason to value.[7] To understand more of what an economics of provision actually offers, we may examine how an economics of property and an economics of provision would answer the following questions:

1. How are the ethical and the economic related?
2. What is the economy's purpose?
3. What is the basis of economic relations?
4. What is the relationship of commerce, society, and the civic?
5. Who organizes the economy?
6. How do you calculate value?
7. What is a corporation?
8. How can we change the economic system?
9. Who has the power to change the economy?

Table 1.1 summarizes the differences outlined in this chapter between an economics of property and an economics of provision. To understand an economics of property today, we need to make the distinction between its theory and its practice. In many cases, the practice makes more sense than the theory, which is why things are not worse off than they are. On the other hand, the theory has also prevented changes in practice that could have moved us toward a just and sustainable economy. In Table 1.1, the first two columns show some of the differences between theory and reality in an economics of property. The third and fourth columns pertain to the economics of provision, detailing its theory and how it could be implemented. Brief explanations of the nine key differences between the two frameworks follow.

I. THE ETHICAL AND THE ECONOMIC

In an economics of property, the invisible hand of the market maintains relationships, so the moral dimension of economic relationships is suspended. The only ethics is that of the virtues of the private

---

[7] Amartya Sen, *Development as Freedom* (New York: Alfred A. Knopf, 1999), p. 74.

Table 1.1 *Economics of property and economics of provision*

	The economics of property		The economics of provision	
	The stated theory	The reality	The theory	Its implementation
1. How are the ethical and the economic related?	The economic is self-regulating and self-contained. Does not need ethics.	The belief in self-organizing systems suspends the moral dimension of economic systems.	*Recognizes the moral dimensions of human relationships in systems of provisions.*	*Ethics of purpose examines the good that any system is aiming for. Ethics of protecting examines a system's fairness. An ethics of provision examines a system's inclusion and improvement.*
2. What is the economy's purpose?	Increase personal and national wealth.	Ensure the protection of the privilege of property.	*Make provisions, protect providers, and create a worthwhile purpose.*	*Protect providers from exploitation and degradation.*
3. What is the basis of economic relations?	Impersonal relationships of property (labor, land, and money).	Owners of property are privileged as traders of labor, land, and money.	*Civic sphere is recognized as the basis for economic relations. Land, labor, and money treated as provisions.*	*Citizens exchange provisions of land, labor, and money based on civic norms of reciprocity and moral equality, plus responses to supply and demand.*

Table 1.1 (cont.)

	The economics of property		The economics of provision	
	The stated theory	The reality	The theory	Its implementation
4. What is the relationship of commerce, society, and the civic?	The social is privatized, and the commercial defines the civic.	The commercial causes and maintains social inequalities, and dominates the civic.	The civic serves as the platform on which citizens re-organize the commercial to alleviate social divisions.	All persons are recognized as having the human right of moral equality and the civic right to live in relationships of reciprocity.
5. Who organizes the economy?	Organized by system dynamics ("invisible hand").	Organized by the elites in business and government.	Organized by citizens through representative civic deliberations on how to live together.	Civic conversations in many different settings use persuasion, incentives, and regulations to organize the economy.
6. How do you calculate value?	Determined by price in market transactions.	Determined by both price and structures of privilege.	Determined by a combination of reciprocity and market price.	Laws such as a "living wage" set floor for wages, while demand determines supply of goods and services.

7. What is a corporation?	The corporation belongs to owners, and should be managed for profit.	Corporations are seen as powerful agents in control of earth's future.	The corporation is also a human community designed to provide goods and services.	Corporations collaborate with other agents in civic systems of provision to make provisions for all.
8. How can we change the economic system?	Change individual preferences.	Random change occurs with new technology, profit-making adventures, advertising, and government regulation.	Three ways to change systems: • Laws and regulations • Incentives • Persuasion.	The public and private agents in a system of provision collaborate to change the system through government regulations, incentives and disincentives, and a shared vision of their civic obligations.
9. Who has the power to change the economy?	Changing the economic system is not necessary. Power resides in consumer choices.	Corporate change is limited by the "business case," which requires that any change will not limit the profitability of corporations.	Citizens have the power through collaboration in private and public agencies to define the civic obligations of all members of various systems of provision.	In different settings, citizens need to create the circumstances for civic deliberation about the best courses of action.

individual. In light of the civic ethics of Aristotle, which we will be using throughout the book, this amounts to a privatization of ethics. By contrast, an economics of provision recognizes the ethical dimension of relationships among providers and the provided, which includes considering the good that any economic system should provide, the protection from harm that providers deserve, and the justice of any distribution of provisions.

2. THE ECONOMY'S PURPOSE

In a property-based economy, purpose resides in individuals who are motivated by self-interest to increase their property through trade. The economy itself as a system is largely invisible (Smith's invisible hand) and its "purpose" is to facilitate the accumulation of personal and national wealth through trade. An economics of provision returns to the original meaning of economics – household management – and restores the purpose of the economy to that of making provisions for families and communities.

3. THE BASIS OF ECONOMIC RELATIONS

A property-based economy treats labor, land, and money as commodities, and recognizes only property owners as decision-making participants. The problem here is that the sources of wealth are not really commodities. Land is part of a living, natural system that provides us life. Labor is the work of women and men providing for themselves and each other. Money provides credit to the creditworthy so they can improve their conditions. An economics of provision not only reveals the true character of these providers of wealth, but also highlights the implicit civic sphere that has been made invisible by Smithian economics. It is global citizenship not property ownership that serves as the basis for economic transactions. All groups that have a stake in economic transactions should be represented in the decision-making process of how to manage the economy. This means that the economy is for all stakeholders, not just for property owners.

4. COMMERCE, SOCIETY, AND CIVIL SOCIETY

In the economics of property, there are only individuals and markets. Ignoring the social, of course, does not make it disappear. Indeed, markets are embedded in social relations – relations of class, gender, race, age, and so on. These social divisions shape the participation of different groups in the market, as well as creating different perceptions of everyday life. An economics of provision recognizes the reality of social divisions and conflicts and facilitates their mediation by high-lighting the civic sphere in which all people are recognized as global citizens with equal civic rights. The civic, in other words, creates a context for both the social and the commercial.

5. WHO ORGANIZES THE ECONOMY?

The Smithian tradition sees the economic system as self-organizing and self-regulating. Given this assumption, it makes sense to protect it from government intervention, just as we should protect the self-organizing dynamics of the biosphere from too much interference. This assumption, however, is false. The economy is not a natural system. It is organized and maintained by individuals and organiza-tions. It is currently organized mostly by business and government elites. The economics of provision calls for a deepening of democratic attitudes that would encourage citizens, at different levels of involve-ment, to participate in organizing the economic system.

An economics of provision suggests that we think of a stake-holder economy in which all persons and groups that have a stake in economic activity are represented in the processes of organizing how the economy provides for families and communities.

6. THE DETERMINATION OF VALUE

In an economics of property, price determines value. At least that is the theory. If you get only 8 cents an hour for your labor, that is because of supply and demand. Other people will work for that amount so why should you get more? The reality is quite different. People without property, who depend on wages for their existence, have little choice but to work for whatever wages they can get. Property owners, on the other hand, can demand salaries that match their control of property, which is determined not by supply and demand, but mostly by structures of privilege. In contrast to this process, an economics of provision uses civic norms such as reciprocity to determine value. People who participate in the creation of wealth and/or profit should be compensated commensurate with their contribution, which should be determined by representatives of all stakeholders.

7. WHAT IS A CORPORATION?

The modern corporation is usually seen as the property of its owners. Senior managers, in this framework, essentially serve a function similar to hotel managers: keep the rooms filled, keep the place safe and clean, and maintain good relations with the community. The master/servant legal tradition supports this view of the corporation. An economics of provision, on the other hand, recognizes the civic status of workers and looks at the corporation as a human community designed to provide goods and services. This view would require changes in the law to support workers' civic rights and to support a view of the corporation as a provider within systems of provision.

8. CHANGING ECONOMIC SYSTEMS

An economics of property holds – in theory – that consumers change the economy by changing what commodities they prefer to buy. Actually, the market changes continually due to the development of new products, new profit-making adventures, extensive advertising to entice consumers to consume, and sometimes new government regulation. In an economics of provision, one can intentionally change the system by using the three strategies of incentives, regulations, and persuasion, which match the three means of maintaining a community – making provisions, giving protection, and creating a worthwhile purpose.

9. THE POWER TO CHANGE ECONOMIC SYSTEMS

In an economics of property, the property owners control the market – and those who own more control more. In an economics of provision, membership in civil society – not ownership – provides the basis of market control. As citizens, we all have a right through direct and representative government to determine the civic obligations of corporations in the system of provision in which they operate.

CONCLUSION

No one knows all the consequences of switching from an economics of property relations to an economics of provision based on civic relations. Others may see things through these lenses that I have not seen. The new frame proposed here does offer a new vision of an economic system in which workers would be treated with dignity, the natural environment would be treated as a living source of life, and the credit/debt function of money would be protected. It also grounds the modern economy in a civic sphere and re-establishes our political stewardship of the economy. By framing the economy as a stakeholder economy, we can ensure that all persons can be represented in the civic conversations that will guide the direction of the economy. These conversations may occur in neighborhoods, cities, workplaces, voluntary organizations, and the halls of Congress. All stakeholders, in other words, should have a voice in deciding how we will live together.

At the center of all these changes is a civic agenda to remove property relations as our economy's foundation and to replace them with civic relations. This would be the next step in a historical progression of replacing property rights with civic rights as the foundation of our life together.

Those individuals and organizations that will resist this agenda cannot be discounted. Many have vested interests in maintaining things as they are. Their power to resist change, however, ultimately depends on the collective belief that continually reinforces the "reality" of the status quo. Our civic agenda is to change this belief system.

This book seeks to serve that end. Part I of the book exposes the deep flaw at the very center of the economics of property, illustrated by Adam Smith's silence about the slave-based tobacco trade in his treatise on wealth creation. It then offers an alternative narrative of human communities that provide, protect, and make life worthwhile for all. Part II explores the relationship between the civic and property rights; reveals the civic as the implicit foundation of market economies; restores civic norms, such as reciprocity; and argues that market competition actually requires a civic foundation. Part III highlights the differences between treating labor, land, and money as commodities and as provisions. Part IV examines the world of systems, presents an ethics of economic systems, and explores how to create systems of provision that we can direct toward a just and sustainable future. Part V, the conclusion, outlines the civic obligations of corporations and then provides a framework for creating the circumstances for civic conversations that will enable us to make the changes we need.

Moving through the book's five parts represents a journey from where we are now – an economy that disconnects our provisions from their living sources and that values property rights over civic rights – to where we must move if we want to create a just and sustainable economy. Such an economy will be one in which all stakeholders are represented and participate in directing it toward providing basic needs for everyone and in protecting future generations from our excesses. To really make this change we must change the stories and images in which we live. Some people believe that we cannot talk our way out of our current global mess, but talking is, in fact, the only way out.

Part I Creating a new economic framework

2 Adam Smith's silence and an economics of property

Now that we have some idea of the differences between the economics of property and an economics of provision, we can begin the journey of moving from one framework to the other. That is not as easy as it seems. But if we agree that we have a moral obligation to direct our economy toward justice and sustainability, then we must take on the task. The current economic framework will simply not allow us to go where we need to go. The next chapters recount the full reality of the economics of property, which grew out of the Scottish Enlightenment, and then propose a model of how human communities should provide for one another. We begin with the economics of Adam Smith's Scotland.

THE CREATION OF WEALTH IN EIGHTEENTH-CENTURY SCOTLAND

Most visitors would have considered Scotland a rather undeveloped country at the beginning of the eighteenth century. Its union with England in 1707, however, proved to be a boon. Scottish merchants profited from the English Navigation Acts that required all goods from the British colonies to be exported on British ships and sent to British ports. They also profited from the Spanish and English wars, because the port of Glasgow was far enough north to serve as a safe place for shipments from the colonies. By the 1750s, the Scottish merchants of Glasgow dominated the tobacco trade, importing even more tobacco than London or other English cities. In 1775, for example, the tobacco trade represented no less than 38 percent of total imports for Scotland and 56 percent of total exports. Imported from the slave-based plantations in Virginia and Maryland, millions of pounds of tobacco flowed into Glasgow and was eventually exported to the European continent. The historian Kenneth Morgan wrote this of the trade's impact:

> Glasgow rose from being a small port in 1700 to become one of the great commercial cities of eighteenth-century Europe, and this was achieved largely by generating new marketing strategies and productivity advances in tobacco shipment ... By carrying the most valuable staple product grown in North America to continental European markets, Glasgow produced dynasties of tobacco lords that laid the economic foundation for the growth of trading activity on the Clyde.[1]

The Glasgow merchants who controlled the tobacco trade – William Cunninghame, John Glassford and Andrew Cochrane were perhaps the most noteworthy – earned the title "tobacco lords" and became some of the richest men in Europe. Cunninghame's home is now the Gallery of Modern Art in Glasgow. Cochrane served as provost of the University of Glasgow when Adam Smith taught there as a professor of moral philosophy.

The wealth that the tobacco trade created enabled these men to become instrumental in the development of other industries in Scotland, through the banks they established and through new businesses in which they invested. For example, Glasgow merchants founded the Smithfield ironworks, which primarily made hoes and spades for the slaves in Maryland and Virginia. They also started the Glasgow tannery, which made saddles and shoes for the plantations. Finally, they expanded the Scottish linen industry, which made linen shirts for slaves in the American colonies, the Caribbean, and the West Indies. The next time you see a picture of eighteenth- or early nineteenth-century slaves dressed in linen shirts, recognize it as a source of Scottish wealth. Slaves in the colonies were both the providers of products to Scotland and the consumers of products from

---

[1] Kenneth Morgan, *Slavery, Atlantic Trade and the British Economy, 1600–1800* (Cambridge: Cambridge University Press, 2000), p. 86.

Scotland. All this benefited the city of Glasgow. As T. M. Devine has written: "Glasgow's success was built on tobacco, sugar, and cotton, all commodities produced by slave labour."[2]

Clearly, the tobacco trade benefited Glasgow, but what of the rest of Scotland? After his own investigations, the Scottish historian T. C. Smout wrote this about Devine's earlier work on the impact of the tobacco trade on Scotland:

> T. M. Devine's careful studies have led to the broad and cautious conclusion that "while not directly responsible for accelerated growth in the later eighteenth century," the tobacco trade was "among the series of influences which helped to raise the impoverished economy of the early 1700s to the threshold of industrialization" and was "crucial to the emergence of the west-central region to a dominating position in the Scottish economy."[3]

There were certainly other emerging industries in Scotland, such as the linen industry, but even this was helped by the exportation of linen to the plantations. In any case, Adam Smith's knowledge came from the tobacco lords, not the "linen lords," if there were any.

The tobacco trade also spurred the economies of Virginia and Maryland. The growth of the tobacco trade in Virginia depended on several conditions: increased consumption of tobacco; availability of capital for increasing production; and access to the tools, clothing, and other supplies for slaves. Scottish industries satisfied the plantation owners with all of these requirements. Scottish merchants set up stores along the rivers in Virginia and Maryland, and through the stores they would purchase the plantation owners' tobacco. The planters could then buy Scottish imports of tools and other needed supplies to grow their business. Daniel Defoe is quoted as saying of Virginia: "If it

---

[2] T. M. Devine, *Scotland's Empire & the Shaping of the Americas 1600–1815* (Washington, DC: Smithsonian Books, 2003), p. 244.

[3] T. C. Smout, "Where Had the Scottish Economy Got to by 1776?" in *Wealth and Virtue: The Shaping of Political Economy in the Scottish Enlightenment* (Cambridge: Cambridge University Press, 1983), pp. 49–50.

goes on for many years more Virginia may be rather call'd a Scots than an English plantation."[4] More than anything else, economic growth depended on the growth of the slave population. As Mike Davey has said: "Without slavery there would not have been a global tobacco trade. In the tobacco region of Maryland, for example, the slavery population grew from 7% to 35% between 1690 and 1750."[5]

Slaves were more than a source of labor in the colonies; they were assets for obtaining loans. Since slaves were seen as property, plantation owners used their slaves as collateral to secure capital for enlarging their businesses. Many of these loans came from Scottish banks founded by the tobacco lords. So the increase in capital benefited everyone – except, of course, the slave population.

As the tobacco trade grew, so did the wealth of Glasgow and the colonies, organized not by Smith's "invisible hand," but by the Glasgow merchants, the slave traders, and the Virginia plantation owners. It was this world – the world of the tobacco trade – in which Adam Smith collected materials for writing *The Wealth of Nations*.

Between 1751 and 1764, Smith was a resident of Glasgow, a professor of moral philosophy at the university, and, without a doubt, a witness to Glasgow's economic growth. But Smith would have much more than just an onlooker's understanding of the source of the city's good fortune. During his tenure at the University of Glasgow, Smith belonged to a "political economy club" that met regularly to discuss economics. The club included some of the tobacco lords, such as John Glassford, George Kippen, and Andrew Cochrane. One Smith biographer, Ian Simpson Ross, writes that Smith probably used their information about America to develop his critique of mercantilism and his advocacy of free trade. Another biographer, Thomas Rae, writes that Smith acknowledged to Thomas Carlyle his debt to Cochrane for information about trade and commerce when he was collecting

---

[4] Quoted in Devine, *Scotland's Empire*, p. 95.
[5] Mike Davey, "The European Tobacco Trade from the 15th to the 17th Centuries," the James Ford Bell Library, University of Minnesota, http://bell.lib.umn.edu/Products/tob1.html (retrieved on November 4, 2009).

materials for *The Wealth of Nations*. Perhaps Arthur Herman best summarizes the importance of these tobacco merchants for Smith:

> It was by watching the city's tobacco trade that Adam Smith, professor at the University of Glasgow from 1751 to 1764, made his first real acquaintance with large-scale business enterprise, and with the businessmen who run it. Smith struck up a close acquaintance with John Glassford, who kept him informed of events in America and also took a keen interest in Smith's progress with his *Wealth of Nations*. Glasgow Provost Andrew Cochrane organized a Political Economy Club, whose members included Smith, Glassford, and another wealthy tobacco merchant, Richard Oswald. Cochrane even presided over a special session of the Glasgow Town Council on May 3, 1762, when Professor Smith was made an honorary burgess of the city.[6]

These tobacco lords, in other words, were a source of Smith's knowledge about the world of commerce, and yet he never tells us about them, or what he learned from them, in his book on the creation of wealth. One can imagine that the tobacco trade would have provided great examples for Smith's theories. There was certainly a division of labor on tobacco plantations, which could have illustrated his theory of the productivity of the division of labor. Instead of this true story, however, he uses the "trifling" example of a pin factory.[7]

Wealth creation may have been due, as Smith says, to "the propensity to truck, barter, and exchange one thing for another."[8] What he does not say is that it was the exchange of slaves and the trading of products produced from slave labor that promoted wealth in Scotland. If he had written about this, of course, he would have had to abandon the notion of an invisible hand directing the economy. It was

---

[6] Arthur Herman, *How the Scots Invented the Modern World* (New York: Three Rivers Press, 2001), pp. 162–165.

[7] Adam Smith, *The Wealth of Nations*, ed. Edwin Cannan (New York: The Modern Library, Random House, 1994), pp. 4–5.

[8] *Ibid.*, p. 14.

not the invisible hand that coordinated the production and distribution of tobacco (among other goods), but the whip of the slave driver, the helping hand of the Scottish merchant, and the imperial hand of the British government that protected and maintained a very lucrative Atlantic commerce. Without the invisible hand, Smith's whole view of human progress would require a major review. The story he did tell us, in other words, was in large measure a fabrication.

The real story of economic growth during early capitalism is a harsh one. It certainly is not the optimistic tale one reads from some contemporary economists. Today, the driving economic trend is globalization, but that actually had its beginnings in the eighteenth-century triangular trade between Africa, the Americas, and Europe. That trade marked an economic system that worked to the benefit of some and the utter degradation of others. Once the gap between what Smith said and what he knew is acknowledged, one wonders how he kept these two stories isolated from each other. In fact, there are places in *The Wealth of Nations* where what he did not write affects what he did write. Reviewing some of these places will help us understand how he maintained his silence as well as give us clues about his reason for doing so.

THE SILENCE IN *THE WEALTH OF NATIONS*

If we judge only by the text of *The Wealth of Nations* then there is scant evidence that Smith witnessed the economic growth of Glasgow or that he learned much about it from the tobacco lords. He does write about the tobacco trade in the context of his arguments against the Navigation Acts, which were British policies that forced all exports from the colonies to be transported on British ships to British ports. He believes that these regulations increased the price of tobacco not only for European consumers, but also for consumers in England.[9] For Smith, the Navigation Acts hindered the free flow of goods, which led to higher prices. This discussion of the tobacco trade, however, does

---

[9] *Ibid.*, p. 646.

not offer a clue that it was a source of wealth for Scotland or that it was based on slavery.

In another of the few passages on the tobacco trade, Smith makes the following remark in comparing the tobacco and sugar plantations:

> I have never even heard of any tobacco plantation that was improved and cultivated by the capital of merchants who resided in Great Britain, and our tobacco colonies send us home no such wealthy planters as we see frequently arrive from our sugar islands.[10]

Frankly, this is difficult to believe. Plantation owners did acquire loans from Scottish banks that were founded by the same Glasgow tobacco lords who, with Smith, belonged to the political economy club. The Virginia planters' debt to Scottish banks, in fact, was well known at the time of the American Revolution, so one wonders why Smith claims to be ignorant of it.

There are other places in *The Wealth of Nations* that seem reasonable until one begins to read with the knowledge that Smith had long been involved in conversations about the slave-based tobacco trade. For example, Smith writes the following about the relationship between population growth and prosperity:

> But though North America is not yet so rich as England, it is much more thriving, and advancing with much greater rapidity to the further acquisition of riches. The most decisive mark of the prosperity of any country is the increase of its number of its inhabitants. In Great Britain, and most other European countries, they are not supposed to double in less than five hundred years. In the British colonies in North America, it has been found, that they double in twenty or five-and-twenty-years.[11]

In a footnote, Smith refers to documentation that supports his assertion about the increase in population: "In 1703 the population of Virginia was 60,000, in 1755 it was 300,000, and in 1765 it was

---

[10] *Ibid.*, p. 182.   [11] *Ibid.*, p. 80.

500,000." What Smith does not say is that a large part of this population increase in Virginia was due to the increased slave population. T. M. Devine writes that in the Chesapeake alone, which would include much of Virginia and Maryland, the number of slaves increased twentyfold, from 7,000 in 1690 to 150,000 in 1750.[12] In the census of 1790, Virginia had a total population of 747,550, and 292,627 were slaves.[13] That is just under 40 percent. The wealth of Virginia, in other words, was not primarily due to European migration during this period, but to the increased number of slaves working on the tobacco plantations. Smith surely would have learned about this from his frequent meetings with the tobacco lords of Glasgow.

Another passage, just as revealing of Smith's silence about the slave-based economy of the colonies, is the following statement about the reasons for the colonies' prosperity:

> But there are no colonies of which progress has been more rapid than that of the English in North America. Plenty of good land, and liberty to manage their own affairs their own way, seem to be the two great causes of the prosperity of all new colonies.[14]

Why only land and liberty here? Smith is explicit elsewhere that the three sources of wealth are land, labor, and capital. The labor of the colonies was, of course, slave labor. So why was that labor not recognized? For Smith, slaves were not a source of wealth because they did not sell their labor in the marketplace, but, instead, slaves themselves were sold in the marketplace. Slaves were the property of the plantation owner, and like the owner's other livestock they were not seen as laborers.

It is true that Smith complains about slavery in *The Wealth of Nations*. In fact, he is seen today as an advocate for ending slavery. But in light of what we now know about his silence, his complaint seems

---

[12] Devine, *Scotland's Empire*, p. 101.
[13] www.virginiaplaces.org/population/index.html
[14] Smith, *The Wealth of Nations*, pp. 616–617.

quite faint. In fact, when Smith addresses the productive use of slavery, his complaints seem faint indeed:

> In all European colonies the culture of the sugarcane is carried on by negro slaves ... But the success of the cultivation which is carried on by means of cattle, depends very much upon the good management of those cattle; so the profit and success of that which is carried on by slaves, must depend equally upon the good management of those slaves, and in the good management of their slaves the French planters, I think it is generally allowed, are superior to the English.[15]

Comparing the management of cattle and of African slaves, of course, expresses the full meaning of "chattel slavery," since *chattel* has the same root as *cattle*. Just as one does not count cattle as laborers, even though they are productive, so one would not count slaves as laborers. This does not mean, however, that slaves were not part of the economic picture. As Gavin Wright points out in *Slavery and American Economic Development*:

> Slaves produced crops for markets governed by complex systems of law and credit, products designed for consumers that were affluent and industries that were advanced by the standards of the day. Distasteful as it may seem to modern readers, slave economies functioned through elaborate legal and financial channels, as fully developed and in some ways more fully developed than their counterparts in the free-labor states. In a word, they were systems of property rights.[16]

In Smith's story of economic progress, however, he omits the misery of the African slaves. Instead of a story about this slave-based economic system, one finds in *The Wealth of Nations* a narrative of how the new world contributed to economic growth. The way Smith constructs this narrative requires us to read it at length because it demonstrates how

---

[15] *Ibid.*, pp. 633–634.
[16] Gavin Wright, *Slavery and American Economic Development* (Baton Rouge: Louisiana State University Press, 2006), p. 12.

Smith's book bolsters the optimistic economics that has dominated so much of our economic thinking.

> The discovery of America and that of a passage to the East Indies by the Cape of Good Hope, are the two greatest and most important events recorded in the history of mankind ... What benefits, or what misfortunes to mankind may hereafter result from those great events, no human wisdom can foresee ... To the natives, however, both the East and West Indies, all the commercial benefits which can have resulted from those events have been sunk and lost in the dreadful misfortunes which they have occasioned. These misfortunes, however, seem to have arisen rather from accident than from any thing in the nature of those events themselves.
>
> ... Hereafter, perhaps, the natives of those countries may grow stronger, or those of Europe may grow weaker, and the inhabitants of all the different quarters of the world may arrive at the equality of courage and force which, by inspiring mutual fear, can alone overawe the injustice of independent nations into some sort of respect for the rights of one another. But nothing seems more likely to establish this equality of force than that mutual communication of knowledge and of all sorts of improvements which an extensive commerce from all countries to all countries naturally, or rather necessarily, carries along with it.[17]

In other words, colonization (and globalization) has benefited some and harmed others, but this belongs to a larger process of global development that will "naturally, or rather necessarily," raise all boats. One must remember that this was written in 1776, when global trade between the Americas and Europe relied on the enslaving of millions of Africans, the continued destruction of native populations, and the privatization of the American continent.

---

[17] Smith, *The Wealth of Nations*, pp. 675–676.

In his popular book *The End of Poverty*, Jeffery Sachs offers a contemporary version to Smith's silence in the section where he surveys the rise of economic growth in Great Britain.[18] Sachs begins by asking the important question: "Why was Britain first?" His answer includes such factors as its social mobility, institutions of liberty, scientific discoveries, its geographical advantages, its military power, and its coal. He makes no mention of the economic contributions of slavery to British economic growth. In fact, Sachs' only mention of slavery comes when he is providing examples of how people have taken up the challenge to improve things. In this context, he describes the struggle of Wilberforce and others who brought about the end of the British slave trade in 1807. It does seem odd that Sachs can use the halt of the slave trade to support an optimistic view of change, without ever recognizing the seminal contribution of slavery to the economic growth of Britain in particular and Europe in general. Contrary to what Sachs says about the beginning of the modern economy, Britain was not first. The Atlantic trade among the peoples of Europe, Africa, and the Americas was first. If globalization refers to the economic integration of different parts of the world through trade, it began with the triangular trade of the Atlantic.

How can one explain the fact that current free-market thinkers seem unable to see the misery of the sweatshop, the destruction of the biosphere, or the suffering caused by oil wars? Like Adam Smith, they seem to be trapped in a narrative of economic progress that allows them to dissociate the accumulation of wealth from the consequences it has on those who provide the wealth, whether that be other humans or the planet itself. Escaping from this legacy will take more than pointing out Smith's omissions in *The Wealth of Nations*, although that should give some people pause. We need to look at what shaped his thinking. It would be a mistake to say that Smith remained silent because he favored slavery. He actually believed it to be a miserable practice. But what kept him silent – what prevented him from telling

---

[18] Jeffery Sachs, *The End of Poverty: Economic Possibilities for Our Time* (New York: Penguin Books, 2005), pp. 33–34.

about the real providers of wealth – was the thing he believed in even more strongly: the primacy of property.

THE ECONOMICS OF PROPERTY

In a sense, behind every theory resides some narrative or story. Behind the theory of wealth creation in *The Wealth of Nations* is the story of property and property relations. The story's main theme is how changes in property accumulation brought about changes in the role of law and government and an increase in social refinement. Intellectuals of the Scottish Enlightenment, including Adam Smith, believed that mankind had evolved through four stages in history: the earliest, savage stage, with its hunters; the pastoral stage, with its herdsmen; the agricultural stage, with its farmers; and the civil or commercial stage, with its traders and merchants.

These four stages were widely used during the Scottish Enlightenment. They served to show connections between progress, property, and the role of government, which was to protect private property. Smith's friend and mentor Henry Home, Lord Kames sums up the tenor of the time when he wrote: "Without private property, there would be no industry, and without industry, men would remain savages forever."[19]

Smith uses these four stages not only to tell the story of European history, which moved from the stage of savagery to the stage of civility, but also to distinguish Europeans from the peoples of Africa, parts of Asia, and the Americas. In other words, the four stages functioned as a story of progress and as a framework for conceptualizing contemporary differences. All peoples started out as savages. The Europeans had progressed through all the other stages to civil society, the Africans, Asians, and Americans had not. The Americans, at least in Smith's eyes, had not advanced beyond the earliest stage. They were still savages, because they had neither accumulated property nor developed laws to protect it. As David L. Blaney and Naeem Inayatullah point out

---

[19] Quoted in Herman, *How the Scots Invented the Modern World*, p. 105.

in their article "The Savage Smith and the Temporal Walls of Capitalism," the four stages gave Enlightenment thinkers a framework to neutralize the differences between themselves and the savages.

> The temporal distance between Indians and Europeans, previously bridgeable only by the activities of the missionary, could now be understood within an "abstract and philosophical" scheme that locates the American Indian at the very beginnings of human society. The differences suggested by the Indians are rendered benign as superceded ways of life.[20]

These four stages play a major role in the construction of Smith's *The Wealth of Nations*. In the very first pages, he makes an extensive comparison between the savage stage, the stage of the hunters, and the stage of commercial society or what he calls "civilized and thriving nations."

> Such nations [savage nations], however, are so miserably poor, that from mere want, they are frequently reduced, or, at least, think themselves reduced, to the necessity sometimes of directly destroying, and sometimes of abandoning their infants, their old people, and those afflicted with lingering diseases, to perish with hunger, or to be devoured by wild beasts. Among civilized and thriving nations, on the contrary, though a great number of people do not labour at all, many of whom consume the produce of ten times, frequently of a hundred times more labour than the greater part of those who work; yet the produce of the whole labour of the society is so great, that all of them are often abundantly supplied, and a workman, even the lowest and poorest order, if he is frugal and industrious, may enjoy a greater share of the necessaries and conveniences of life than it is possible for any savage to acquire.[21]

---

[20] David L. Blaney and Naeem Inayatullah, "The Savage Smith and the Temporal Walls of Capitalism," retrieved as PDF file, December 1, 2007. Also available in *Classical Theory in International Relations*, ed. Jahn Beate (Cambridge: Cambridge University Press, 2006), p. 151.

[21] Smith, *The Wealth of Nations*, p. lx.

This passage, like others we have reviewed, demonstrates again that abstract theory could easily override actual facts in *The Wealth of Nations*. Many Native Americans were actually doing quite well before the European invasion. Furthermore, as we have shown, slavery was a key economic basis for the "civilized and thriving nations." How "civilized" was that? If civil society had moved beyond the rudeness of early stages, then how could property owners derive their wealth from slave labor? How civil can a society be if it is dependent on the terrorism that slavery always entails?

In such a case, a society's civility depends on keeping slavery out of sight and out of mind. Smith's notion of the "invisible hand" begins to take on a different meaning. What was invisible in Smith's account of wealth creation was the role of slavery. The slave trade, however, was an important part of the global economic world in which Smith lived. Trading slaves, in fact, was a very visible market.

> Like other pieces of property, slaves spent most of their time outside the market, held to a standard of value, but rarely priced. They lived as parents and children, as cotton pickers, card players, and preachers, as adversaries, friends, and livers. But though they were seldom priced, slaves' values always hung over their heads. J.W.C. Pennington, another fugitive, called this the "chattel principle": any slave's identity might be disrupted as easily as a price could be set and piece of paper passed from one hand to another.[22]

One could make a distinction between two markets: an international market where people from Africa were sold in American ports, and a domestic market where slaves were sold by one American slaveholder to another. The domestic market continued until the Civil War and involved the movement of over 1 million slaves from the upper to the lower Southern states.[23] Smith, of course, would have known more about the international trade from the tobacco lords of Glasgow. The

[22] Walter Johnson, *Soul by Soul: Life Inside the Antebellum Slave Market* (Cambridge, MA: Harvard University Press, 1999), p. 19.
[23] *Ibid.*, p. 5.

international slave trade, if one can make comparisons, was probably the more brutal of the two. In fact, the international slave trade had a long and savage history.

> In the four centuries of that triangular trade, ten to eleven million people – fifty or sixty thousand a year in the peak decades between 1700 and 1850 – were packed beneath slave ship decks and sent to the New World. Indeed, up to the year 1820, five times as many Africans traveled across the Atlantic as did Europeans. And those numbers do not include the dead – the five percent of the human cargo who died in crossings that took three weeks, the quarter who died in crossings that took three months. Behind the numbers lie the horrors of the Middle Passage: chained slaves forced to dance themselves into shape on the decks; the closed holds, where men and women were separated from one another and chained into the space of a coffin; the stifling heat and untreated illness, the suicides and slave revolts, and dead thrown overboard as the ships passed.[24]

Smith certainly did not support the slave trade, as John Locke did, but neither did he talk about it.[25] His silence is the issue here, because of its consequences. The silence did not leave a void. Silences seldom do. Instead, it allowed a different story to be told, a story that made it that much more difficult to tell the truth. Smith's optimistic economics simply had no place to acknowledge that slavery was part and parcel of the creation of wealth in eighteenth-century capitalism. How could you fit the economics of slavery into a passage such as the following?

> Human society, when we contemplate it in a certain abstract and philosophical light, appears like a great, an immense machine, whose regular and harmonious movements produce a thousand agreeable effects.[26]

---

[24] *Ibid.*, p. 4.

[25] See the Appendix for an account of Locke's investment in the slave trade.

[26] Adam Smith, *Theory of Moral Sentiments* (Mineola, NY: Dover Publications, Inc., 2006), p. 316.

Furthermore, Smith believed that the role of government was to protect property, not to protect persons. As he writes in *The Wealth of Nations*:

> In every country where the unfortunate law of slavery is established, the magistrate, when he protects the slave, intermeddles in some measure in the management of the private property of the master; and, in a free country, where the master is perhaps either a member of the colony assembly, or an elector of such a member, he dare not do this but with the greatest caution and circumspection.[27]

In other words, from an economic point of view – that is, from the point of view developed by an economics of property – the plantation slaves are property. Add, to this view of slaves as property, the common view of government as the protector of property, and you begin to understand why Smith did not write that the slave-based tobacco trade was a major source of the wealth of his nation. Whatever the reason for Smith's silence, he left us with an economic framework that is blind to the misery of human providers and to the degradation of nature's provision.

If Smith had told the truth, we might have an economics today that would serve as an adequate framework for assessing current global issues. We might have an economics that would make the connections between the poverty of the many and the wealth of the few; the connection between the early twentieth-century prosperity of people in North America and the widespread use of the US Marines in South America; a connection between the increased consumption by the middle class in the United States, the increase of workers in the Maquiladoras across the Mexican border, and the increased unemployment in the United States.

Perhaps if economists in this Smithian tradition had known the untold story behind Smith's work, they could have transformed Smith's legacy into an economics that recognized the providers of

---

[27] Smith, *The Wealth of Nations*, p. 634.

wealth, both human and non-human, as deserving of respect. This has not happened. Instead there has been a steady denial of the ethical dimension of market relations. Where would you find any moral questions among pieces of property or between commodities? If market transactions are merely the exchanges of commodities, then what could be ethical or unethical about engaging in transactions to the fullest? Supply and demand is all you would need. That is the old story. The new story, which will be told in the following chapters, recognizes that the market exists in human relationships – relationships that are largely controlled by human hands, not invisible ones. In other words, market relationships are moral relationships. The recognition of the ethical or moral aspect of market relationships is the first step toward civilizing the economy. The step is actually bigger than one might suspect. First we need to make some preparations, which is the task of the next chapter.

3 Reclaiming the notions of provision and family

We need an economy that recognizes and includes the living providers of wealth instead of one that ignores them or treats them as nothing but property. We need an economics that recognizes the ethical relationship between providers and the provided for. In our current economic framework, the ethical is largely located either in individual persons, or in relationships among persons outside of the market. Inside the market, one can trust the invisible hand, or "the miracle of the market," to move us in the right direction. The relationships of supply and demand, in other words, are not seen as moral relations, but as property relations. As long as we interpret persons and the planet as property, we will continue to lose valuable time that we need to redirect our economy toward a just and sustainable future.

This chapter attempts to restore the ethical dimension of economics or, more precisely, to change our thinking so that economics and ethics belong together. There are several ways to do this. In this chapter we will restore the human dimension of the relationship between providers and the provided. We will then turn to restoring the family and community as the center of economic action instead of the individual entrepreneur or "economic man" of our current property-based economics.

In the tradition of an economics of property, economic action is the effort of the isolated individual or economic man, who acts on his self-interest or preferences and tries to maximize his good fortune. As an alternative for an economics of provision, I offer Virginia Held's suggestion that the image of the mother and child more correctly represents our human nature.[1] This image highlights a relationship

---

[1] Virginia Held, *Feminist Morality: Transforming Culture, Society, and Politics* (Chicago and London: The University of Chicago Press, 1993).

of attachment, instead of isolation, and allows us to acknowledge the labor of the parent in making provisions for the child. Furthermore, it imagines a relationship of mutual identity, rather than one based on each individual's self-interest.

If we reflect on our experiences, it becomes obvious that we do not exist as isolated individuals disconnected from families and friends as much current economic theory assumes. Instead we exist in significant relationships with others, and these relationships give our actions most of their meanings. Our concerns for each other can easily be interpreted as our wanting to provide for each other, or at least to ensure that people have what they need to provide for themselves. An economics of provision, in other words, appears to fit with our experiences. This instant reflection, however, raises another question: "Why have we not heard of this type of economics before?"

There are a number of reasons, but two seem particularly important for recovering the story of human provisioning: the limited notion of provisions and the exclusion of the family. As Nancy Folbre argues in her book *The Invisible Heart*, the family has been largely eliminated from economic thinking, and yet the family is the primary location where we provide and care for one another.[2] True, individuals do want to provide for themselves, but we do this in community with others. Economics, in other words, is not simply about individuals, but about individuals in communities. To restore this dimension of economics, we can return to Aristotle's understanding of the relationships among the household, the village, and the city. In Aristotle's "economics" we will find some things we do not agree with. He accepted slavery and a patriarchal society, but his description of the relationships among families, clans and the civic can be very useful in understanding the civic and ethical aspects of the relationships among providers and the provided.

---

[2] Nancy Folbre, *The Invisible Heart: Economics and Family Values* (New York: The New Press, 2001), p. vii.

When we focus on the relationship between providers and the provided, we need to acknowledge that sometimes we have been as silent as Adam Smith about the misery of the real providers of our prosperity. Some of us may have even used the notion of God's providence as a way to ignore the work of the actual persons who provide things for us. Furthermore, this idea of God's providence has been linked with Smith's notion of the invisible hand, in such a way that it is easy to overlook the human and ethical aspect of the relationships among various actors in our economic life. William E. Connolly has described the linkage as follows:

> Such a link between markets and providence initially assumes that things will take care of themselves as long as the system is not interrupted much by state regulation and receives large state subsidies. But when things turn sour, supporters of the equation can easily turn ugly. The equation between markets and providence fosters denial and can easily devolve into aggressive fatalism. This tendency is reflected in the stories of Fox news that previously denied global warming and now assert that it is too late to do anything about it.[3]

When abstract theories prevent recognition of the actual human interactions that happen on the ground, so to speak, then we need to change the theories. Such is the case not only with the abstraction of the invisible hand, but also with the abstraction of God's providence. We need to restore the ethical dimension of making provisions before we can take full advantage of Aristotle's notion of the economic movement from the family to the village and city. In order to do so, we first examine how the notion of God's providence has sometimes led to a suspension of the ethical, and then we will return to the family and civic community as the basis for economic activity.

---

[3] William E. Connolly, *Capitalism and Christianity, American Style* (Durham, NC and London: Duke University Press, 2008), p. 101.

GOD'S PROVIDENCE AND THE SUSPENSION OF THE ETHICAL

If we could visit the Atlantic trading community in the eighteenth century, we would overhear two quite distinct conversations. One conversation would be about trade and economics. The other would be about how God's providence guided the settlement of the colonies. Although one was secular and the other was sacred or theological, both largely prevented the privileged classes from recognizing the misery of those who provided their wealth. Furthermore, just as we live today with the legacy of Smithian economics, we also live with the legacy of eighteenth-century theology. Therefore, just as we explored the narrative behind the economic theory in the previous chapter, we will here explore the narrative behind this theory of divine providence

Many British colonists assumed that their temporal existence was under the tutelage of God's providence. This was true for intellectuals on both sides of the Atlantic. For the settlers of the colonies, the theme of God's providence served as a justification for their immigration to the new world. The early British and Dutch colonists, both the Puritans in Massachusetts and the members of the Virginia Trading Company in Jamestown, used the notion of God's providence to understand their actions as well as to persuade others to leave Britain and join them. When the colonies later separated from Britain to form their own nation, as one would expect, the notion of God's providence also changed. As Nicholas Guyatt has written:

> In fact, American separatism emerged from a shared Atlantic understanding of God's involvement in politics, and history, an understanding that was widely evident in religious and political rhetoric but which started to unravel in the years after 1763 ... While Britons struggled to spin their history into a single thread of providential favor, Americans cultivated the story of their founding and rearranged their history to exclude Britain and to invent a providential purpose.[4]

[4] Nicholas Guyatt, *Providence and the Invention of the United States, 1607–1876* (New York: Cambridge University Press, 2007), p. 93.

Instead of examining the political and economic reasons for the revolution, in other words, the colonists clung to the notion of God's providence as a justification for this event. Not everyone used the idea in this way, of course, but it did continue to influence future events in the new country. A few years after the colonies gained independence, the notion was used to justify a new project – the transfer of freed Africans living in the United States to Africa. In the 1820s, prominent politicians and civic leaders formed the African Colonization Society, which founded the colony of Liberia and transported black Americans who wanted to return to Africa. All of this was seen as part of God's providence. In the words of Lyman Beecher, God "called us to colonize Africa, as significantly as he called our fathers to colonize at Plymouth."[5] The effect of the plan, had it totally succeeded, of course, would have been to make the United States a nation for whites. The politics of removal – of not only Africans but also Native Americans – loomed large and played a major role in the 1830s and 1840s. It seems that God's plan for the United States was a plan only for white Europeans, not for people of color.

As the crisis between the Northern and Southern states deepened in the 1850s, the notion of God's providence was stretched once more. Some people in the South regarded slavery as part of God's providence. That being the case, they argued men should not interfere with God's plan by ending slavery, but should wait until God's intentions become clear. One Southern leader, James Buchanan, argued that slavery was a "divine trust" that had been transmitted to the South by God.[6] Antislavery leaders, on the other hand, argued that slavery was against God's providence, and that the nation must abolish it or would receive God's wrath.[7] Once the Civil War began – and especially when the North was assured of victory – the war itself became part of God's plan to redeem the nation.

In examining the use of providential language to interpret the meaning of the Civil War, Guyatt points out that the focus on God's

---

[5] Quoted in *ibid.*, p. 193.   [6] Quoted in *ibid.*, p. 251.   [7] *Ibid.*, p. 256.

providence prevented many from seeing that freeing the slaves was a moral issue. As a result, the question of how to integrate blacks and whites was not seen as a moral challenge.[8] Instead, whites celebrated the end of slavery as assurance that their special place in God's providence had been restored. Just as Smithian economics created a blind optimism by omitting the story of slavery, the notion of divine providence silenced the moral question of whether it was right to exclude former slaves from the national story.

Frederick Douglass was one of those who articulated this moral mistake. In a speech entitled "The Mission of the War," he said: "It is cowardly to shuffle our responsibilities upon the shoulders of Providence."[9] I think he is right. If we are to develop an effective economics of provision, we need to understand the difference between theological and ethical interpretations of provisioning. There is no better place to explore this difference than in the scriptural story of God's providence: the story of Abraham and his son Isaac in the book of Genesis.

In the story, God tells Abraham to sacrifice his son Isaac as a sign of Abraham's obedience. So Abraham ties up his son, builds an altar, and begins to place his son on it. God intervenes and tells Abraham not to harm his son, since he has shown his obedience. Abraham finds a ram in a nearby thicket and sacrifices the ram as a burnt offering instead of his son. The story ends by Abraham naming the place where this occurred, "God will provide" (Genesis 23: 9–15). It is clear that what God provides – the ram in the thicket that can be used for the offering – is provided as a means for satisfying God's demand for a burnt offering.

What does this story mean for us today? How can we find a meaning that is true to the original context and has relevance for us? Today, for example, most of us would find it insane for a father to say he was going to sacrifice his son because God told him to. And yet, that is the heart of the Abraham story. So how can we find meaning in this

---

[8] *Ibid.*, p. 261.   [9] Quoted in *ibid.*, p. 416.

story for us? Perhaps the nineteenth-century Danish theologian Søren Kierkegaard supplies the best answer. He believed that the right under-standing of the story required what he called "the teleological suspen-sion of the ethical."[10] Since the story so confounded our moral sensibilities, Kierkegaard argued that it was meant to transport us from an ethical response where we think about right and wrong to a religious response where we open ourselves to God. The purpose of the story, in other words, was not to give us something we could apply to our moral life together. Kierkegaard was a theologian who tried to free the notion of "God" from our grasp, so we could be confronted by the divine presence. This makes sense, but it also runs the risk that we never reinstate the ethical that we have suspended for the sake of the theological.

An economics of provision is based on moral and ethical standards and we need to clear away those ideologies that hide these standards, whether it is the invisible hand or God's hand. This does not mean that there is not a place for speaking of God's providence. Today, however, I do not believe we can afford to let the notion of God's providence prevent us from facing the real misery of our providers. People certainly have valid notions of God's involvement in our every-day life, but God's involvement should not blind us to the involvement of the actual persons who provide our families and communities with what they need.

We need to be watchful when theological answers obscure eth-ical questions. At the same time, the theological dimension of provi-dence reminds us that we do not live by bread alone. While our economics of provision should focus on the provision of our well-being or human flourishing, it does not cover the whole story of human existence. Actually, we can never cover the "whole story." What we want is a story that rings true with our experiences – or, perhaps I should say, one that allows our experiences to ring true.

---

[10] Søren Kierkegaard, *Fear and Trembling* (New York: Wilder Publications, 2008).

If we return to the ethical questions about how we should relate to one another, we can begin to look at how human communities actually provide for their members. As we said earlier, the primary location for making provisions for each other is the family. To restore the economic significance of the family, we now turn to Aristotle's view of economics.

ARISTOTLE'S VIEW OF THE FAMILY, THE VILLAGE, AND THE CITY

Perhaps one of the stranger aspects of the Enlightenment's four-stage view of history is its exclusive focus on male individuals. Men were first hunters, then shepherds, farmers, and then traders. Where are the women, the families, and the clans? The legacy of this tradition dominates much of microeconomics today, focusing on individual preferences, individual self-interest, and individual rational choices.

Aristotle begins his "history" with the "elementary associations" of male and female, and master and slave. From these associations come the family or household, which includes children, as well as animals and land to provide for the family's subsistence. The household also included slaves. (Aristotle did not oppose slavery as Smith did; but he also did not deny the role of slavery in the household, which Smith did.) Families or households joined together to form the next unit of association – the village. In the confines of the village different households could barter with one another. The final association was the city or polis, where the masters of the households join together, as Aristotle writes, "for the sake of a good life."[11]

The city, for Aristotle, was the natural end of human associations or communities. Although it existed only after the household and the family, in terms of human purpose it was prior to both because it was what humans naturally aimed for. Only in the city, Aristotle believed, did humans reach their goal of self-sufficiency.

[11] Aristotle, *The Politics of Aristotle*, ed. and trans. Ernest Barker (London, Oxford, and New York: Oxford University Press, 1946), p. 5.

> The man who is isolated – who is unable to share in the benefits of political association, or has no need to share because he is already self-sufficient – is no part of the polis, and must therefore be either a beast or a god.[12]

The emergence of the city or the civic from the family and village associations entails a transformation from associations based on making provisions to an association based on concepts of justice and human happiness. Or, to put it another way, the civic provides the opportunity for human fulfillment because humans speak and think about what is right and wrong, good and evil, and how we should live together. In contrast to the Smithian perspective, which tries to wall off the economy from government, Aristotle places the economic inside the political. The economic is a part of the larger whole of civic life. The civic, in other words, becomes a condition for the development of the economic. A central aspect of the economic is what Aristotle calls the art of acquisition.

ARISTOTLE'S "ART OF ACQUISITION"

At one level, the art of acquisition is simply getting the things necessary for running the household. The household must have the provisions it needs. Another aspect of this art, however, goes beyond making household provisions. It acquires things to make exchanges. Aristotle gives the following example:

> We can take a shoe as an example. It can be used both for wearing and for exchange. Both of these uses are uses of the shoe as such. Even the man who exchanges the shoe, in return for money or food, with a person who needs the article, is using the shoe as a shoe; but since the shoe has not been made for the purpose of being exchanged, the use which he is making of it is not its proper and peculiar use. The same is true for all other articles of property.[13]

---

[12] *Ibid.*, p. 6.   [13] *Ibid.*, p. 23.

So the shoe can either be used to provide someone foot protection or it can be treated as property that can be traded. In Aristotle's vocabulary, the distinction is between a property's "use value" and "exchange value." Its use value, for him, is its natural or proper function, while its exchange value, as he says, is not necessary.

Aristotle was aware, of course, that things were made not only for members of the household, but also for members of the village and beyond. Early trade among different households in the village would have been done mostly through barter. As people began to exchange goods beyond the village, however, money was instituted as a medium of exchange. (This view of money will be addressed in future chapters.) For the most part, Aristotle saw money as a commodity that could be used to measure the worth or value of other commodities. In time, he suggests, money took on a second meaning. It became something to accumulate. People acquired money both to make exchanges for the household and to accumulate money. In the first instance, wealth would measure the quality of household provisions; in the second, wealth measured the amount of money. As Scott Meikle points out, for Aristotle, true wealth consists in the things one has that are useful for the household, not in the accumulation of property or money.[14] Wealth, in other words, resides in the making of provisions, not in the accumulation of property.

Aristotle has given us a place to begin our new narrative – the formation of human families. And he has identified an ideal to move toward – the emergence of civil society. Even though many of his notions of household management begin with classical patriarchal assumptions and are embedded in an economics of property, his connection between the family and economics does have significance for us. True, he does not see household slaves or women as providers. For him, economics (household management) includes making provisions for the family, but the members of the family are not seen as providers. Here, as in most of Western culture, the male is seen as superior to

[14] Scott Meikle, *Aristotle's Economic Thought* (Oxford: Clarendon Press, 1997), p. 48.

women and slaves, so it would be hard to see women and slaves as the key providers of the male's household. Just as we need to overcome the suspension of the ethical by looking beyond the notion of God's providence, we need to overcome the blindness in patriarchal cultures by recognizing all members who actually provide for the household. The construction of a narrative for an economics of provision in the next chapter will begin with the family, as Aristotle suggests, but it will recognize and honor all providers, which includes women as much as men.

How easy it is to favor the abstract or the metaphorical over the concrete and the actual. If we can say that things happen as they do just because (you can add whatever abstraction you want), then we have escaped the work of considering if things could have been otherwise. At the very bottom of the idea of human freedom is this possibility: the possibility that things could have been otherwise. As Aristotle said, we only deliberate about what could be different. Although the Enlightenment taught us much about individual freedom, we have also inherited from Smithian economics and eighteenth-century theology a kind of fatalism that needs to be suspended, even discarded, so we can become fully engaged in the work of organizing an economy that is sustainable and just.

4 Making provisions in a dangerous world

The usefulness of a story or narrative is that it not only makes sense out of the past, but also serves as a framework for moving into the future. The Enlightenment story of the four stages of history performed these functions quite well until recently, at least for the storytellers. As long as this story is not questioned, it appears as the one true story. Today, however, we live in a pluralistic society where there are multiple stories and multiple perspectives of the world. I continually observe some of these differences in my classes when I ask students to write a one-page story of the United States. In most classes, some students tell a story of freedom – how the Puritans came to the Americas to enjoy religious freedom. Others tell the war story, which continues to be a popular narrative of the United States. It involves a list of the wars, from the Revolutionary War through the Civil War to World War One and Two and finally to the Vietnam and Iraq wars. Depending on who is in the class, we might also hear the story of the destruction of Native American culture and land, or the story of slavery, or the story of women struggling for equal rights, and so on. What is fascinating is that all these stories are true, and yet the official story seldom has room for all of them. Just as the Scottish Enlightenment story of the four stages of human history prevented the inclusion of slaves in the fourth stage, most stories tell some of the truth but not the whole truth.

No one story about economic development will tell the whole truth. Still, I think we should talk about what we know. Since every story ends up serving some purposes and not others, we need to be clear about the purpose of the story behind an economics of provision, which is quite simply to enable the creation of a just and sustainable economy.

We begin with the assumption that all human communities must do three essential things: provide for themselves, protect themselves, and find ways to express the meaning of their life together. Like other primates, early human communities must have provided for and protected one another, or they would not have survived. Early on, and especially with the development of language, our ancestors would have found ways to identify the significance of their lives through gesture, ritual, and story. Humans were participants in a much larger drama than just their human families and communities. Just as there was a need to provide and to protect, there was a need to identify the meaning of the world in which they lived. At some time, after humans gained the capacity to speak and reflect, they began to ask questions. As far as we know, no other primate asks questions, especially questions about the meaning of things. "Why did this happen?" "Why do we do it this way?" "Why is there suffering?" We are not humans because we can ask why, but we would be a different kind of animal if we could not. At the heart of this question lies the larger search for purpose. "What is the purpose of doing this or that?" The notion of purpose must be added to the activities of provide and protect if we are to understand the full meaning of managing a household – the full meaning of economics.

Managing a household does not take place in isolation. Early human communities saw themselves as a part of nature, not apart from nature. The natural world was a source of abundance and scarcity, and it could be just as fickle as any person in granting gifts or making demands. The economy of early communities always belonged to a natural world, as Figure 4.1 indicates.

Provide, protect, and purpose parallels the three terms that Kenneth Boulding used in analyzing the organization of systems and power relations. Boulding writes that all human systems have what he calls "three faces of power," which he calls the powers of making exchanges, giving treats, and promoting integration.[1] Integration refers to common meanings or beliefs that unite communities (creating

[1] Kenneth E. Boulding, *Three Faces of Power* (Newbury Park, CA: Sage, 1989)

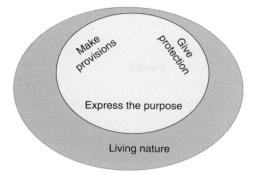

FIGURE 4.1 The economy of human communities

purpose), threat refers to laws or rules that ensure punishment if violated (giving protection), and exchange refers to incentive systems that provide good consequences for particular behaviors (making provisions). All human systems, he claims, will have some balance of these three faces of power. We will look at different versions of this triad throughout the following chapters, but here we want to use them to help us to understand the basic dynamics of early human communities.

Recent anthropological research supports this triad and offers an alternative to the Scottish Enlightenment view of the first, or savage, stage of human history. It now appears that hunting was not the earliest activity of human communities. We were not the hunters, but the hunted. Anthropologists Donna Hart and Robert Sussman have offered persuasive arguments based on empirical data that our earliest ancestors were not aggressive hunters, but rather were gatherers and perhaps scavengers, who spent much of their energy protecting themselves from predators.

> Were our ancestors gentle savages or bloodthirsty brutes? They were social animals; they were primates; they were complex beings in their own right who were not necessarily headed in a foreordained direction. They were trying to adapt to their environment and reproduce successfully. Most primate societies and individuals exhibit cooperation as a social tool, not aggression. Success is not

synonymous with brutality; it comes through finesse and friendship.[2]

From Hart and Sussman's portrait of our ancestors, we can begin to tell a story that shows provisioning as a primary process of human systems. The story begins with our ancestors acting much like other primates. But they were different because they had moved to the edge of the forests, where they became bipedal (walking on two legs) and began to speak (probably at first to warn family members of approaching predators). As one would suspect, they spent most of their time making provisions for their everyday life, and watching out to make sure they were not someone's dinner.

One can imagine that, in the process of securing provisions, some family members would protect the more vulnerable, such as infants, small children, the elderly, and the incapacitated. Perhaps males took on this role, since they were probably larger and were not as necessary for making provisions. This would explain the male propensity to protect. It would also give us a new way of seeing male aggression as a response to a threat and motivated by fear. In fact, if danger was a constant, primal concern for human communities, then male aggressive behavior might be more correctly understood as arising from insecurity rather than from an instinct to conquer or control. This is significant because our assumptions about our ancestors seem to have a strong influence on our ideas about human nature. In the picture we are drawing, what needed protection were the providers and the community provisions, rather than anyone's property.

Small human communities may have lived for thousands of year at this stage of gathering food, making provisions for one another, and protecting each other. With the development of language, we can assume that they added a third element to their patterns of communication: a way of naming and verbally participating in the events they were experiencing. This third element – the element of

---

[2] Donna Hart and Robert W. Sussman, *Man the Hunted: Primates, Predators, and Human Evolution* (New York: Westview Press, 2005), p. 117.

language – made all the difference in the world. Language actually created the world in the sense that now human communities could construct a world through song, ritual, and narrative. It allowed them to create a purpose for things. With language, human communities could understand and reflect on their own practices as never before.

A good case study for our exploration of these different dimensions of primitive cultures are the Ohlone Indians, who lived in the San Francisco Bay area for about 10,000 years before the arrival of Europeans. Because of the abundance of plants, animals, and fish, they remained a hunter/gatherer society. In Malcolm Margolin's study of the Ohlone Indians, he describes their daily life as filled with supernatural powers and spirits. Margolin writes:

> To pass beyond ordinary consciousness and cultivate a special relationship with one or more of the animal-gods was a more or less constant activity for the Ohlones, as it was for other California Indians. Virtually all people (not merely shamans) needed at least some spiritual help to defend themselves against enemies, protect themselves on strange trails, avoid poisons, win at gambling, have successful love adventures, avoid rattlesnake bites, cure minor ailments, hunt and fish well, or live a long life.[3]

The world of early human communities, in other words, was a world of multiple meanings and levels of reality. It was a world of spirits who played multiple roles in the communities' life. Again, Margolin's description of the Ohlones is instructive:

> The Ohlones often sought out the animal-gods as healers or advisors, but at the same time they were also deeply afraid of them. For these were still the animal-gods of the myths: amoral, unpredictable, greedy, irritable, tricky and very magical. Cultivating such helpers was a complicated, exasperating, and often dangerous undertaking.[4]

---

[3] Malcolm Margolin, *The Ohlone Way: Indian Life in the San Francisco-Monterey Bay Area* (Berkeley, CA: Heyday Books, 1978), p. 137.
[4] *Ibid.*, pp. 138–139.

For the Ohlone, in other words, the world was a fearful and dangerous place. They were not the aggressive hunters or savage type that fits with the economics of property. Rather they were a careful and mindful people who sought help to survive in a world they did not control. They were gatherers as well as hunters, which meant that some of the group brought provisions for others. In his study of early tribal societies, Karl Polanyi has suggested that there were two processes of sharing provisions that predated the household – reciprocity and redistribution.[5] (As we shall see later, these became norms for civil society.) Margolin's description of the Ohlone hunter sharing his kill with his community is a good example of both norms:

> When a man killed a deer, for example, he did not bring the meat home, dry it, and store it for personal use. Acquisition was not an Ohlone's idea of wealth or security. Instead the hunter kept very little, perhaps even none of the meat, but rather distributed it along very formal lines to family and community. The people in turn gave him great honor. The women treated him with respect, the men listened to his advice in the sweathouse, and everyone praised him as a good hunter and a generous, proper man.[6]

In this description, we first see the redistribution of the meat to family and community, and then reciprocity that returns good for good, offering respect and recognition of the hunter as a "generous, proper man."

Although reciprocity belongs to the activity of providing, it also relates to the third community activity of expressing purpose. Reciprocity is a moral relationship between persons rather than an impersonal relationship between commodities. It exists in communities that see their activities as belonging to a larger whole or purpose. We can see this in Margolin's description of the Ohlone life during the harvesting of oak acorns, which he calls "the staff of life" for the community.

---

[5] Karl Polanyi, *The Great Transformation: The Political and Economic Origins of Our Time* (Boston, MA: Beacon Press, 1944), p. 49.
[6] Margolin, *The Ohlone Way*, p. 89.

Throughout the year the people held various feasts, festivals, and religious dances, many of them tied to the biological rhythms of the oak trees. Time itself was measured by the oaks. The acorn harvest marked the beginning of the new year. Winter was spoken of as so many months (moons) after the acorn harvest, summer as so many months before the next acorn harvest. The rhythms of the oak trees marked the passage of the year and defined the rhythms of Ohlone life.[7]

As these early human families felt and reflected on their interactions, they would experience their support for each other as worthwhile and meaningful. These experiences of and reflections on the meaning of their communal life would motivate them to provide for and protect each other. The purpose of providing and protecting, in other words, was grounded in their experiences of caring for each other. It was this way of life that led Margolin to conclude that the key virtue of the Ohlones – and I think of many early peoples – was generosity.[8]

This world was certainly not a perfect world. In some ways it was desperate. Survival could never be taken for granted. There was certainly much to worry about and much to manage. On the one hand, the Ohlone were very generous and hospitable to others. On the other hand, they were also deeply suspicious. Margolin writes of this tension:

> Thus the relationship between the different tribelets was marked by the strongest of attractions and at the same time the strongest of repulsions. The people were generous and hospitable, yet underneath they often seethed with suspicions. Their dislike of each other kept the Ohlones apart: forty or so independent tribelets, speaking eight to twelve different languages. Yet their intimate family, trading, and other economic ties kept their dislike in check.[9]

Not so different from human relationships today, especially when we encounter strangers. At the same time, we must admit that a major

[7] *Ibid.*, p. 41.   [8] *Ibid.*, p. 89.   [9] *Ibid.*, p. 101.

transformation of human relationships separates us from this early community of reciprocity and redistribution. We don't know exactly how the transformation happened, but we know its results. They are visible in Aristotle's description of household management. By the time of Aristotle, men are the masters and owners as well as the protectors and providers, and the focus on making provisions has been overshadowed by the drive to accumulate property. Maybe this happened when human societies became dependent on hunting and men became more necessary as providers for the group. The Ohlone Indians are especially interesting here because they were both hunters and gatherers. The acorn harvest was as central to their life as the game that the hunters brought home. Both men and women were providers, but men were the traders with other tribes. As trading developed, one can imagine that the dominance of men increased. This would have been further promoted when the purpose of trading changed from the making of provisions to the accumulation of property.

We may not know all the dynamics involved in these early transitions, but the results are clear. Women became the property of men and the trading of women – especially daughters who were attached to dowries – became a means to accumulate property. These transactions were embedded in rituals and stories – language can both reveal and conceal the truth – but in the end they were structures of inequality and domination, which continue to this day in spite of the many movements for equal rights for women. As Michelle Goldberg has recently documented, no country is not involved in such struggles today.[10] Any story of provisioning worth telling today must take these struggles into account and include them in the framework of moving toward a just and sustainable economy. Family relationships must be recognized as subject to the same requirements for morally equal relationships as any other human relationships. Privacy, in other words, should not be allowed to serve as a cover for domination. This

---

[10] Michelle Goldberg, *The Means of Reproduction: Sex, Power, and the Future of the World* (New York: The Penguin Press, 2009).

brings us to the next stage of our story – the rise of the civic sphere. It will eventually become the sphere where all people – women, children, and men – are seen as global citizens with equal civic rights.

THE EMERGENCE OF THE CIVIC SPHERE

Almost by definition, human families and small clans were able to provide for themselves or they would not have survived. These families may have joined together in villages, as Aristotle suggests, but even then they probably remained in family clans. When they encountered other families, however, the story becomes much more complicated. In general, when different groups face one another, they can respond in one of four ways: They can withdraw, give, take, or trade.

When we remember the insecurity of our earliest ancestors, it would not be surprising if they developed patterns of withdrawing. At the same time, the standard norms of reciprocity and generosity among members of the same tribe may have been extended to strangers. Hospitality was a key virtue of many traditional tribes. When the Native American tribes encountered European explorers, for example, the Europeans were often treated as guests. They received things to make them feel welcome. The Europeans, on the other hand, acted much more like invaders, taking rather than giving.

The response of taking is seen as normal by many who exist within the tradition of the economics of property. In his recent book on why some nations are wealthy and some are poor, David S. Landes writes about the taking by Europeans in the new world. "Where one group is strong enough to push another around and stands to gain by it, it will do so. Even if the state would abstain from aggression, companies and individuals will not wait for permission. Rather, they will act in their own interest, dragging others along, including the state."[11] This statement seems to assume that humans are naturally aggressive and exploitive. I hope our story of provisions has provided a more

---

[11] David S. Landes, *The Wealth and Poverty of Nations: Why Some Are So Rich and Some So Poor* (New York: W. W. Norton & Company, 1999), p. 6.

reasonable assumption. Whether one group pushes another around, it seems to me, depends not only on their relative strength, but also on their beliefs. Just as Europeans used the four stages of history to justify their treatment of Americans and Africans, one could imagine that a different story would engender different treatment. In other words, it is not only the desire for gain, but also the stories we live in, that determine whether one group takes from another group or not.

An alternative to taking, of course, is trading. This fourth possibility requires that both sides have an interest in making a good deal, and that there exists the possibility of each side improving its situation – of increasing their provisions for themselves and their families. The reciprocity practiced within the Ohlone clans would now need to be extended to relationships between different people. Whether such situations are sustainable, of course, depends not only on people's understanding of one another, but also on the trust that develops between them – a trust that eventually is treated as valuable not merely because of its utility, but also because of its intrinsic worth.

Trading with strangers, when it is free from compulsion, requires that the parties trust one another. One can imagine that such trust developed from trading experiences, because without it continual trading would have been impossible. In the West, at least, trading associations developed with the rise of cities, and what held them together was common membership of the city, or citizenship. This move from the family and village to the city is recorded in Aristotle's *Politics*, in which he argues that the civic sphere, while last to develop, was first in importance because it allowed the complete flourishing of humans.[12]

If we take the civic sphere as the basis for exchanges or market transactions and as the location for conversations about human flourishing, then we can envision a new formulation of the three essential tasks of human communities – to provide, protect, and find a worthwhile purpose. In the economy of cities, the task of creating a worthwhile purpose emerges as civic deliberation about how to live together,

---

[12] Aristotle, *The Politics*, p. 2.

FIGURE 4.2 The economy of cities

the task of protecting providers is transformed into the enactment of laws, and the task of making provisions becomes the work of organizing markets. All this occurs, as before, in the living biosphere (see Figure 4.2).

The story of provisioning has one similarity with the Enlightenment story of property relations. Both tell of the transition from tribal communities to civic communities. They are also very different. The Enlightenment story ignores the losses of the transition to modern economics, such as the loss of a living relationship with nature and the loss of reciprocal relationships with providers. The Enlightenment story concludes with the commercial dominating the civic instead of the civic providing the context for the commercial. The story of provisions includes women and men who work together to provide, protect, and create meaning for their families and communities instead of focusing on the behavior of abstracted self-interested individuals. There are more differences that will become apparent as we continue to explore all the characteristics of a civic economics of provision.

It is not really necessary to believe in the story of provisioning. What is necessary is for us to have some other place to ground our ideas than in the Enlightenment story of the emergence of property and property relations. This is one alternative; perhaps there are others. The point, which will be explored in the next chapter, is to have the capacity to replace property relations with civic relations as the foundation for economic activity.

Part II The civic option

5   From property relations to civic relations

Switching from the language of an economics of property to the language of an economics of provision is an essential step in civilizing the economy, but it is not enough. We also must replace the economy's current foundation of property relations with a new foundation of civic relations. To do that, we need to develop an adequate understanding of the civic.

The following chapters explore the civic meaning of property, the relationship between the civic, the commercial, and the social, the civic norm of reciprocity, and civic competition. These explorations should give us a broad enough view of the civic to understand how it might function as the foundation for a just and sustainable economy. We will be building on what we have already said about the civic sphere, which can be summarized as shown in Figure 5.1.

As we outline the move to a civic view of the economy, it will become clear that some changes will be more difficult than others. Many conversations about economic options seem to be limited to the alternatives of capitalism or socialism. Most economies, of course, contain a mixture of the two, but this mixture seldom is taken seriously. Too often, the terms are simply used as trigger words to smear an opposing point of view. This book's approach is civic, instead of socialist. It imagines the economy in the hands of citizens; not in the hands of invisible forces that protect either privileged groups or government bureaucracies. A civilized economy is not one in which some groups control other groups, but one in which all groups participate in the various processes of developing an economic order. A civilized economy does not require the end of property rights or the denial of ownership. It does require that we recognize the civic realm that already underlies our current economy and that we restore its character as the foundation for human flourishing.

> The civic sphere is:
>
> • beyond relationships of family and clans;
>
> • a foundation of trust for exchanges among strangers;
>
> • a location for ongoing conversations about how members of cities (citizens) should organize their life together.

FIGURE 5.1 The civic sphere

THE CIVIC ASSUMPTION BEHIND PROPERTY RELATIONS

In the Smithian theory of economics, the value of something depends on how much money it can fetch in the market. Its value, in other words, is known only when it becomes a commodity or property. When something – even something as fundamental to life as water – becomes scarce, this tradition of economics says that we should treat it as a commodity. What does that mean? It means that someone can own that commodity, and can sell it to those who need it. If water were really scarce, then it would be very valuable. It would fetch an even higher price. The price would allow us to know the true value of water and not to waste a drop. What more could you want?

What happens then to those who cannot afford to pay the price? If our relationships with water are completely based on price, then those without water and without any property to exchange for water will get none. They will die of thirst. Do ownership economists really support the death penalty for those without property? I doubt it. My guess is that property advocates take for granted that governments will prevent people from dying of thirst. Behind the talk of property relations, in other words, lies a hidden assumption that civic relations would prevent society from falling into chaos. So, maybe the journey from property relations to civic relations is not such a long one after all. We may just need to recognize the invisible civic sphere that property advocates would appear to tacitly acknowledge. In fact, these civic aspects of markets have a much longer history than one might imagine. Before the advent of the ideology of price-based market relations, traditional communal rights guided how people traded with each other. They participated in what could be called communal markets.

COMMUNAL MARKETS

Prior to the emergence of capitalism in the West, most British markets were local and dominated by men and women who brought surpluses from their households to swap with others. Here is an example of the civic rules of a market in Wiltshire, England, in 1564:

1. Before the market starts the sellers of grain are to agree with the local justices what the price should be.
2. No transactions may take place before 9 a.m. when a bell will be tolled 20 times.
3. When the market opens, purchases must be for the customer's own use and be limited to 2 bushels of grain.
4. After 11 a.m. (when the bell is again tolled 20 times), grain may be bought by those who will resell it (eg. bakers, brewers, and badgers).
5. Those buying the grain to resell must be licensed by a Justice of the Peace.
6. Grain may only be bought on market day.
7. No person may buy grain in the market if she has sufficient of her own.[1]

What a contrast with commercial markets today where prices are determined by supply and demand – at least in theory. In traditional communal markets, there were few if any middlemen. People traded directly with each other. Only with the growth of cities and transportation did traders and merchants replace the household members as the dominant actors in market transactions. In Smith's account of the market, we read nothing about families or households, but a lot about merchants. As he writes: "Every man thus lives by exchanging, or

[1] Mark Overton, *Agricultural Revolution in England: The Transformation of the Agrarian Economy 1500–1850* (Cambridge: Cambridge University Press, 1996), pp. 135–136.

becomes in some measure a merchant, and the society itself grows to be what is properly a commercial society."[2] It may well have been the tobacco merchants of Glasgow who served as a model for his economic theory. His writing certainly shows how far his world was from the early communal markets.

Karl Polanyi called this shift from a communal market to a commercial market the "great transformation" – a transformation that we are still living with today.[3] Central to the transformation were the British enclosure enactments that radically changed the use of land and the rights of village peasants. These enclosures changed basic relationships not only between people and land, but also between masters and servants.

ENCLOSURES AND COMMON RIGHTS

For Smith, there are three sources of wealth: labor, rent, and stock (or money). Parallel to these are three sorts of people: people who live by wages, by rent, or by profit. "These are the three great, original and constituent orders of every civilized society, from whose revenue that of every other order is ultimately derived."[4] This order of society only emerged in the eighteenth century, or, perhaps more accurately, it was still emerging in the eighteenth century, at least in Britain, and its emergence was largely caused by the enclosure of land and the abolition of common rights.

"Common rights" described those rights enjoyed by the commoners or peasants. They included the right to access the fields and forests around villages for grazing livestock, gleaning leftover grain, and gathering fodder for animals, as well as the right to wood and other materials for fuel. With these rights, many commoners (some owning land themselves, others belonging to villages, and some landless) were able to provide for their families, by sharing land with others and taking on extra work when they needed to.[5] The enclosure enactments

---

[2] Smith, *Wealth of Nations*, p. 24.   [3] Polanyi, *The Great Transformation*.
[4] Smith, *Wealth of Nations*, p. 285.
[5] J. M. Neeson, *Commoners: Common Right, Enclosure and Social Change in England, 1700–1820* (Cambridge: Cambridge University Press, 1993), p. 42.

resulted in the loss of these rights and many commoners became dependent on wages. They became laborers.

The enclosures of the commons were a series of government policies that occurred primarily between the fifteenth and the eighteenth centuries. They resulted in the exclusive use of the land by the owner. It became his private property. Many of the commoners who had had access to the land now could not survive in their villages and had to move to cities for work or immigrate to the colonies. So when Smith writes that labor was a primary source of wealth, we need to remember this: that many of these laborers may have been quite satisfied as commoners, and they may have had no choice but to leave their villages to work in the industrial mills. Just as we learn nothing from Smith about the slaves that produced tobacco for the Glasgow merchants, we learn very little about the origin of the working class that in his theory was the primary source of wealth. In any case, the enclosures allowed land and labor to be treated as property that could be bought and sold in the market. Their value was determined, at least in theory, by supply and demand.

The movement into capitalism, thus, can be seen as a movement from the notion of common rights to the notion of private rights. This may sound benign until we remember that the movement represented a life-changing loss for commoners and a huge boon for those who held property – the landowners. These landowners became part of "civil society," which the early Enlightenment defined as a refined way of living. But civil society included only owners of property. The workers were seen as servants of masters, not as citizens. This relationship of master and servant was based on the property rights of the master. The servant lost the common rights that allowed an independence from living on wages and the master gained an exclusive right to control property. Most of contemporary business law, at least in the United States, continues to be based, for the most part, on this master/servant relationship.

The extension of civic and human rights to workers, women, and even children during the twentieth century has made this property-based relationship between employees and employers seem out of place in democratic societies. Workers, like managers, are citizens and they should not be required to leave their civic rights or expectations at the workplace door. Internationally, the rights of workers have been recognized for a long time. In the United Nations Declaration of Human Rights, for example, one reads the following:

1. Everyone has a right to work, to free choice of employment, to just and favorable conditions of work and to protection against unemployment.
2. Everyone, without any discrimination, has a right to equal pay for equal work.
3. Everyone who works has the right to just and favorable remuneration insuring for himself and his family an existence worthy of human dignity, and supplemented, if necessary, by other means of social protection.
4. Everyone has the right to form and to join trade unions for the protection of his interests.[6]

These human rights are based on the dignity of the person, not on whether the person has property to sell for wages. This does not mean that market interactions have no effect on employment opportunities. But it does mean that market interactions should originate from and respect civic norms. Our focus on the civic rights of workers also gives us a new understanding of the meaning of property. It too belongs to a civic context.

THE MEANING OF PROPERTY

What effect does an economics of provision have on property? For the most part, the only change is that we can more easily recognize the actual character of property in modern societies. Contrary to popular opinion, property is not an economic institution, but a political one. As the Peruvian economist Hernando DeSoto has pointed out, people may

---

[6] W. Laqueur and B. Rubin, *The Human Rights Reader* (New York: New American Library, 1979), p. 200.

have assets, but if they do not have a legal title to them, these assets will not count as property.[7] DeSoto has tried to get governments in South America to give property titles to people living in homes they have built on the edges of cities so they could use them as collateral for obtaining credit. As he points out: Without a legal title, one is without property rights.

DeSoto's observation actually contradicts one of the basic tenets of traditional capitalism – private property. Property is essentially public. It would not exist without laws and law enforcement. Membership in the legal community, in other words, is the precondition for ownership of property. Whereas the theory of an economics of property holds that ownership is prior to civic membership, an economics of provision acknowledges the reality that even more fundamental than private ownership is civic membership.

Now one might worry that if we admit that property is actually a political institution, the government might try to tell me what I can do with my property. Actually, this does happen. Perhaps the biggest government take-away of property in the United States occurred during the Civil War. In an 1860 speech, Abraham Lincoln estimated the value of the slave population in the United States as not less than $2,000,000,000.[8] The war was a "civil" war because, in part, it was between citizens about property rights. Contests among citizens about property rights will continue as long as our democracy exists. In the political judgment of most people, giving and protecting some property rights is beneficial to society. The question is really about the meaning of property, not its elimination. To explore this question, we can think about the different aspects of a dwelling.

WHAT IS A DWELLING?

The dwelling in which a family lives can be considered a home, a house, or a piece of real estate. As a home, it is a place where families

---

[7] Hernando DeSoto, *The Mystery of Capital: Why Capitalism Triumphs in the West and Fails Everywhere Else* (New York: Basic Books, 2000), p. 157.

[8] Wright, *Slavery and American Economic Development*, p. 72.

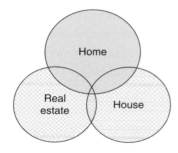

FIGURE 5.2 A dwelling

provide for one another. As a house, it was built from natural and technological resources, provides shelter and enclosure, may be pleasing to the eye, uses energy, and emits wastes. It belongs to a natural and urban environment. As real estate, it can be sold or used as collateral for credit. An economics of property ignores the making of provisions in the home and the house's relationship to the natural and urban environment. It focuses on the real estate aspect alone. An economics of provision, on the other hand, recognizes all the meanings and puts the property aspect in its rightful place. So, when we think of economics as household management, it needs to include at least the three aspects shown in Figure 5.2.

All three aspects of any dwelling belong to larger units or systems. The home belongs to extended families or clans, to social systems, and to the civic realm. The house belongs to various ecosystems, such as the water cycle or the carbon cycle. And the house as real estate belongs to both political and market systems.

These various aspects of a dwelling resonate well with my experiences on our family farm in Nebraska. My parents owned the farm. They had a title to it. They farmed the land to make a living, and to provide a home for the family. We also heard stories about the land. How it had been part of the Great Plains, with buffalo herds larger than our farm. How the sod was broken and wheat was planted. We also participated in our family's efforts to drill a well and begin to irrigate the land, making it more productive and us wealthier, or at least so we thought. At the time we did not talk about the finite resources of the underground aquifer that contained the water we used. Today, it is 70 percent empty and farmers in the Great Plains states may soon have to return to dry farming.

If we can distinguish between a farm and the land, we can see a difference between property and a living provider. We are still learning what this means. My family had a legal right to use the water, to fertilize the land, to use genetically engineered seeds, and to keep others off our property. We lived, for the most part, within the parameters of an economics of property. Today, given the shrinking amount of underground water, given our knowledge of the serious health effects of using pesticides and fertilizers, and given the moral responsibility to preserve the fecundity of the land for future generations, we need to see the land as more than property. It is a living provider that needs protection from abuse. It also needs farmers to gather its provisions for all of us. To give a property title to the farmer gives the "owner" the right to make a living and to bring the farm's produce to market. But it does not give the farmer the right to destroy the land for future generations. Perhaps the best way to think about this is to see property as a concession.

PROPERTY AS A CONCESSION

The *American Heritage Dictionary* defines a concession as "A grant of a tract of land made by a government or other controlling authority in return for stipulated services or a promise that the land will be used for a specific purpose." The word can also refer to a business itself as in "an ice-cream concession in the subway system."[9] The term has a varied history. During the colonial period, it designated land that a strong nation had a weaker nation concede for its use. There are remnants of this tradition in the Shanghai districts of the "French Concession" or the "British Concession." The only similar concession existing today is the US presence in Guantanamo Bay on the island of Cuba. If we look

---

[9] *The American Heritage Dictionary of the English Language,* third edition (Boston: Houghton Mifflin Company, 1962), p. 391.

beyond colonization, and to a suitable notion of concession for an economics of provision, an "ice-cream concession" in a public park serves as a good model. This business occupies public or civic space to perform a specific service. The ice-cream concession could not change into a hotel without permission from the park commission.

In a similar vein, farmers could see their "ownership" as a concession to use the land for a specific purpose. And who would give the concession? The government. And in a democracy, it would be the people as represented by their government – the citizens. Membership in the city or the civic realm would be the necessary condition for gaining the right to property, to ownership. We will return to the notion of concession in Chapter 10 on the meaning of land.

This civic framework could also apply to the property of other businesses. Of the several aspects of a modern corporation, one is that it can be bought and sold. It is property. People who "own" the property, however, own it only because they have title to it, and, as we said before, a property title is a political institution. Ownership can be seen as a concession, which gives the owners the rights of ownership and the responsibilities of belonging to the civic realm. The implications of this will become apparent later when we explore the idea that a corporation has civic obligations.

If property rights are essentially political rights and property ownership is derived from civic membership, then it does seem possible to place our feet on a civic foundation for our reflections on an economics of provision. Whether there are good reasons for doing so and how we might organize such an economy are the topics of the following chapters.

6   Society, civil society, and the market

The civic sphere is not a stranger to our current economy. As we have seen, the civic undergirds market transactions, serves as the foundation for correcting market failures, and provides a platform for granting property rights. Still, we have not recognized its function as a foundation for providing, protecting, and creating a worthwhile purpose for human communities. To do so, we need to gain a fuller understanding of the social, civil society, and the market. This chapter highlights the character of the civic by contrasting it with the commercial, as well as with the social, and then develops the notion of civil society as our ongoing civic conversations about how we should live together.

THE CIVIC AND THE COMMERCIAL

How should we view the civic and the commercial? Are they similar or quite different? The legacy of Enlightenment economics views them as quite similar, if not identical. Aristotle, on the other hand, presents them as quite different. Let us examine both viewpoints and see which one seems more useful today.

Remember the four stages of history posited by many writers of the Scottish Enlightenment? The final stage of development – the commercial stage – was also the stage of the civic or civil society. Adam Smith and most other Enlightenment scholars consider this identification of the commercial with the civic as a natural development. But at least one of Smith's friends, Adam Ferguson, had some serious misgivings. Ferguson worried that uniting the commercial and the civic would result in replacing the public spirit of civic sacrifice with the private interest in individual gain. In his book *An Essay on the History of Civil Society* (1767), Ferguson draws a sharp contrast between the political civic and the commercial civic. He writes:

> To the ancient Greek, or the Roman, the individual is nothing, and
> the public every thing. To the modern, in too many nations of
> Europe, the individual is every thing, and the public nothing.[1]

The focus on individual gain was not Ferguson's only worry. He was
even more worried about the withering of the classical civic spirit of
heroic sacrifice and its replacement by the more mundane virtues of
the merchant. With the rise of the commercial, Ferguson believed that
something was lost in what we might call the domestication of the
civic.

> The commercial and lucrative arts may continue to prosper, but
> they gain an ascendant to the expense of other pursuits. The desire of
> profit stifles the love of perfection. Interest cools the imagination,
> and hardens the heart; and, recommending employments in
> proportion as they are lucrative, and certain in their gains, it drives
> ingenuity, and ambition itself, to the counter and the workshop.[2]

At the same time, as a member of the Scottish Enlightenment,
Ferguson recognized that the change in the civic represented an
improvement:

> The trader, in rude ages, is short-sighted, fraudulent, and mercenary;
> but in the progress and advanced state of his art, his views are
> enlarged, his maxims are established: he becomes punctual, liberal,
> faithful, and enterprising; and in the period of general corruption, he
> alone has every virtue, except the force to defend his acquisitions.
> He needs no aid from the state, but its protection; and is often in
> himself its more intelligent and respectable member.[3]

The improvement in manners or etiquette was the new meaning of the
civic. To be civilized was to be tolerant. What could be wrong with the
idea that commercial relations might increase tolerance? Nothing in

---

[1] Adam Ferguson, *An Essay on the History of Civil Society*, ed. Fania Oz-Salzberger
(Cambridge: Cambridge University Press, 2006), p. 57.
[2] *Ibid.*, p. 206.   [3] *Ibid.*, p. 138.

itself. As we know, however, the Enlightenment foundation for this new etiquette was based on turning a blind eye to the plight of slaves and others who provided the means for this civility. What was civic, in other words, was only the social world of enjoying provisions, not the social world of the providers.

Seeing the commercial as civic may have been an attempt, as Richard Boyd has argued, to overcome what commercial society considered to be "uncivil groups."[4] After the religious wars of the seventeenth century in Europe, one could certainly understand the desire to find a stage for human interaction that was not dependent on religious conviction. Still, what a mind-boggling world where religious fanaticism is seen as uncivil, but slavery is not. In fact, slave owners, and those whose wealth depended on slaves, saw themselves as quite civilized. They represented a refined and polite society. Michael Warner, in his *The Letters of the Republic*, writes the following about the meaning of *polite* for the eighteenth-century gentlemen:

> The power of the term – especially for Americans, for whom it legitimated trade rather than nobility – came in part from its ability to establish two things at once: a norm of subjectivity, since it implies a special kind of experience and a set of prescribed behaviors to go with it; and a way of thinking about commerce, such that the normal interaction of trade will be seen to have a meliorative, civilizing outcome.[5]

Why not be polite? For property owners, who enjoyed the protection of the law, access to government, and the possibility to engage in trade with other property owners, politeness would indeed seem to be the right stance within their social group. Is not this part of the legacy of Adam Smith's omission of the real providers of wealth? If we are to

---

[4] Richard Boyd, *Uncivil Society: The Perils of Pluralism and the Making of Modern Liberalism* (Lanham, MD: Lexington Books, 2004), p. 137.

[5] Michael Warner, *The Letters of the Republic: Publication and the Public Sphere in Eighteenth-Century America* (Cambridge, MA: Harvard University Press, 1990), p. 132.

have an integrative economy we need an integrative civic sphere. Limiting the civic to the commercial realm seems not only to deny the status of citizen to those who are not property owners, but also to limit the goals of the good life to the goals of commerce. In Aristotle's writings, we find a much different view of the civic and a different view of the civic and the commercial.

ARISTOTLE'S NOTION OF THE CIVIC

As we already know, Aristotle believed that the city or civic emerged from the evolution of families and villages. Households began dealing with one another and discovered that it was to their mutual advantage not only to engage in trade, but also to establish norms and processes for dealing with conflicts. These conflicts could arise from a variety of sources, including differing opinions about what was a good deal. In any case, they found that it was to their mutual advantage to establish what the classical scholar Bernard Yack calls a "political community."[6] It provided a context and a language for talking about conflicts, and for talking about what constituted the good life. The language was a language of justice and friendship. By engaging in conversations about their obligations to each other (civic friendship) and their dealings with each other (justice) they could formulate how they should live together. Yack provides us an interesting contrast between the conversations of the Athenian political community and a community of players in a card game.

> Given the very specific and limited purpose of their association, game players require merely that all follow some set of rules so that they can get on with the pleasure – or profit – that comes from playing the game. No demand for intrinsically valuable or correct standards, apart from the formal obligation to play by the rules of the game, follows from their communal activities. As a result, game

---

[6] Bernard Yack, *The Problems of a Political Animal: Community, Justice and Conflict in Aristotelian Political Thought* (Berkeley: University of California Press, 1993), p. 55.

players spend relatively little time debating the best rules of the game ... Members of political communities, in contrast, devote a great deal of attention to determining what they think are the intrinsically correct standards of mutual obligation. Consequently, they are disinclined simply to delegate the power to make, interpret, and enforce these standards to a third party. Instead, they compete for this power or look for individuals with the appropriate substantive qualifications for exercising it.[7]

For Aristotle, this talk about the rules is precisely what makes humans human. He draws out the implication of recognizing that humans are talking animals in his *Politics*:

> Nature, according to our theory, makes nothing in vain; and man alone of the animals is furnished with the faculty of language. The mere making of sounds serves to indicate pleasure and pain, and is thus a faculty that belongs to animals in general; their nature enables them to attain the point at which they have perceptions of pleasure and pain, and can signify those perceptions to one another. But language serves to declare what is advantageous and what is the reverse, and it therefore serves to declare what is just and what is unjust. It is the peculiarity of man, in comparison with the rest of the animal world, that he alone possesses a perception of good and evil, of the just and unjust, and of other similar qualities; and it is association in a common perception of these things which makes a family and a polis.[8]

For Aristotle, the political community provides the space for conversations about the good life, about justice and fairness. Such conversations enable humans to become fully human in the sense that they can realize their highest abilities. As Aristotle declares: "Man, when perfected, is the best of animals; but if he is isolated from law and justice he is the worst of all."[9]

---

[7] *Ibid.*, p. 58.   [8] Aristotle, *Politics*, p. 6.   [9] *Ibid.*, p. 7.

Even though the political community is based on mutual advantage, it acquires a meaning clearly beyond individual self-interest. By participating in conversations about different views of justice and how people should live together, persons are able not only to live, but also to participate in a good life.

The civic, for the Greeks, was the true location for human fulfillment. The commercial was seen as providing the necessities of life, but not life's fulfillment. Commercial activity was necessary for a thriving community, but not sufficient. A thriving community also had to be a place where participants would join together in debates about justice and human happiness, and recognize each other as just and virtuous citizens.

The civic, in other words, was seen as the location (a location created and maintained by continual conversations) that is not only independent of, but also serves as a basis for, the commercial. To see how this could manifest itself today, we need to understand the meaning of the social, and the relationship between the social and the economic.

THE CONCEPT OF THE SOCIAL

The original notion of the social was that of association. One still finds the term used in this way in such titles as, for example, the "Society of Business Ethics." In the modern period, however, the social has acquired a broader meaning and refers to our life in various groups or collectives or what we today call "society." People have also used the term to refer to the plight of workers. In Germany, for example, "the social question" arose in the nineteenth century as a concern about unemployed or poorly employed workers. This concern initiated the labor movement, socialist parties, social programs and various social services around the world. Programs such as social security or social welfare are grounded in this third aspect of the meaning of social.

The idea of the social as a problem coincides with the rise of capitalism and the emergence of a class of persons dependent for their survival on wages over which they had little or no control. Socialism was, among other things, an attempt to free people from that dependency. It is easy to agree with the basic compassion of socialism for the misery of workers, but in many cases socialist solutions can be seen today as remaining within the framework of an economics of property.

Socialists believed that if the workers or government owned the means of production instead of the capitalists, then a new age would become available. Well, the new age has not become available in part because the battle over ownership did not address the underlying economic issue, which is: How should we organize ourselves to provide for everyone? The control of owners over non-owners may have been the problem, but changing who controls whom is not the solution. Civilizing the economy offers a course of action that places civic relations, not property relations, as the foundation of economics. From a civic perspective, the social takes on a broader reference that includes all the groups that compose modern society.

Even though the social emerged with the modern market economy, it has now become a set of relationships in which the market is embedded. What makes the social important for economics today, in other words, is that markets are part and parcel of the social. In contrast to the Smithian tradition of economics, which assumes that the market is its own self-organizing system, in fact, the market is mostly organized around social differences. Bankers do not get million-dollar salaries while janitors get less than a living wage because of some insulated market dynamics, but rather because of the social classes in which these different workers belong. Your place in society, in other words, will shape your opportunities to engage in market transactions and the likelihood of your success. The particular socio-economic groups into which we were born and raised not only influence our access to provisions, but also how we perceive our world, others, and ourselves.

THE SOCIAL FOUNDATION OF PERCEPTIONS

The discipline of sociology, developed in the nineteenth century, took up the issue of how one's participation in various social groups influenced one's self-understanding as well as one's opportunities for fulfillment. Research has shown that how people behave in specific situations depends not only on their personal beliefs, but also on

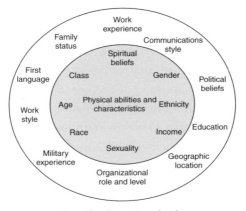

FIGURE 6.1 The diversity wheel

their interpretation of what society expects of them.[10] In a situation where people are expected to consider the interests of others, for example, people are much more likely to do so than in a situation where people are expected to act only on their self-interest. In other words, whether we follow such norms as reciprocity, fair play, or beneficence largely depends on our interpretation of social expectations. What we expect from others, and from ourselves, depends on our assumptions about the society in which we live.

As a Western protestant white male, I see the world much differently than most of the global population. And others see the world differently than I do. This does not mean that I or any other particular individual caused these social differences. Neither did they come about "naturally," like changes in the weather. No, there are several causes, and certainly the history of the Atlantic trade continues to influence our local and global societies. The significance of these social differences has been recognized recently in the field of diversity awareness and training. One popular means of exploring our diversity has been to use the diversity wheel (Figure 6.1).[11]

[10] Cristina Bicchieri, *The Grammar of Society: The Nature and Dynamics of Social Norms* (New York: Cambridge University Press, 2006), p. 125.
[11] From www.Loden.com/Site/Dimensions.html (retrieved on September 10, 2009).

The inner circle of the wheel represents "primary" social categories and the outer circle "secondary." The primary categories are more or less given while the secondary are more or less chosen, or at least are easier to change. Individuals, of course, belong to several of these categories and as individuals may identify more with some than with others. The diversity wheel does not tell us much about any particular individual, but it does tell us something about society; namely, society is just as much about what divides us as what unites us.

If we look at the secondary set of categories – from family status to geographic location – we can imagine that great differences make for strong divisions. In the year 2000, for example, the world's richest 225 people had a combined wealth equal to the annual income of the poorest 47 percent of the world's people.[12] The United Nations Development Program's 2005 Human Development Report recorded that "One-fifth of humanity live in countries where many people think nothing of spending $2 a day on a cappuccino. Another fifth of humanity survive on less than $1 a day and live in countries where children die for want of a simple anti-mosquito bednet."[13] None of us, of course, choose which fifth of the world's population will be our birthplace, but we can choose whether or not we will recognize that we all belong to the same generation.

As we have seen, the Enlightenment view of different stages of history allowed the Europeans to believe that their commercial/civic stage existed in a more advanced time than the savages on other continents. Different people were seen as living in different times. When we think of future generations, however, this division is no longer viable. It is no longer possible to separate the fate of "our" children and grandchildren from the fate of the children and grandchildren of "others". We will either save one planet with one people or

---

[12] Des Gasper, *The Ethics of Development: From Economism to Human Development* (Edinburgh: Edinburgh University Press, 2004), p. 2.

[13] Kevin Watkins, "International Cooperation at the Crossroads: Aid, Trade, and Security in an Unequal World," *Summary Human Development Report 2005* (New York: United Nations Development Program, 2005), p. 17.

we will not save any. Almost by necessity, we all belong to this generation that faces the challenge of creating a just and sustainable economy. To be contemporary, to live in this world rather than in some make-believe world, of course, is always a challenge. To say we are all of the same generation may give us reason to acknowledge our common challenge, but it does not really bridge our differences. To bridge the differences, we need to civilize the social, or to recognize a common identity as global citizens belonging to a civil society.

THE CHARACTER OF CIVIL SOCIETY

Those of us constructing an economics of provision face a dilemma; we are always located in some social groups rather than others. If we remain within the "social," we remain within our social divisions. The solution lies in the civic. For just as the civic sphere functions as a foundation for trade among strangers, it can also serve as a foundation for mediating between our social divisions. Civil society, in other words, represents a broader human context that could hold us together, despite our social differences. Jeffery Alexander's definition of civil society is particularly relevant for us.

> It is the we-ness of a national, regional, or international community, the feeling of connectedness to "every member" of that community that transcends particular commitments, narrow loyalties, and sectional interest. Only this kind of solidarity can provide a thread, not of identity in the narrow sense, but of a kind of mutual identification that unites individuals dispersed by class, religion, and ethnicity, or race.[14]

If our economics of provision is to fulfill its promise, we need to ground it in this kind of civil society – a civil society based on solidarity with others. This notion of civil society is quite different from the notion of "civil society organizations" – nonprofit or voluntary organizations

---

[14] Jeffery C. Alexander, *The Civic Sphere* (New York: Oxford University Press, 2006), p. 43.

such as the Red Cross. These groups are independent from both corporate and government domination, and their mission is usually to protect social groups and the natural environment from being harmed by the economics of property. Although many of these groups are engaged in projects that could be models for an economics of provision, their separation from the economic and the governmental has resulted in viewing civil society as outside of the mainstream rather than the common ground that holds the mainstream together. The view of civil society developed here has been articulated quite well by, once again, Jeffery Alexander:

> Civil society – and the groups, institutions, and individuals who articulate their "interests" in civil society terms – pulls together these inputs according to its own normative and institutional logic. That is to say that the solidarity sphere we call civil society has relative autonomy and can be studied in its own right. It is homologous with, to some degree independent of, and sometimes a match for the other "societies" that constitute the subject of contemporary social science – the economic, the political, the familial, the ethnic, and religious.[15]

Alexander opens a way to make our way from social divisions to civic solidarity by offering a civic sphere that is connected to the social and yet is not bound by it. This zone of civic life can serve as a container or context for the commercial market, which gives businesses a civic obligation to cooperate with market and non-market agencies in a common effort to make provisions for all. Civil society, in other words, would function as the foundation for human relationships in the economy.

One could propose that we should focus on notions such as human dignity or individual rights instead of civil society. The risk with the language of human rights is that it allows us to overlook our social nature. If we see human rights as a means of protecting

[15] *Ibid.*, p. 54.

individuals in a network of relationships, then the tradition of human rights and the notion of global citizen would support each other. We are members of society, and if we are to move beyond the divisions of social groups, then we need membership someplace else. That place can be civil society, where again we are members and we are related to one another. This time, however, we are related to one another as citizens.

One's role as a citizen, to quote the political theorist Sheldon Wolin, "provides what other roles cannot, namely an integrative experience which brings together the multiple role activities of the contemporary person and demands that the separate roles be surveyed from a more general point of view."[16] When I see the other not only as a factory worker, a computer expert, or a farmer, but also as a citizen, then I begin to recognize this other person as having multiple roles and relations as I do. Our different social roles, in other words, are integrated under a common membership in civil society. As the original meaning of the word implies, a citizen is one who belongs to a city. One cannot be a citizen alone. It is a relational term. It is a term for all who belong to civil society.

CIVIL SOCIETY AS A CONTEXT FOR THE MARKET

Creating a civil society does not mean that we take the market out of social relations and transport it into civil society. It does mean that the social relations in which market transactions occur are seen as contained and shaped by the relational identity and normative standards of civil society. As Figure 6.2 shows, civil society would function as the context for the social relations in which global markets are embedded.

The illustration in Figure 6.2 shows the contextual relationship between commerce and civil society, but does it not yet include the government. Without government, civil society is impossible. Just as market systems require stability and security, so does civil society. As

---

[16] Sheldon Wolin, *Politics and Vision: Continuity and Innovation in Western Political Thought*, expanded edition (Princeton, NJ and Oxford: Princeton University Press, 2006), p. 389.

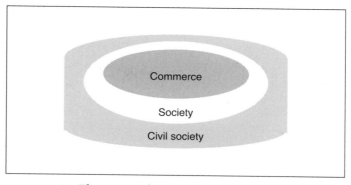

FIGURE 6.2 The context of commerce

we have said before, in an economics of provision, the primary role of government is to protect the civic foundation of trade. We can now expand on this to say that government protects everyone's membership in civil society and enforces the basic civil relationships among members when necessary. In the United States, of course, we have a long history of struggle in recognizing everyone's civic identity in society, from the Civil War in the nineteenth century to the civil rights movement in the twentieth.

Government needs to protect not only the civic sphere, but also the civic character of market competition. This does not simply happen by wishing. When necessary, government should develop standards of corporate conduct to ensure that workers and others are treated as citizens. Government can also create an even playing field for business competitors by developing environmental and social standards that all competitors must follow. Given these multiple functions of government in civilizing global markets, a more complete picture of the contextual character of civil society and commerce would look like Figure 6.3.

While government can protect and in some cases promote the civic nature of civil society, it cannot by itself create or maintain it. Civil society finally depends on the everyday practices of extending trust to one another, recognizing each other as citizens of the same generation, and engaging in conversations around common issues and

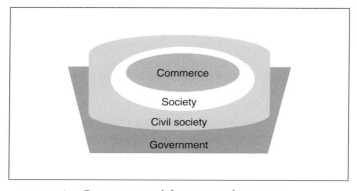

FIGURE 6.3 Government and the context of commerce

controversies. These conversations provide a civic identity to the participants and support civic norms for making decisions. The question of civic norms moves us from the description of how civil society can help us overcome or at least mediate social divisions to the question of what moral standards should guide interactions among citizens. In the next chapter, we take up the most crucial civic norm for markets, the norm of reciprocity.

7   Restoring reciprocity

The previous chapter emphasized the inclusive character of civil society. Civil society includes all of us as global citizens. This chapter examines the civic norm that holds civil society together: reciprocity. If we are to replace property relations with civic relations, then we need to replace the exclusive focus on individual gain with a relational notion of reciprocity as the basis for the economy. We need to restore reciprocity as the moral foundation for making provisions. No better place to begin than with the following from the *Analects of Confucius*:

> Zigong asked: "Is there any one word that can serve as a principle for the conduct of life?" Confucius said: "Perhaps the word 'reciprocity': Do not do to others what you would not want others to do to you."[1]

Confucius' definition of reciprocity will remind Western readers of the Golden Rule: "Do unto others what you would want them to do to you." One finds reciprocity practiced in many cultures as a principle for human relationships. In most formulations, what I want or do not want serves as a guide for treating others. This assumes that everyone is more or less the same – others will want or not want the same as I would. In traditional cultures, this assumption worked quite well, but it has some limitations in our pluralistic culture. People from different cultures and backgrounds have different expectations and different wants. Thus we must modify our traditional forms to honor the diversity of the global community; we need to ask about and listen to cultural differences. At the same time, reciprocity still directs our

---

[1] Roger T. Ames and Henry Rosemont, Jr., trans., *The Analects of Confucius: A Philosophical Translation* (New York: Ballantine Books, 1998), XV: 23.

attention to an essential aspect of civic relations in our neighborhoods, workplaces, cities, and global communities – we do expect that others will respond appropriately to us as human beings. Human relationships, in other words, are essentially moral relationships. To understand how reciprocity can help us understand the obligations these relationships entail, we will look at three different manifestations of reciprocity: the reciprocity of exchange, the reciprocity of participation, and the reciprocity of deliberation.

THE RECIPROCITY OF EXCHANGE

In the Western tradition, we find the classic definition of reciprocity of exchange in Aristotle's *Ethics*. In the fifth book, which addresses questions of justice, he writes that reciprocity is the form of justice that deals with exchanges.

> But in associations that are based on mutual exchange, the just in this sense constitutes the bond that holds the association together, that is, reciprocity in terms of a proportion and not in terms of exact equality in the return. For it is the reciprocal return of what is proportional (to what one has received) that holds the state together.[2]

Two aspects of Aristotle's understanding of reciprocity seem worth highlighting. First, reciprocity is a form of justice. This gives it a normative dimension, since justice is not about how we *do* treat one another, but how we *should* treat one another. Second, reciprocity requires fair exchanges based on proportionality. If a homebuilder, for example, were to make an exchange with a shoemaker, the exchange should not be one house for one pair of shoes, but should be in proportion to the relative value of the house and the pair of shoes. How would one determine what the proportion would be? Both could be translated into money, which would serve as a common coin to represent the proportional value of the house and the shoes. The house would

---

[2] Aristotle, *Nicomachean Ethics*, trans. Martin Ostwald (Englewood Cliffs, NJ: Prentice Hall, 1962), p. 124.

certainly cost more than the shoes, but how much more? Aristotle's answer is that we would need to find the right proportionality between the house and the shoes to answer that question.[3] And the answer would differ in each particular case. In all cases, however, each receives according to the value of what one has provided, and that value is determined by its proportional value to other provisions. Reciprocity, in other words, requires that each receive according to the contribution she or he has made. The reality of supply and demand may certainly help determine value, since no exchange will take place unless someone demands what another has supplied. On the other hand, if a person provides a service or product that meets a need – there is a demand for it – then the provider and the provided should be seen as existing in a relationship of reciprocity, where the provider receives in terms of his or her contribution.

From a civic perspective, exchanges would be grounded in moral relationships of reciprocity. This aligns with Lawrence Becker's view of reciprocity as a *deontic* virtue. For him, a virtue is a disposition to act in a certain manner, and a deontic virtue is a disposition to obey a moral obligation. In the case of reciprocity, the obligation is to return good for good, and to resist evil.

> The concept of reciprocity that I shall defend may be summarized in the following maxims: that we should return good for good, in proportion to what we receive; that we should resist evil, but not do evil in return; that we should make reparation for the harm we do; and that we should be disposed to do those things as a matter of moral obligation.[4]

In contrast to an older view of reciprocity that says "an eye for an eye," Becker does not include negative reciprocity in his definition, because he sees reciprocity as a moral virtue.[5]

---

[3] Meikle, *Aristotle's Economic Thought*, p. 27.
[4] Lawrence C. Becker, *Reciprocity* (Chicago, IL and London: The University of Chicago Press, 1986), p. 4.
[5] *Ibid.*, p. 49.

> Clearly, since the whole idea of reciprocity is to return *good* for good, the return of evil for it will by definition be unfitting, as well be a return of something valueless. Further, since the point of being disposed to reciprocate is to create and sustain balanced social relationships, the good returned will have to be good *for the recipient* and (eventually) *perceived* by the recipient both *as a good* and *as a return*.[6]

The key phrase here is "balanced social relationships." Such relationships require at least that each person receives what he or she is due, which should be related to the value of their contribution. This principle, of course, does not tell us exactly what each should receive, but it does offer some guidelines. First of all, reciprocity would exclude exchanges where some people benefit at the expense of others. This principle is similar to John Rawls' famous difference principle of justice, which states that inequalities must be arranged so they are to the advantage of the most disadvantaged: "While the distribution of wealth and income need not be equal, it must be to everyone's advantage, and at the same time, positions of authority and offices of command must be accessible to all."[7] While this aspect of reciprocity keeps people from being exploited by others, it does not give us a clear idea of what one is due. Consider the following case.

Several years ago, women from sewing factories in the Dominican Republic visited college campuses in the northeast United States to tell students that they received eight cents for each baseball or college cap the students bought for around twenty dollars.[8] The eight cents was not enough to pay the family bills for the month, so their children ate less at the end of the month, until the next paycheck. The women could have asked the students to pay eight cents more for the caps, which would have doubled their wages. But

---

[6] *Ibid.*, p. 107. Italics in original.
[7] John Rawls, *A Theory of Justice* (Cambridge, MA: Harvard University Press, 1971), p. 61.
[8] Bob Herbert, "Sweatshop U in Dominican Republic," *New York Times*, April 12, 1998.

they did not. With eight cents more they would not have become rich, but they would have had enough for their month's expenses. Would any students have objected? I assume not. So why don't companies simply pay a living wage to workers and pass the increased cost on to the consumer? Because companies do not view these women as providers of caps, but only view their work as commodities to be paid the minimum that the labor market will allow. If they were seen as providers, as well as global citizens, then the relationship between the working women and the company would be one of reciprocity, which would require that these women receive a living wage for providing caps to the college bookstores.

One could argue, of course, that these women would rather work for subsistence wages than be unemployed, which makes the current arrangement one of mutual advantage. Reciprocity, however, demands more for at least two reasons. One reason is that this arrangement does not sustain balanced social arrangements, which we acknowledged as the goal of reciprocity. The second is that it does not recognize workers as a part of the business of making college caps, as participants in this enterprise. To comprehend the meaning of this second reason, we turn to the second form of reciprocity: reciprocity of participation.

THE RECIPROCITY OF PARTICIPATION

Most people do not have a choice whether to participate or not in various economic markets. Participation is the only way to survive. Most of us, in fact, must participate in the labor and housing markets, as well as the education and health-care systems, all in order to provide for our families and ourselves. We will explore the nature of these systems in future chapters, but here we can reiterate that persons in these systems should be regarded as citizens. The necessity of participation, in other words, should not lessen the civic claim for reciprocal relationships.

Carol Gould's framework for connecting freedom and reciprocity can help us understand what is at stake here. In *Rethinking Democracy*, Gould argues that freedom has two aspects: freedom as the capacity to make choices and freedom as "the exercise of this capacity in the form of self-development."[9] If freedom is to have any meaning, she argues, it must include the making of choices about one's self-development, and the conditions necessary to realize them. Furthermore, these conditions are essentially social. The exercise of freedom, therefore, depends on social relations that provide the necessary conditions for persons to carry out "those actions that express one's own purposes and needs."[10] Now, if we assume that everyone has an equal right to freedom, which Gould does, then every moral agent participating in these social relations has an equal right to self-development, which means that these social relations should be relationships of reciprocity. As Gould puts it:

> Equal rights to the conditions of self-development require a certain form of social relations if they are to be realized … it would require the recognition by each individual of the equal freedom of the others. Such a relation is therefore one of reciprocal recognition of their equal agency.[11]

In contrast to non-reciprocal relationships such as oppression or exploitation, relationships of reciprocity allow persons to count on mutual recognition of the need for provisions that are necessary for a human life.

If we apply this notion of reciprocity to the case of the college caps, we see that the current arrangement – which simply offers the workers more than they would have if they were unemployed – is not enough. In terms of the reciprocity of participation, they deserve wages that would enable them to create the conditions for their self-development, which would require not only a living wage, which is already supported by the reciprocity of exchange, but also the opportunity to participate in determining the conditions necessary for

---

[9] Carol C. Gould, *Rethinking Democracy: Freedom and Social Cooperation in Politics, Economy, and Society* (Cambridge: Cambridge University Press, 1988), p. 45.
[10] *Ibid.*, p. 47.   [11] *Ibid.*, p. 72.

maintaining balanced social relationships – relationships based on reciprocity.

For Gould the reciprocity of participation is most fully realized in democratic practices. "The reciprocal recognition and respect for the other which defines social reciprocity is most fully realized in the direct or face-to-face interactions which characterize participatory forms of decision-making."[12] If we were to apply this form of reciprocity to the workplace, workers could say, "No production without representation."

"No taxation without representation" was one of the most stirring and significant demands made in the American Revolution. The idea is clear: If I pay taxes to fund the government so it can carry out policies that affect me, then I should have a say in the determination of those policies. My views should be represented. This is the basic civic claim of democratic practices. Similarly, if we are serious about recognizing the civic sphere as the foundation for exchanges, then this principle should guide the design of all organizations, including modern corporations. All employees of the corporation, for example, would have representation in the process of deciding the distribution of that corporation's income – how much to research and development, to bonuses, and so on – to ensure that the distribution reflects both what different groups in the organization have contributed and what creates and maintains balanced social relationships in the organization. The reciprocity of participation can be fully exercised only when it extends to our third form of reciprocity – the reciprocity of deliberation.

THE RECIPROCITY OF CIVIC DELIBERATION

Deliberation is the hallmark of civic life. It emerges from the realization that things could be otherwise – could be different than they are. People deliberate when they have choices. In fact, the presence of choices makes civic deliberation quite different from some other forms of discourse.

---

[12] *Ibid.*, p. 89.

The root of deliberate is "libra," which refers to a scale, so to deliberate is to weigh the merits of different views. This fits with reciprocal relationships, since it gives each side of a controversial issue its due. Those arguments that have better reasons would receive more attention and the argument with the best reasons would receive the strongest support. That's the theory. It gets a bit more complicated in practice, however, because to weigh the merits of different views, one must understand them. Making one's reasons understandable to others, it turns out, is not as easy as it sounds. One way to explore this is to make a distinction between private mediation and civic deliberation.

Although it might seem odd to speak of private mediation, there is a widespread practice of conflict mediation that more or less fits with this notion. Perhaps the most famous model of conflict mediation is the process outlined by Fisher and Ury in their book *Getting to Yes*. In this model of resolving conflicts, the mediator asks the parties involved to "focus on their interests."[13] The mediator then tries to clarify each party's real interests and find a "win/win" situation. The parties are not asked to examine their interests or to justify them, because they are essentially private. Interests are like preferences; we are entitled to have preferences without permission from others. So the best solution to any conflict – the win/win – is one that satisfies each party's preferences as much as possible.

The reciprocity of civic deliberation is quite different, primarily because it is based on public reasoning rather than private preferences. People come together not as consumers with preferences, but as citizens with values. They are calculating not how to win as much as they can, but how to find a solution that matches their values and aspirations. A shared commitment to such civic values of reciprocity and fairness underpins their conversation. Furthermore, they aim not at mutual satisfaction, but at joint action. The question addresses what "we" should do together.

---

[13] Roger Fisher and William Ury, *Getting to Yes: Negotiating Agreement Without Giving In* (New York: Penguin Books: 1983), p. 41.

So what about the workplace? Can workers and managers engage in civic deliberation? They certainly have conflicts, but are these conflicts based on different interests? In the economics of property business model they are, since the conflict is about the value or price of different properties (labor, land, and money) or conflicts between the owners of different types of capital (money, fixed, human, intellectual, and so on). But if we switch to an economics of provision that is based on civic relations, the picture looks much different. First of all, the role or purpose of the business organization changes from return on investment to that of making provisions. In this model, all members of the organization are "employed" to fulfill the mission of providing quality goods and services. They may disagree about the best means of doing that, but not about the company's purpose. In fact, this common purpose gives them a shared vision that enables them to deliberate on how best to realize it. If we see businesses as aiming at making provisions, the workers could certainly deliberate about to achieve this goal. Before we can say for sure that deliberation is possible in the workplace, we need to know more about its main characteristics.

The model of civic deliberation for many of us in the United States is the town-hall meeting. People come from their homes or places of business to engage in a discussion on controversial issues that need action. Let's use this model to examine the key characteristics of civic deliberation. A town-hall meeting occurs when people come together to address a common need. At the meeting, they explore different courses of action and the reasons that support them. In the course of the meeting, people are bound to misunderstand each other's positions and will need further explanation of the course of action being advocated. This brings us to a key point: All speakers need to make their views available to others as much as they can.

In civic deliberations, one's private interests need to be translated into public values – values that belong to the organization in which one is participating. Making one's reasons available to others does not presume that others will agree, but rather that they will understand. Listeners should be able to say, "If I saw the situation as this speaker does, then I would agree with her conclusions." Some may believe that this focuses too much on rationality. After all, people arrive at their beliefs through intuition, gut feelings, religious teachings, and so forth. One could argue, "Since we did not arrive at many of our opinions through reason, how can we be expected to have 'reasons' for them now?" But this point overlooks the difference between acquiring an opinion and presenting it for others. Civic deliberation is concerned not so much with how one acquired an opinion or belief, but with showing others how the opinion makes sense. Public reasons, in other words, are located in *public*, in the context that a group or collective constructs as it deliberates about what should be done.

Instead of examining why one believes something through introspection, civic deliberation asks people to examine why something should be believed by appealing to the different reasons that have some currency within the public context. A prime example of this phenomenon in the United States is the separation of church and state. Members of different religious communities may have different reasons for believing in equal rights for all persons, and yet when they speak to one another, they appeal to reasons for equal rights that belong to the civic realm rather than to their particular religious communities.

Appeal to reason, however, should not exclude feelings and emotions from the arena of civic deliberation. In classical rhetorical theory, the three sources for developing reasons for public speaking were the speaker's character, the audience's beliefs, and the logic of the argument – *ethos*, *pathos*, and *logos*. The speaker's character (or *ethos*) included experience, authority, and position. Reasons based on *ethos*, for example, could take advantage of the speaker's trustworthiness, her expertise, or her experiences. All can be good reasons for acknowledging what she has to say. Reasons based on *pathos* could elicit people's hopes, expectations, fears, and values. Finally, reasons based on *logos* would appeal to the validity of one's arguments or the connections one has drawn between different events or ideas. For civic deliberation to fulfill its own possibilities, it needs to strike a balance among the three. It needs the whole packet: the logic of the argument, the character of the speaker, and the beliefs of the audience.

These three sources for civic deliberation seem to omit what we talk the most about: the facts. What an omission. After all, this is the information age. Yes, but information alone does not constitute an argument. It has little meaning by itself. Instead, the meaning of information depends on who we are (*ethos*), what we believe (*pathos*), and how we think (*logos*). In other words, only when information is connected to the public sources for the development of reasons does it become persuasive. In our everyday life, we constantly exchange information relying on, and yet usually unaware of, this background. Information about what is happening is not unimportant, but its importance depends on our beliefs and our ability to make connections – our rational abilities.

Civic deliberation can occur in many different settings. One imagines it naturally in Western civic institutions, such as town-hall meetings, but it occurs in many other places as well. For example, we may not think that Native American tribes engaged in something close to civic deliberation – especially if we accept the Enlightenment's distinction between the civilized and savage nations – but written accounts prove otherwise. In fact, Native American oral tradition holds that the Iroquois Federation predates the arrival of the European colonists (though there is some disagreement about its origins). The Federation originally included five tribes – the Mohawks, Oneidas, Onondagas, Cayugas, and Senecas – who joined together to cease fighting among themselves and to promote their common advantage. They maintained their union through the Great Law of Peace, which outlined their agreements. Male delegates and deputies were elected by each clan's mother to represent the clan's position at the Grand Council. In contrast to the patriarchal culture of the colonists, these Native American tribes were matriarchal. The clan mothers not only selected, but could also remove a delegate if he had not fulfilled his responsibilities. At the council sessions, the delegates engaged in deliberation about matters that concerned their common interests. James Adair, in 1775, wrote of their sessions:

> The Indian method of government ... in general ... consists of a federal union for mutual safety ... The Indians, therefore, have no such titles, or persons as emperors, or kings, or an appellative for such ... They can only persuade or dissuade the people, either by the force of good nature and clear reasoning, or by coloring things, so as to suit the prevailing passions ... They are very deliberate in their councils, and never give an immediate answer to any message sent to them by strangers, but suffer some nights first to elapse. They reason in a very orderly manner, with such coolness and good-natured language, though they may differ widely in their opinions.[14]

Sounds like a very successful town-hall meeting, and a good illustration of the reciprocity of deliberation. This type of conversation would have been quite surprising to those in the Scottish Enlightenment. How could savages have engaged in such reasonable and civic discourse? But of course, civic deliberation does not depend on the ownership of property; it simply requires human relationships of mutual respect and reciprocity.

This third form of reciprocity – the reciprocity of deliberation – helps us understand the prior two forms – reciprocity of exchange and participation. The practice of weighing the merits of different reasons for different courses of action is like weighting the contribution of different provisions or the weighting of the benefits for participating in organizations. In each case, the relationship is one of fairness or justice so people receive their due. To receive their due in exchanges requires that their reward be in proportion to their contribution. Deciding what this proportion would be in concrete cases hinges on the reciprocity of participation, which means that all participants would be represented in making that decision. Finally, the reciprocity

---

[14] Quoted in Donald A. Grinde and Bruce E. Johansen, *Exemplar of Liberty: Native America and the Evolution of Democracy* (Los Angeles: University of California, 1995), pp. 17–18.

of deliberation would ensure that these decisions were based on good reasons that are accessible and persuasive for all involved in the conversations.

With the restoration of reciprocity, we have laid the groundwork for civilizing the economy. It replaces price as the means for determining the value of a provider's contribution to our communities and families. It does not replace the market itself; supply and demand play important roles in determining what people need and value. Mark Brown has suggested that we could think about this relationship in terms of deliberation setting boundaries for acceptable results and acceptable treatment of participants in market interactions, and then within these boundaries competition would determine price.[15] This would be one way to civilize the market – there may be others as well. Success in installing reciprocity as the basis of market relations depends on whether we can engage in civic deliberations in many different settings in which we live and work.

Whether civic deliberation is possible depends on the circumstances in which we live, and some circumstances are more open to such practices than others. We will return to the question of circumstances and civic deliberation in the final chapter. For now, we can take the civic norm of reciprocity as the key characteristic of a civic economics of provision and in the next chapter use it as a framework for understanding market competition.

[15] Personal conversation with Mark Brown.

8 Civic norms and market competition

If we restore reciprocity as the foundation for market transactions, what will happen to competition? Is not competition the real source of energy that keeps the economic motor purring? Take it away and the whole business of business will grind to a halt. Like competitive sports, business thrives on the possibilities of winning and losing. Besides, it is how we sort out the best from the also-ran or even the quite good. If we establish an economics of provision rather than property, won't it need a healthy dose of competition to keep it humming? All this may be true, but what kind of competition belongs to market transactions: the competition on the battlefield, of the playground, or in the realm of ideas? As we shall see, competition in an economics of provision does not disappear. It just becomes civilized.

Although the moral value of competition has rarely been questioned in traditional economics, Frank H. Knight, one of the founders of the Chicago School of Economics, wrote a fascinating essay in 1923 on the ethics of competition. He pinpointed many of the concerns we still have today.

Knight explores the ethics of competition in the context of the following definition of economic activity: "Economic activity is *at the same time* a means of want-satisfaction, an agency for want-and-character formation, a field of creative self-expression, and a competitive sport."[1] Using this definition as a guide, he explores the moral meaning of each aspect of economic activity. Regarding the first aspect, the means of want-satisfaction, Knight writes,

[1] Frank Hyneman Knight, *The Ethics of Competition* (New Brunswick, NJ: Transaction Publishers, 2004), p. 39.

the wants which the economic system operates to gratify are largely produced by the workings of the system itself. In organizing its value scale, the economic order does far more than select and compare wants for exchangeable goods and services; its activity extends to the formation and radical transformation, if not the outright creation, of the wants themselves; they as well as the means of their gratification are largely products of the system.[2]

Does market competition, in other words, create wants that have no other purpose than the maintenance of the market system? This question is answered in Knight's second aspect of economic activity: It tends to create individuals who mirror the dynamics of economics. He puts it this way:

> The competitive economic order must be partly responsible for making emulation and rivalry the outstanding quality in the character of the Western peoples who have adopted and developed it. The modern idea of enjoyment as well as achievement has come to consist chiefly in keeping up with or getting ahead of other people in a rivalry for things about whose significance, beyond furnishing objectives for the competition itself, little question is asked. It is surely one function of ethical discussion to keep the world reminded that this is not the only possible conception of values and to point out its contrast with the religious ideals to which the Western world has continued to render lip-service – a contrast resulting in fundamental dualism in our thought and culture.[3]

Considering how our consumer-based culture has continued to expand since the 1940s, I imagine that Knight would see his warning as having had little effect.

Knight's third aspect of economics as a "field of creative self-expression" and his fourth aspect of economics as "a competitive sport" refer more directly to the competitiveness of the market. He

---

[2] *Ibid.*, p. 38.   [3] *Ibid.*, p. 39.

argues that business leaders are motivated not merely by satisfying their wants, but by winning. Look at those who continued to remain involved in economic activities once all their material needs were met. Knight suggests that they are motivated by "a joy of activity not dependent on any definite use to be made of the results."[4]

> Economists and publicists are coming to realize how largely the efficiency of business and industry is the result of this appeal to intrinsic interest in action; how feeble, in spite of the old economics, is the motivation of mere appetite or cupidity; and how much the driving power of our economic life depends on making and keeping the game interesting.[5]

Business, in other words, offers an outlet for self-expression similar to the sports arena or even the battlefield.

In the 1920s, when Knight wrote this essay, it was clear that only a few had access to this field of possibilities. He puts it this way: "Economic production has been made a fascinating sport *for the leaders*, but this has been accomplished by reducing it to mechanical drudgery for the rank and file."[6] This inequality in participation in economic competition raises ethical questions for Knight, but I don't think it is his main point in the exploration of the ethics of competition. Instead, he seems to focus on the question of whether ethics must offer some value or ideal other than the economic value of competitive activity. If there are no other values, then we are left with what he calls "an ethics of power."

> It is in terms of power, then, if at all, that competitive economics and the competitive view of life for which it must be largely accountable are to be justified. Whether we are to regard them as justified at all depends on whether we are willing to accept an ethics of power as the basis of our world-view.[7]

---

[4] *Ibid.*, p. 51.   [5] *Ibid.*, p. 53.   [6] *Ibid.*, p. 59.   [7] *Ibid.*, p. 60.

The problem for Knight is that an ethics of power is not an adequate guide for a social life. In fact, he fails to find any ethical justification for seeing competitive economics "as a basis for an ideal type of human relations or as a motive to action."[8]

At the same time, he is not sure if there exists a better alternative. As he says, the radical critics of economic competition vastly underestimate "the danger of doing vastly worse."[9] It seems like his purpose in this essay is not to offer a better way, but rather to explore the way things were going – and he finds that direction deeply troubling.

What troubles Knight is that the excellence produced by market competition has become disconnected from – even contradictory to – the traditional social, aesthetic, and spiritual values of Western culture. Although it is not explicit, one can easily read in his essay a plea that ethics will somehow bring economic activities back into connection with these traditions. The next generation of the Chicago School of Economics, of course, moved in the opposite direction, working to ensure that market competition would be free from government interference or changing social norms. Especially in the years of Reaganomics, the battle cry was simply "Let the games begin." We are growing painfully aware how this aggressive global competitiveness has moved us toward the destruction of our planet. To see such destruction as a "sport" may seem obscene, but many people have no problem seeing market competition as a sport.

MARKET COMPETITION AND SPORTS

The United States, particularly, seems to promote the strong analogy between competitive sports and competition in the marketplace. A company competes to be Number One (national champion), develops its brand to have the most loyal customers (fans), and tries to recruit top managers (stars). It is all a game, and the only goal is to win, without violating the rules. There may be a strong similarity between winning a game and accumulating more property. But is engaging in

[8] *Ibid.*, p. 66.   [9] *Ibid.*, p. 50.

Competition	Contest	Quarrel	Grapple
Rivalry	Confront	Dispute	Race
Jealousy	Challenge	Encounter	Join issue
Struggle	Conflict	Spar	

FIGURE 8.1 Terms for tension among persons

market transactions really a sport, or is there a more helpful notion of market competition that will align itself closer with an ethics of provision? I think that if we want to change from an economics of property to an economics of provision, we will have to make distinctions between different types of competition instead of allowing competition to define very different kinds of human activities.

People say life is competitive, but is it competitive like the competition between hot and cold air currents or the competition between men and women? The problem is that if we use one term to refer to so many different things, we miss what is unique about each instance, and the term itself loses its meaning. Look at the list of terms for tensions between persons and groups shown in Figure 8.1.

Clearly these terms have vastly different meanings, and to limit us to one term for all these differences signals a serious poverty of the imagination. It is interesting that the word *compete* originally meant to seek or strive together. The com- of compete functions like the com- of *compassion*, which means to suffer with or to share suffering. Competition, in other words, originally meant doing something together instead of doing something to defeat or destroy the other. Today, it has a broad range of meanings, from the competitiveness of war to the competitiveness of ideas. Perhaps we can gain some clarity about the term and its relationship to the market by placing different forms of competition on a continuum, as in Figure 8.2.

At one extreme we could find war, in which one side tries to destroy the other side within broad rules of war, and at the other extreme we find the idea of a dialogue, in which participants explore topics together. They suspend their judgment of the merit of each

War	Sports	Private mediation	Civic deliberation	Dialogue
Destroy the enemy	Winners/ losers	Win/win	Aims for joint action	Generate new ideas
Fear & domination --------------------------------Safety & equality-----------				

FIGURE 8.2 The competitive continuum

other's ideas and explore the hidden assumptions behind them. Between these extremes we could place most other forms of competition, but we will highlight only three: the competition of ideas in civic deliberation, the competition of interests in private mediation, and the competition of individuals and teams in competitive sports. To understand how market competition fits within this continuum, we can ask: "Is market competition more like the competition of sports, interests, or ideas?"

Let's look first at the competition in sports and see how it compares with market competition. Knight clearly sees the economy as a sport for the wealthy and privileged. And so it has been. The wealthy have the chips, so to speak, to play the game. For most of us, however, the market economy is not a sport at all. Struggling to find work or to find food that one can afford is not a sport. Sports are forms of entertainment. One can decide to play or not. Losing is not something you need to take home with you. It is only a game. Losing a job is not a sport. You have to go home without the paycheck.

Sports competition is also different from the competition of ideas (civic deliberation). In boxing, for example, the rules of the game allow one person to attempt to throw a knockout blow to the opponent's jaw, something that would be considered quite uncivil in civic deliberation. Different sports have different rules, of course, and some games are closer to civic norms than others. The point is that sports allow the suspension of civic norms for the sake of the game. There is nothing wrong with this, at least for most sports. In fact, sports are very enjoyable and clearly people love to play and watch them. The point is that the competition of sports is not the same as either market competition or the competition of ideas.

If market competition is not like competitive sports, is it closer to the competition of interests or of ideas? On one level, the difference between the competition of interests and of ideas may be one of language. What are interests if not what we value, and what are our values if not our ideas about what is important? So there may be little difference. On another level, as we learned earlier, there is a decisive difference between seeking win/win situations that are of mutual advantage and seeking joint actions that are based on shared norms and purposes. Perhaps in the real world, market competition swings back and forth between seeking to satisfy individual interests and relying on civic norms to move us beyond our self-interest to what is good for the whole. There probably is a push and a pull here. The push is our motivation to gain what is best for us and the pull is to do what is best for the whole. The strength of the pull depends on our recognition of the civic foundation of market transactions, and that our actions will either strengthen or weaken it. If we include in our definition of the civic the notion of solidarity, as was recommended earlier, then we can agree with Peter Ulrich's argument in his book on integrative economics: "The solidarity of the winners and losers in competition must thus be seen as an integrative precondition and not as contrary to the liberal idea of order."[10] Competitors in the market, in other words, should have one foot in the civic sphere of cooperation as they compete with the other foot in the market of making provisions.

MARKET COMPETITION AND CIVIC NORMS

If we remember that all markets exist in social relations, then the sport analogy is not just inaccurate. It is worse. It prevents us from

---

[10] Peter Ulrich, *Integrative Economic Ethics: Foundations of a Civilized Market Economy* (Cambridge: Cambridge University Press, 2008), p. 244.

recognizing how millions of people actually experience the economy. By ignoring the daily misery of workers and consumers who must enter markets to survive, the sport analogy for business continues the legacy of dissociative economics that we uncovered in Adam Smith's *Wealth of Nations*. Market competition is only a sport for those who can easily afford to choose whether or not to play.

To create a market economy that includes all the providers, then, we need to recognize and expand its civic foundation. A civic foundation would give market participants – workers, investors, and consumers – the right to talk about what they deserve. They could appeal to both reciprocity of exchange and reciprocity of participation. They could enter into debates about whether they are receiving their due for their contribution. These conversations would not only appeal to price, which has some relevance in assigning value, but they could also appeal to justice: the justice of reciprocity. To engage in this type of conversation, they would have to move beyond their own social category and form an identity as a member of civil society and as a global citizen. Severyn Bruyn's definition of civil markets would seem to include this understanding of reciprocity:

> By civil markets, we mean systems of exchange in which competing actors agree to standards for the common good and are capable of enforcing them. This means situations in which trade, professional, labor, and community associations set codes of conduct, require certification procedures, and establish neutral observers (monitors) and regulatory systems that are authorized to issue penalties for members who break contracts. For a "free market" to operate with civility, it must be based on certain principles of justice and rules of fair competition.[11]

As Bruyn points out, progress has been made in developing a civil economy. The establishment of the International Organization for

---

[11] Severyn T. Bruyn, *A Civil Economy: Transforming the Market in the Twenty-First Century* (Ann Arbor: The University of Michigan Press, 2000), p. 207.

Standardization in 1947, the United Nations Conference on Trade and Development in 1964, and the Coalition for Environmentally Responsible Economies in 1989 marks some of this progress. These developments, as well as other forms of responsible corporate activities, provide evidence that markets can become civil. Integrating the civic norm of reciprocity into their decision-making will not only lead corporate leaders to make responsible actions, it will also support the development of the civic realm.

Although our identity as citizens is grounded in this civic sphere, we should not discard that identity when we enter competitive markets as workers, managers, consumers, or investors. If we are to civilize markets, then business leaders at all levels must see themselves also as citizens – citizens who identify with the civic norms of moral equality and reciprocity.

As a civic foundation for market competition, the notion of reciprocity can provide a cooperative basis on which we can compete. Relationships can be based on civic rather than property relations. Once we make this move to a new ground on which to stand, so to speak, we can then begin to understand that the basic sources of wealth – labor, land, and money – are not really properties, but providers.

For Adam Smith, labor, land, and money or capital were "naturally" properties, because they existed for him within the framework of an economics of property. If one moves out of this framework, they are clearly not commodities. To treat them as commodities one would have to make what the early twentieth-century economist Karl Polanyi called a "great transformation" of their actual meaning.

> The crucial point is this: labor, land, and money are essential elements of industry; they also must be organized in markets: in fact, these markets form an absolutely vital part of the economic system. But labor, land, and money are obviously *not* commodities; the postulate that anything that is bought and sold must have been produced for sale is emphatically untrue in regard to them. In other

words, according to the empirical definition of a commodity they are not commodities. Labor is only another name for a human activity which goes with life itself, which in its turn is not produced for sale but for entirely different reasons, nor can that activity be detached from the rest of life, be stored or mobilized; land is only another name for nature, which is not produced by man; actual money, finally, is merely a token of purchasing power which, as a rule, is not produced at all, but comes into being through the mechanism of banking or state finance. None of them is produced for sale. The commodity description of labor, land, and money is entirely fictitious.[12]

Is Polanyi correct? It all depends on our viewpoint. If we look at labor, land, and money from a civic perspective, they clearly appear to us as providers, not properties. In the following chapters, we explore the significance of this civic view of the providers of wealth.

[12] Polanyi, *The Great Transformation*, pp. 75–76.

Part III A civic view of labor, land, and money

Labor: employment as engagement

In Parts I and II, we have offered an alternative to the dissociative economics of an economics of property – an economics of provision – and an alternative to property relations as the foundation of economic interactions – civic relations. In the next chapters, we continue the work of civilizing the economy by exploring three sources of wealth – labor, land, and money – from the perspective of the civic economics of provision. These explorations should not be taken as conclusive, but rather as attempts to give new directions for conversations about the multiple meanings of these sources of wealth. We begin with labor and an exploration of employment as self-merchandizing versus employment as engagement.

EMPLOYMENT AS SELF-MERCHANDIZING

Of the three sources of wealth – land, labor, and money – Adam Smith believed that only labor could really increase the amount of wealth, because a group of workers could become more productive through the division of labor. Labor, in other words, was the only cause of economic growth for Smith. Few agree with Smith's view of labor as the sole source of value creation today. Still, Smith's view of free labor remains a central tenet of the economics of property. As we already know, Smith did not consider slaves to be laborers, since they were the property of their owners. Laborers, on the other hand, "owned" themselves, or, we should say, owned their labor. They could then sell it for wages. For all practical purposes, workers were seen as involved in self-merchandizing. Patricia Werhane explains Smith's view as follows:

> Because that property [one's productivity] is one's own, to which one
> has a perfect right, and because productivity is exchangeable, one

should be free to exchange this commodity, and others should be free to employ it. Thus one can sell one's labor productivity (but not one's strength and dexterity) without thereby selling oneself into serfdom. If one is not paid for one's productivity, one's property rights will be violated. Worse, because one's productivity is an outcome of one's own labor, if it is not recognized as an exchangeable commodity, one thereby will be treated as a slave.[1]

Free labor, in other words, refers to anyone who can choose to sell his or her productivity in exchange for wages. This idea closely resembles today's notion of entering the "job market" to find work, which combines two features of labor in an economics of property: Laboring is a commodity that a laborer can sell, and a laborer is free to sell it or not.

Many students in my business ethics classes seem to share these assumptions. A common reason they give for going to school, for example, is to improve their skills and knowledge so they will get a better (higher paying) job. They have their eyes on the job market and want to have as much to offer as possible. When I ask them how much they are worth in the current job market, they respond by saying it depends on the available jobs, the competition, and the pay that people can command in similar jobs. That is what determines the value of commodities. I then ask them how merchandizing themselves differs from selling a commodity such as a car or a bicycle. This seems to them like an odd question. They did not see themselves as commodities, but they do not really have a language to say how they are different from commodities when they go into the job market. Without really answering, many will typically reply that at least they will have a choice whether to take a job or not.

What many of my students fail to realize is that most people in the world lack the privileges of college and an array of choices about their careers. In fact, most people in the world did not freely choose to work, in any meaningful sense, but must work in order to provide for

---

[1] Patricia Werhane, *Adam Smith and His Legacy for Modern Capitalism* (New York and Oxford: Oxford University Press, 1991), p. 135.

FIGURE 9.1 Two ends of the boat

themselves and their families. Furthermore, as we noted earlier, laborers did not just somehow appear in the eighteenth century look-ing for work. Until the enclosures of land in the seventeenth and eighteenth centuries, there were not many laborers. The enclosure movements forced the commoners, many of whom had been able to make a living without wages, to leave the land and enter the cities, where they depended on wages for their survival. Their choice was that they were free to work for wages or to starve. Millions of workers today have this same "freedom of choice." The cartoon in Figure 9.1 aptly illustrates the actual "work situation" of most laborers.[2]

It is not difficult to identify the owners of the boat, nor the laborers. From an economics of property perspective, the laborers should be grateful to be in the boat. At least they have work. Better in the boat than in the water. From a civic economics of provision, the picture looks quite different. The people on the dry end of the boat depend on the workers for their survival. Even more importantly, all four people are in the same boat. They are participants in the same boat ride.

[2] Source unknown.

If one is desperate for work to provide for one's self and family, it makes little sense to separate one's productivity from one's self or from one's relationships with others, as we find in the economics of property. And yet, this is the basis of most employment in the United States, and nowhere is it better expressed than in the doctrine of "employment at will."

EMPLOYMENT AT WILL AND THE ECONOMICS OF PROPERTY

The idea of at-will employment first appeared in a treatise on master-servant relations by H. G. Wood in 1887. The traditional master-servant relationship was primarily about hierarchy and control, but it contained customs of mutual obligations, such as the notion that when someone was hired it would be for one year. Employment at will allows either party – the employer or the employee – to ignore this tradition and to end the employment "at will." As Patricia Werhane says in her study of employment at will (EAW):

> EAW has been interpreted as the rule that employers whose employees are not specifically covered by statute or contract "may dismiss their employees at will ... for good cause, for no cause or even for causes morally wrong, without being thereby guilty of legal wrong."[3]

There are many reasons for being critical of employment at will, and Werhane covers many of them. She also points out that there is really no good reason for treating private employees differently than public employees, and yet employment at will applies only to private employees. She writes:

> "Public" employment, that is, employment in local, state, and national government departments and their agencies, falls within

---

[3] Patricia H. Werhane and Tara J. Radin with Norman E. Bowie, *Employment and Employee Rights* (Malden, MA: Blackwell Publishing, 2004), p. 55, quoting Lawrence Blades, "Employment at Will vs. Individual Freedom: On Limiting the Abusive Exercise of Employer Power," *Columbia Law Review*, Vol. 67, p. 1405.

the providence of the Constitution and federal oversight. "Private" employment, on the other hand – employment in non-government-owned entities, such as for-profit corporations – remains virtually immune to Constitutional considerations and many legislative strictures.[4]

Public employees, in other words, are protected by the Fourteenth Amendment to the Constitution, which states that no state shall "deprive any person of life, liberty, or property, without due process of law." What is curious is that this right to due process applies only to public employees. The court's justification for the distinction is not that public employees are recognized as citizens and private employees are not, but rather that public employees are seen as having a "property interest" in their employment and private employees do not have such an interest. The status of both types of employees, in other words, is based on property relations, not civic relations. So what is a property interest and how come private employees do not have it?

There is some fuzziness about the notion of property interests, and it varies from state to state. In general, it recognizes some connection between one's work and one's self. For example, public employees may have an interest in maintaining a good reputation for quality work. If so, then a termination without cause would damage their interest, and, in a sense, take away their property – their reputation for quality work. Therefore, public employers cannot terminate public employees with giving them due process to protect their property interests.

Private employers have no such constraint. They can terminate employees at will. (Since both public and private employees can leave their work without due process, the issue is not really about the employee's will, but the employer's.) Private employers have greater latitude because they are masters of their servants, and it turns out that the master is the one who has a property interest in the employee. The

---

[4] *Ibid.*, p. 35.

master controls the employee, as he controls his other property. From a civic perspective, this is all rather confusing. But what is noteworthy is that property rights, not civic rights, determine who gets protection under the Fourteenth Amendment in these situations.

If we are to successfully switch from property relations to civic relations as the basis for our economy, we will have to do some major rethinking in the arena of employment, which could begin with evaluating the meaning of due process for all employees as citizens.

Historically, one could argue that the "employment-at-will" doctrine signaled an advancement for employers and employees when it was instituted in the nineteenth century. It did free both groups from some of the customs of the master-servant tradition. At the same time, by grounding work relationships in property relations, it granted privileges to property owners that people dependent on wages did not have. In today's world, the disparity between worker and employer has become more severe because it is often a relationship between a human person and a "legal person" – a large business corporation. As legal persons, corporations can make contracts and choose to employ people or not, but they do not support families, get depressed, or worry about grandchildren. They are not living, breathing persons. Still, the language of employment-at-will assumes the employment arrangement is among equals. This assumption only makes sense in an economics of property, where the human dimension of life is extinguished. A civic economics of provision offers other possibilities of interpreting the relationship among persons at work. It looks at labor not as a way of merchandizing skills and talents, but as a way of becoming engaged in the processes of making provisions.

EMPLOYMENT AS ENGAGEMENT

The difference between labor as employment and labor as engagement harks back to the distinction made earlier between the "economic man" and the "parent and child" images. Once again, these ideas are guided in part by a feminist interpretation of human relationships and in part by the failure of the economics of property to protect the real providers of wealth – labor, land, and money. The question here is not whether one has sympathy for the suffering of others, but whether one organizes the economy so providers are protected. Perhaps no one understood this issue better than Karl Marx. Here, he criticizes Adam Smith's proposal for separating laboring from the laborer:

> First, the fact that labour is *external* to the worker, i.e., it does not belong to his essential being; that in his work, therefore, he does not affirm himself but denies himself, does not feel content but unhappy, does not develop freely his physical and mental energy but mortifies his body and ruins his mind. The worker therefore only feels himself outside his work, and in his work feels outside himself. He is at home when he is not working, and when he is working he is not at home. His labour is therefore not voluntary, but coerced; it is *forced labour*. It is therefore not satisfaction of a need; it is merely a *means* to satisfy needs external to it. Its alien character emerges clearly in the fact that as soon as no physical or other compulsion exists, labour is shunned like the plague. External labour, labour in which man alienates himself, is a labour of self-sacrifice, of mortification. Lastly, the external character of labour for the worker appears in the fact that it is not his own, but someone else's, that it does not belong to him, that in it he belongs, not to himself, but to another.[5]

In the last sentence, we can see how the word *belong* has changed from being used as a term of personal relations to being a term of property relations. For Marx, this represented an alienation of the self from itself, because *what we do* cannot be totally divorced from *who we are* without damage to our essential integrity.

A good example of the alienation of the self from itself in an economics of property is the case of surrogate motherhood. Let's say a woman agrees to give birth to a child (labor) and then gives the child to

[5] Karl Marx, "Economic and Philosophic Manuscripts of 1844," in *The Marx-Engels Reader*, ed. Robert Tucker (New York: W. W. Norton & Company, 1963), p. 60.

a couple for money. In a sense, the mother treats her baby as a commodity. She disconnects – alienates herself – from the baby so she is selling not herself, but her baby. In other words, the mother no longer belongs to the baby, and the baby, as a commodity, belongs to no one, until the buyer takes possession. They now own the child. (There are probably instances where surrogate motherhood does not involve the commoditization of the baby, but these are probably among people deeply connected, rather than disconnected, with each other.)

Belonging has a double meaning. It can mean ownership, as when I say, "This belongs to me." It can also mean membership, as when I say, "I belong to this family." This double meaning of belonging corresponds to and exposes the difference between seeing labor as property and as a provider. If I see what I provide as property – as a commodity – then the best I can do is to separate myself from it so that I do not become property as well. If I see what I provide as a provision, then the work of providing includes both who I am and what I do. My work becomes an engagement of myself in making provisions. In an economics of property, to see myself identified with what I do is to lose my self, since what I do is treated as property. In an economics of provision, on the other hand, when I identify with what I provide for others I see myself involved in a process of making provisions for others that can make my work meaningful.

If we are to change our approach to work from self-merchandizing to engagement, the workplace itself will also need to change. One change would be that we shift from property relations to civic relations as the basis for relationships among employees and employers. The move to civic relations would allow us to recognize the workplace as a place to make provisions, and as a work community. This means that we could understand ourselves as workers not in terms of what we own and can sell on the job market, but in terms of the work community to which we belong.

Developing such a work community requires a high degree of security. If employers can arbitrarily terminate one's employment, such security is simply impossible. Only when workers are granted

Table 9.1 *Two views of labor*

	Self-merchandizing	*Engagement*
Foundation	Property relations	Civic relations
Self-identity	Ownership	Membership
Security	Employment at will	Due process
Control	Hierarchical	Democratic

the basic civic right (not property right) of due process will the work-place become safe enough for workers to actually become involved in their productivity. To achieve this type of security, employees must be able to count on reciprocal relationships, including the reciprocity of exchange, participation, and deliberation. As we noted before, such reciprocal relationships mean that workers will be represented in the process of designing the policies of their organizations. Table 9.1 sum-marizes these requirements for employee engagement by contrasting labor as self-merchandizing and labor as engagement.

Which view of labor is practiced in a particular workplace depends in large part on management. One's view of labor is only the other side of one's view of management. If the managers manage as property owners, then laborers will, at least in most situations, be left only with the option of self-merchandizing. If the workplace is man-aged as a civic community, on the other hand, then workers can become engaged in their work.

In many cases, the most challenging aspect of creating work-places for employee engagement is the issue of control. If we are to civilize the workplace we must move from the current hierarchical master-servant arrangement where workers submit to their employers as subjects submit to their ruler, to a workplace that recognizes the moral equality of all. This would mean a democratization of the work-place, which does not require one-person one-vote, but rather that workers are treated as citizens, not subjects, and participate in the design of their workplace.

EMPLOYEE ENGAGEMENT AND WORKPLACE DEMOCRACY

Workplace democracy is a topic too broad to cover here in detail, but some ideas from discussions about it can help further clarify the direction that civilizing the workplace would lead us. Workplace democracy can range from workers participating in discussions about work design to workers actually owning the means of production, including the financial and physical capital of the firm. Remember that a civic economics of provision recognizes property as a political institution and subject to political policy. This view allows us to separate the control of the workplace – as a community of workers – from the question of property ownership. In many cases, the wise decision will be to grant individuals and groups property rights as they now enjoy them. At the same time, the power to arbitrarily control others by virtue of the ownership of property would be a violation of the civic norms of moral equality and reciprocity.

In the chapter on reciprocity, we saw that the relationship among people at work is a moral relationship, and that people have a civic right to have a say in determining those relationships. That does not mean, of course, that the workplace would be run by majority rule, but rather by civic deliberation. This process could take many forms. Thad Williamson's description of a workplace where democracy is absent gives us some notion of where we need to go to achieve workplace democracy:

> Workplace democracy can be usefully contrasted to work organizations in which employees serve solely at the will of management, in which employees have no collective voice over workplace conditions, in which employees have no voice in management decisions, and in which it is understood that the employee is at bottom a commodity to be deployed (or discarded) as management sees fit.[6]

[6] Thad Williamson, "The Relationship between Workplace Democracy and Economic Democracy: Three Views," paper given at the 2004 Annual Meeting of the American Political Science Association, September 2–5, 2004, Chicago, IL.

Clearly, seeing workers as providers rather than commodities, and as citizens rather than servants, lays the groundwork for workplace democracy. When we place the work of making provisions in its fundamental civic context of providing, protecting, and creating a worthwhile purpose, we can easily envision workplace democracy. In a recent book on the importance of establishing stable and viable communities, the authors describe a democratic community that I believe a civic economics of provision would promote:

> A democratic community should provide sufficient material provision for all its members, minimally, and must ultimately be able to exercise meaningful self-determination over its economic and social life.[7]

In a democratic community, in other words, making provisions is an integral part of living together. Furthermore, all citizens should have a say in how we live together.

In the United States today, workers are recognized as citizens in some cases and treated as servants in others. The rights to unionize, and the protection against discrimination and sexual harassment are based on our civic rights. At the same time, employment at will, management's control over one's work, and the distribution of profits continue to be based, in most cases, on property rights. As we shall see in later chapters, a business can be understood as property and as a work community. We do not need to choose one and ignore the other. We need to clarify their relationship. From a civic economics of provision, community overrides property; property rights must serve the common good. In some organizations, a civic economics of provision already fits better with their practices than a property-based economics. In many other places, and even in classrooms, we face a choice of seeing one's work life either as a life of self-merchandizing or as a life of engagement.

---

[7] Thad Williamson, David Imbroscio, and Gar Alperovitz, *Making a Place for Community: Local Democracy in a Global Era* (New York and London: Routledge, 2002), p. 295.

In the economics of provision, people focus on and identify with the provisions, and a major source for making these provisions is the second source of wealth: the land. As we shall see in the next chapter, the alienation of labor caused by an economics of property has repeated itself with a vengeance in our relationship with the living planet.

10 Land: ownership as a concession

When we discussed the meaning of property in Chapter 5, we said that the idea of property implied ownership and ownership required a legal title. This means that a piece of land is not actually property until someone has a legal title to it, which is a political act. Without the political acts that establish land *as* property, the ownership of land is subject to the will of the stronger.

The status of the land, of course, is always subject to how we define it. Even if we define it as "natural," we usually remain within our understanding of it. To see the land as something beyond understanding, as something else, is difficult. Every once in a while – at the ocean, in the forests, at twilight, or in memories of changing seasons – we recognize "nature" as something not subject to our definition, but as something else. This is something you cannot own, buy and sell. It is something our definitions never totally encompass. It is the aspect of nature that makes it a living system.

The danger we face today is that by determining land as property (a determination does terminate what it defines), we may well kill the breathing of the earth. Perhaps no one has captured this threat more clearly than Aldo Leopold. In his *A Sand County Almanac* (1949), he described the land as a living system:

> Land, then, is not merely soil; it is a fountain of energy flowing through a circuit of soils, plants, and animals. Food chains are the living channels, which conduct energy upward; death and decay return it to the soil. The circuit is not closed; some energy is dissipated in decay, some is added by absorption from the air, some is stored in soils, peats, and long-lived forests;

but it is a sustained circuit, like a slowly augmented revolving fund of life.[1]

With an awareness of the dynamics of the land, or biotic community, Leopold offers the following ethical principle: "A thing is right when it tends to preserve the integrity, stability, and beauty of the biotic community. It is wrong when it tends otherwise."[2] Leopold's view is not that of a romantic, but rather that of a deer hunter who lived with nature rather than apart from it. In the final analysis, humans too are part of the biotic community.

As we face the depletion of farmland, the destruction of wetlands, the loss of biodiversity, the growing shortage of fresh water, and the ever-growing accumulation of waste, even an obsessive rationalist would have to acknowledge the significance of Leopold's view of the land. This does not mean that we should not cultivate the land, nor that we should not allow people to own it, but we do need to do these things from a perspective of civic relations, not property relations. This will require a conversion of our normal way of thinking about the land. To understand clearly what we need to turn away from, there exists no better example than the story of how the Europeans turned the land of the Americas into their private property.

PROPERTY AS THE PRIVATIZATION OF LAND

Within the scope of the Enlightenment's four stages of history is a story of the privatization of land. During the hunting and grazing stages of human history, land remained a commons. During the agriculture stage, cultivated land was considered as belonging to the cultivators, but it stopped belonging to a particular person or family once it was no longer cultivated. Only in the fourth stage does land become something that could be exclusively controlled by the owner, whether it was cultivated or not. At this stage, it becomes private property.

---

[1] Aldo Leopold, *A Sand County Almanac: And Sketches Here and There* (London: Oxford University Press, 1949), p. 2.
[2] *Ibid.*, pp. 224–225.

British colonists used these four stages of history to legitimize their taking of land in the Americas. The native peoples of the Americas, the British assumed, were at an earlier stage of development, because they had not yet taken ownership of the land, which in the British view meant that they were not making it productive. By taking the land and treating it as private property, the colonists believed they were actually civilizing the new continent.

It turns out that many of the East Coast Indians did have cultivated fields, which the colonists viewed as property. In such cases, colonists actually bought the land from the Indians. (Uncultivated land, on the other hand, was seen as not belonging to anyone.) One may well ask, of course, whether these sales were voluntary. Perhaps more importantly, the selling and buying of land meant quite different things for the Indians and the Europeans. For the Indians, selling land meant that the buyers would become an integral part of their social and political network. For the English, the deal meant that they would now have exclusive use of the land and the Indians would have to vacate the land, a concept quite foreign to the Indians.[3]

This severing of the ownership of land from any community relationships or obligations had antecedents in Britain in the enclosure movements of the fifteenth and eighteenth centuries, which we discussed earlier. Stuart Banner describes the similarity between the English enclosure movements and the privatization of land in the Americas this way:

> Enclosure meant the conversion of an ancient system of property rights, in which individuals and groups often possessed rights to use particular resources scattered in various places, into the familiar modern property system, in which individuals possess all the resources within a given area of land ... Indian property arrangements were similar in some respects to the English common fields. The combination of individual planting rights in particular

---

[3] Stuart Banner, *How the Indians Lost Their Land: Law and Power on the Frontier* (Cambridge, MA: The Belknap Press of Harvard University Press, 2005), p. 58.

plots of land and group resource-gathering right in the remainder would have reminded many English colonists of property systems back home.[4]

A similar transformation occurred in Scotland. Between 1780 and 1850, as many as 500,000 Highlanders were displaced from their ancestral homes so the land, on which they had lived for generations, could be used for grazing sheep.[5] Known as the "Clearances," these forced evictions are recognized today as a violation of the ancient property right known as *duthchas*, which was the obligation for clan leaders "to provide protection and security of possession of their people within their lands."[6] For the Indians in the Americas and the Highlanders in northern Scotland, the common right of all to use land as needed was replaced by the right of one to exclude others from the land that he owned. For the most part, we still live in this tradition today.

To overturn this tradition, we can begin by heeding other views of the relationship between land and people, such as that of Vandana Shiva. The founder of Navdanya, a movement for biodiversity conservation and farmers' rights in India, Shiva has written about a partnership with nature.

> Sustenance, in the final analysis, is built on the continued capacity of nature to renew its forests, fields and rivers. These resource systems are intrinsically linked to life-producing and life-conserving cultures, and it is in managing the integrity of ecological cycles in forestry and agriculture that women's productivity has been most developed and evolved. Women transfer fertility from the forests to the field and to animals. They transfer animal waste as fertilizer for crops and crop by-products to animals as fodder. They work with the forest to bring water to their fields and families. This partnership between women's and nature's work ensures the sustainability of

---

[4] *Ibid.*, p. 37.
[5] Ben McConville, "Cleaning the Air on the Clearances," Scotsman.com, September 2005 (retrieved on December 10, 2007).
[6] Devine, *Scotland's Empire*, p. 126.

sustenance, and it is this critical partnership that is torn asunder when the project of "development" becomes a patriarchal project, threatening both nature and women.[7]

In terms of our story of provisions, Shiva's complaint about patriarchal development projects represents a significant protest against the domination of an economics of property and property relations. When land is treated as a commodity, the bonds of nature – which connect all of life, both human and non-human – are severed. We are left with an object that appears to us lifeless even though it is the giver of life. This contradiction in Western thought has many roots, of course, including its tradition of patriarchal religions.

WESTERN RELIGIONS AND THE VITALITY OF NATURE

In the West, the three great religions – Judaism, Christianity, and Islam – spring from the victory of the patriarchal, nomadic Hebrew tribes over the agricultural, matriarchal cultures of the settled communities of Canaan. The contrasts between the Canaanites and the Hebrews were stark. The Canaanites practiced agriculture and worshiped multiple gods and goddesses through fertility festivals and rituals. The Hebrew tribes were nomadic shepherds who worshiped Jehovah, or Yahweh, a single male god. Whereas the Canaanites found vitality in the natural world, for the Hebrews vitality resided in the story of their relationship with their god. The earth, for them, was something to subdue and conquer.

Western culture still lives with this dominance of the male principle of control (or protection) over the female principle of fertility (or providing). Although there have been many variations and oppositions to it throughout Western history, the patriarchal tradition continues to foster the view of nature and land as something at our disposal, for our use. It just seems "natural" to treat land as property.

---

[7] Vandana Shiva, *Staying Alive: Women, Ecology and Development* (London: Zed Books Ltd., 1989), p. 45.

So where does the vitality of life on this earth come from? Today, we know that all energy ultimately comes from the sun. If the sun burned out, the earth would no longer sustain life. Our access to this energy is largely through the cultivation of the earth and the extraction of its energy deposits, such as oil and coal. We will look at the system of the biosphere later when we consider the systems in which we live, but what we can recognize for now is that the land is a biotic system, a living provider of wealth. Although few would want to reinstate the religion of the Canaanites, they were closer to the truth about nature than the early Hebrew tribes.

We could suggest that we should all become nature worshipers, but that is not our plan here. Our aim is to clear the way to recognize land as a provider rather than as property. This means that we need to take seriously our experiences of the beauty and delicacy, as well as of the power and grandeur of the natural world. In the Western religions, we also find beliefs about nature as God's creation and of his presence in nature. Such traditions certainly bring us closer to the kind of attitude we need toward nature if we are to create a just and sustainable economy.

As we watch the patriarchal, property-based narrative of economics destroy species, deplete resources, pollute our waters, and increase global warming, it should be fairly clear that we need a new narrative about the land. In the chapter on economic systems, we will take up this question at a different level, as we explore the difference between biological, linguistic, and social systems. For now, we need to examine what land would look like from a civic perspective.

A CIVIC VIEW OF THE LAND

If we think of the land in terms of the three essential activities of providing, protecting, and creating purpose, the civic perspective would frame the land in such a way that we have access to the land's provisions but also protect it as a living system. Property rights would serve as a means for harvesting the productivity of the land, but not as a license to destroy its fecundity. Land management, in other words, would be grounded in a civic notion of land as a common resource. This means that property rights would be granted to persons by civic governments in tune with the basic activities of making provisions, giving protection, and creating a worthwhile purpose.

Although one could develop more cooperative ways to cultivate land than that of giving property title to individuals and families, such practices will likely predominate in the United States. This title, however, should be seen as a political decision. As DeSoto reminds us:

> The crucial point to understand is that property is not a physical thing that can be photographed or mapped. Property is not a primary quality of assets but the legal expression of an economically meaningful consensus about assets. Law is the instrument that fixes and realizes capital. In the West, the law is less concerned with representing the physical reality of buildings or real estate than with providing a process or rules that will allow society to extract potential surplus value from those assets. Property is not the assets themselves but a consensus between people as to how those assets should be held, used, and exchanged.[8]

The consensus that DeSoto mentions could be based on civic conversations about how to protect the provisionary dimension of land for this and future generations. The right to farm the land would then be a concession to farmers.

LAND OWNERSHIP AS A CONCESSION

Concessions crop up extensively today in developing countries as a type of agreement between governments and global businesses. Long-term projects – such as building and maintaining airports, water systems, roads and highways – often hinge on concession agreements. Nicholas Miranda, in a recent article on concessions in developing countries, defines them as follows:

---

[8] DeSoto, *The Mystery of Capital*, p. 157.

> A concession agreement is an agreement between a government and a private company ("the concessionaire"), in which the government transfers to the company the right to maintain, produce, or provide a good or service within the country for a limited period of time, but the government retains ultimate control of the right.[9]

This may sound like privatization, and in developing countries it has some of the same benefits and dangers. In a study of concessions by the World Bank, J. Luis Guasch points out the following differences:

> Although concessions and privatizations tend to achieve the same objective – securing private sector managerial and operational expertise and investments – they differ in three respects. First, concessions do not involve the sale or transfer of ownership of physical assets, only the right to use the assets and to operate the enterprise. Second, concession contracts are for a limited period – usually 15–30 years, depending on the context and sector. Finally, the government as owner of the assets retains much closer involvement and oversight in concessions.[10]

If we apply the notion of concession to the owning of farms or apartment complexes, for example, we would need to rethink the meaning of ownership. Still, we do have examples of long-term leases on public property, and other forms of private ownership on public property that make this a workable idea. Think of the private homes in national parks or the leasing of public lands for cattle grazing.

Some people may object to seeing land ownership as a concession because they connect the notion of privacy with property ownership. Governments do have a duty to protect personal and familial privacy, and privacy has been recognized as an essential aspect of personal autonomy. Still, a renter in an apartment complex has the

---

[9] Nicholas Miranda, "Concession Agreements: From Private Contract to Public Policy," *Yale Law Journal*, December 1, 2007.

[10] J. Luis Guasch, *Granting and Renegotiating Infrastructure Concessions: Doing it Right* (Washington, DC: The World Bank, 2004), p. 30.

same rights to privacy as any homeowner. Ownership and privacy, in other words, can be separated.

If the land does belong to all of us, or if we all belong to it, and we need to cultivate it to provide for us, then giving farmers long-term concessions seems like a way to remain conscious and responsible for using the land as a provider and protecting it as a living system.

Should we consider all ownership situations as potential concessions? What about the physical assets of a business or corporation? As we shall see later on, a corporation has multiple meanings. It can be treated as a piece of property and as a community. People speak of a corporation possessing various forms of capital: financial, physical, intellectual, human, social, and natural. The physical capital is most clearly property, although, in an economics of property, all of these forms of capital are treated as forms of property. Some can be protected by patents. From the perspective of an economics of property, the corporation as property trumps the notion of the corporation as a community of workers, which means that the property owners control the direction of the corporation. If we switch to an economics of provision and see property rights based on civic relations, we get a very different picture.

Treating property as a concession affects our relationship with both human and non-human communities. For human communities, treating property as a concession changes the location of community control from the property owners to all members of the community. For non-human communities – that is, for the biosphere – treating property as a concession allows us to protect the planet – a living system – from being treated as a commodity. This planet does not belong to our generation. There is no one to give us title to it. It belongs to all generations. We actually belong to it. To find our home in nature, we need to know how to belong to it instead of forcing it to belong to us.

11   Money: commodity or credit

What is money? It has multiple functions in our everyday lives. For most of us, money is something we receive as wages, something to pay our debts, to purchase things, to collect as credit, and to save for the future. In Smithian economics, money is first of all a commodity that can be used in the trading of other commodities. In other words, it is primarily a medium of exchange. Gold coins, for example, are commodities – they can be bought and sold, but they also function as a medium for exchanging other commodities. That is the theory. The theory also holds that money is what Geoffrey Ingham calls a "neutral veil," which means that it merely symbolizes the real exchange ratios between other commodities.[1] Money, in other words, should not be an issue. This view gives us a picture of money as a means for effective transactions. It does not explain how money became such a trustworthy medium of exchange.

Imagine that someone, let's call him Adam, goes into a second-hand shop and sees a used guitar he would like. It is priced at $60. Adam only has $50. The conversation proceeds as follows:

Adam: "I will pay you $50 for the used guitar there."

Shopkeeper: "Sorry, but the guitar is well worth $70."

Adam: "I am not disagreeing with you about the price of the guitar, I just think a dollar is worth more than you do. I think that 50 dollars should buy the guitar, not 60."

Shopkeeper: "I am not selling dollars, I am selling a guitar, and it costs $60."

This conversation is of course, a fantasy. We do not haggle about the value of money that we use to buy and sell commodities. We haggle

---

[1] Geoffrey Ingham, *The Nature of Money* (Cambridge: Polity Press, 2004), p. 33.

about the value of commodities, in this case the used guitar. Money, in other words, functions as a measure of the value of commodities. To fulfill this function, money itself cannot be treated as a commodity whose value depends on supply and demand. This is what Smithian economics failed to understand. The value of money is determined not by the market, but by what is called the "money of account."

THE MONEY OF ACCOUNT

The money of account is the monetary unit that is used in market transactions, such as the dollar or the euro. When we buy and sell commodities, this money of account – the dollar in the case of the second-hand store transaction – serves as a means of measuring the value of the commodity. This seems obvious and yet it is often misunderstood. Let's return to the store again. The shopkeeper and the customer are bargaining about the price of the guitar. It might seem that they are trading money for the guitar, but that is not the case. The customer does have dollars, but the meaning of the dollars cannot be negotiated in the same way as the value of the guitar. Both parties agree on the value of the money. They may disagree on the value of the guitar. If they do disagree, it is because they see the guitar's value differently, which could be for any number of reasons. True, they could disagree about the meaning of the money. The buyer may have attachments to the money that the shopkeeper does not have. Perhaps the buyer has been saving for months to get enough money to buy a guitar. Maybe the buyer received it as a birthday gift. We could imagine different stories about the money as well as about the shopkeeper's desire to sell the guitar. All these differences, however, do not affect money's role in this transaction. It serves to measure the value of the guitar. As Geoffrey Ingham says, money is actually a third entity, used here by both the buyer and the seller.

> Barter exchange of commodities, whatever the complexity of the system, is essentially bilateral; but monetary relations are trilateral. Transacting agents are themselves unable to produce universally

acceptable money at will. Monetary exchange, unlike exchange in general, involves a third party of those authorities that may legitimately produce money. It has been the fundamental error of economic orthodoxy to subsume monetary exchange under the general rubric of pure dyadic exchange.[2]

The provision of a common currency that functions as a third entity, allowing strangers to engage in exchanges, is similar to the function of the civic sphere we detailed earlier. Just as the civic sphere provided a platform on which strangers could make deals to their mutual advantage, money provides a means that both parties can use to assess the value of commodities. Whether we finally agree with this view of money may largely depend on our view of money's origin.

THE ORIGIN OF MONEY

Many people commonly hold the belief that money emerged from exchanges, and that it belongs to the world of commerce. Others hold that governments first issued money, which would place it in the civic realm and the world of politics. We will briefly explore arguments for both views and the significance of this debate.

The argument that money originates from the state stems partly from the early practices of paying obligations to religious or state authorities. As Geoffrey Ingham points out, the primitive notion of *Wergeld*, or "worth payment," referred to a compensation for injuries and damage in communal or tribal societies.[3] He draws the following conclusion from his review of the evidence on the early uses of money:

> All evidence points to the historical origins of money as a means of calculating obligations and debts in pre-market tribal and clan society. Early settled agricultural societies developed a more complex division of labour than the hunters and gatherers,

---

[2] Geoffrey Ingham, "'Babylonian Madness': On the Historical and Sociological Origins of Money," in *What Is Money?*, ed. John Smithin (London and New York: Routledge, 2000), p. 23.

[3] Ingham, *The Nature of Money*, p. 92.

generating a surplus that was distributed unequally. Measures for the assessment of differential social and political obligations were developed. These varied by the nature of the transgression and the status of the injured party, and formed the conceptual basis for money of account.[4]

The first function of money, according to this view, was to pay debts – debts to the state – and the establishment of the money of account was a means to uniformly measure the debt to be paid. This assignment of payment by the state could have easily provided a background for a second early practice: paying taxes. Only later did money function as a medium for the exchange of commodities. Furthermore, its capacity to serve as a medium of exchange was based on its credibility, which was maintained by the state.

Ingham's observations match those of Richard Von Glahn, who points out that during the Song dynasty in China, between the tenth and thirteenth centuries, it was the state that created *paper* money.

> The history of paper money in China does indeed attest to the crucial importance of the state in its fiscal practices in sustaining a viable paper currency. While paper currencies, along with other paper instruments like commodity vouchers, came to play significant roles in the fiscal administration of the Song and its successors, they also served, at certain times and in certain regions, as the primary means of exchange in private trade as well.[5]

The role of money as a medium of exchange, in this case, was secondary to the state's use of money for its own finances. This view differs from the goldsmith story, the traditional textbook explanation of the origin of paper money. Here is the story as told by Baumol and Blinder:

---

[4] *Ibid.*, p. 105.

[5] Richard Von Glahn, "The Origins of Paper Money in China," in *The Origins of Value: The Financial Innovations that Created Modern Capital Markets*, ed. William N. Goetzmann and K. Geert Rouwenhorst (New York: Oxford University Press, 2005), p. 89.

> When money was made of gold it was most inconvenient for
> consumers and merchants to carry it around and to have to weigh
> and assay it for purity every time a transaction was made. So it is not
> surprising that the practice developed of leaving one's gold in the
> care of the goldsmith, who had safe storage facilities, and carrying in
> its place a receipt from the goldsmith stating that Joe Doe did indeed
> own five ounces of gold of a certain purity. When people began
> trading goods and services for the goldsmith's receipts, rather than
> for the gold itself, the receipts became an early form of money.[6]

So goes the first part of the story. The next part is not about the
merchants who now had paper receipts instead of their gold, but
about the goldsmith:

> When goldsmiths decided that they could get along by keeping only
> a fraction of their total deposits on reserve in their vaults and lending
> out the balance, they acquired the ability to create money.[7]

In the first part of the story, the value of the receipts or paper money is
backed by gold – a commodity – and the value of the gold depended on
its weight and purity. (We will get to the second part of the story later.)
One must assume that in time the receipts – the paper money – would
have a value assigned to them, probably in specific dominations, such
as one, five, and ten, so people could trade with them. If I have ten units
of money, for example, I would know that I have ten times more money
than if I only had one unit. This brings us back to the idea of money as a
unit of account – money is used to measure the value of commodities,
but is not a commodity itself. So it seems that if we follow what
happens over time with paper money, the goldsmith story ends with
the money of account. Ingham appears to be correct; money is not a
commodity like other commodities, but a third entity that allows for
the exchange of commodities.

---

[6] William J. Baumol and Alan S. Blinder, *Economics: Principles and Policy*, third edition
(New York: Harcourt Brace Jovanovich, 1986), p. 227.
[7] *Ibid.*, p. 228.

The second part of the goldsmith story – that banks create money – is more complicated. Banks do issue credit and, because of what is called fractional reserve banking, they can offer much more credit than they have deposits. They assume that everyone will not withdraw their deposits at the same time. But does this constitute the creation of money? It would, perhaps, if money is credit and if all credit is money. If money is credit it seems that the government story and the goldsmith story are actually telling the same story – the story of credit and debt. So, even though the goldsmith story begins with the commodity view of money, if we continue its story to its end, we see that the commodity view of money obscures money's actual function – providing credit and paying off debts. What is necessary is that we can trust the value of paper money. Who should we turn to: government or the banks? To more fully understand the relationship between the government and banks, we need to further explore the function of money as credit and debt.

MONEY AS CREDIT AND DEBT

Although you may have money in your billfold and treat it as a thing you possess, its real value exists, for the most part, in the relationship between you as a user of the dollar, and the agency that issued the dollar. This relationship has two aspects. The first aspect involves a promise. As Ingham says, "The credibility of money is now based exclusively on the credibility of promises to pay. The institutional fact of money is now no more than this credibility, as it is established by the rules and conventions that frame and legitimize the acts of borrowing and lending by all the agents in the monetary system."[8] The issuer promises to treat the dollar as a dollar. This may seem like an empty promise, but it has meaning; namely, it allows me to use a specific sum of dollars to pay a debt of the same amount. I can rely on the dollar as I rely on any promise.

[8] Ingham, *The Nature of Money*, p. 136.

The second aspect involves credit and debt. Your dollar represents a "credit" that you can use to pay the "debt" you incur when you purchase something. This may not be so obvious with cash as it is with credit cards. The credit card company has extended to you a certain amount of credit. When you use the card, you create a debt to the credit card company, which you pay later. Credit and debt are two sides of the same coin, so to speak.

When we move from our individual use of money to make purchases, pay debts, and make a living to larger social systems, we find that relationships between credit and debt becomes much more complicated. To explore these relationships, we turn to the famous story of the conflict between Greenbacks and the Goldbugs in the nineteenth century.

GREENBACKS AND GOLDBUGS

During the US Civil War, as in most wars, the government issued money to finance operations. When the war ended, there was a huge supply of government notes (greenbacks) still in circulation. Farmers and laborers from the western and southern states wanted the government to issue more greenbacks to facilitate debt repayment, economic growth, and development. They formed the Greenback political party in the mid-1870s and campaigned for the government to control the money supply so it could adjust the volume of currency in proportion to economic growth.[9] The eastern-based bankers, who became known as Goldbugs, wanted the government to recall the greenbacks and return to a gold-backed currency. The two parties had very different interests. The Greenbacks wanted more credit for the creation of wealth. But an increase in money supply would also increase inflation, which would decrease the value of the banks' loans. So the banks wanted to restrict the money supply. It might look as though the banks were trying to protect the value of money, but remember that

---

[9] Gretchen Ritter, *Goldbugs and Greenbacks: The Antimonopoly Tradition and the Politics of Finance in America, 1865–1896* (Cambridge: Cambridge University Press, 1997), p. 49.

the value of money depends on the money of account, which is maintained by governments, not banks. There are several ways to understand this disagreement over the monetary standard, but I think that Gretchen Ritter's interpretation highlights the issue that was faced then and that we still face today.

> The debate over the monetary standard was about more than mere money. At issue were competing visions of economic development and political change. The choice between greenbacks and gold was a choice between a democratically controlled, national monetary standard and a market-oriented, international monetary standard. Concern with inflation and contraction went beyond prices to matters of class and sectional relations. Beliefs about the value of money and who should control it went to fundamental differences over the relationship between economic and political life.[10]

Money, in other words, is about social relations. Treat it as a commodity, then those who own the money can use it to make more money, which is certainly in the interest of the bankers. Treat it as a provider, or as a means of provision, then those who need credit to finance their endeavors of making provisions for themselves and others will be able to improve their lot. Capitalism, as Ingham has stated, is run by "credit-money."[11]

Money, in other words, already belongs to an economics of provision – money provides credit and the means of paying debts. This function of money, however, has been obscured and sometimes violated in our current economy based on property relations. Banks continue to treat money as property – as a commodity – that they can use to make more money. The 2008 financial crisis and its aftermath have made the decision to begin treating money as a provision even more urgent than ever before. What difference would such a decision make? Look at the kind of conversations it would engender on the domestic and international fronts.

[10] Ritter, *Goldbugs and Greenbacks*, p. 73. [11] Ingham, *The Nature of Money*, p. 107.

THE DOMESTIC FRONT

The financial crisis of 2008 had more than one cause, of course, but a significant trigger was the plummet in housing prices in the United States. This kicked the legs out from under a financial world that had been built largely on sub-prime and other nontraditional mortgage loans. And what a financial world it was – a world of more than a trillion dollars of either bad money or at least risky debt.

This financial world was largely born in the 1990s through deregulation of the banking industry and the promotion of home ownership. A key decision was the 1999 repeal of the Glass-Steagall Act, which had segregated financial institutions according to their business. Thus, commercial lenders could not engage in investment or in insurance activity, nor could they collaborate with such institutions. In the absence of this regulation, banks were allowed to engage in all sorts of financial practices.

Many politicians encouraged the growth of the financial sector. Besides supporting the repeal of the Glass-Steagall Act, Washington also supported NAFTA, which resulted in the integration of the North American financial community, but did little to protect labor or the environment.[12] As Kevin Phillips writes in his recent book *Bad Money*, it appears that the government had decided that the growth of the US economy would depend on the growth of financial services.[13] During this time, the financial sector grew to around 20 percent of gross domestic product, while manufacturing dropped to around 12 percent. And for some years, everyone – from the Bush administration and the Federal Reserve, to local loan officers and to homebuyers – seemed to cooperate to keep the money flowing.

From the perspective in this book, the banks were engaged in turning relationships of provision (credit and debt with promises to pay) into financial products or commodities that could be bought and

---

[12] Jeff Faux, *The Global Class War: How American's Bipartisan Elite Lost Our Future and What It Will Take to Win It Back* (New York: John Wiley & Sons, Inc., 2006).

[13] Kevin Phillips, *Bad Money: Reckless Finance, Failed Politics, and the Global Crisis of American Capitalism* (New York: Viking, 2007), p. xiii.

sold. Instead of keeping the mutual promises implicit in credit and debt relationships, banks enticed people without strong credit to take on a debt that could easily overwhelm them if housing prices ever stalled or fell. The money relationship among citizens, in other words, was replaced by a property relationship among property holders. At the same time, the loan mortgages were pooled and packaged into securities (mortgage backed securities, or MBS). These commodities were bought and sold as though they were corporate stocks and bonds.

Here is the question. Should we treat corporate stocks and bonds differently than we treat mortgages, or government treasury bills and government bonds? A corporate bond is certainly a form of property. The value of the corporate bond depends on the value of the corporation, or perhaps on the value of the bond as a piece of property. Its value is not a concern of the state. Money is a different kind of entity. It is essentially state-legitimized credit. We should therefore have a means (regulations) to prevent it from being treated as property.

From the perspective of an economics of provision, a bank's function is to provide credit, not to amass debt for its own benefit. There are certainly banks that do this very well. This is not an impossible task. ShoreBank, for example, was established in 1973 to promote the economic development of the South Side of Chicago.[14] Because of racial discrimination, many creditworthy residents had not been able to get credit for homes or for starting or improving their businesses. So the bank provided small loans to businesses and families located in South Chicago. Another example is the Grameen Bank in Bangladesh, which was started by Muhammad Yunus, who won the Nobel Peace Prize for his pioneering work in microcredit banking. The Grameen bank has provided millions of people with small loans for economic development. The loans, sometimes as little as 20 dollars, have allowed people to start or improve their small businesses and thereby boost their standard of living.[15] The bank has become a model for

---

[14] www.shorebankcorp.com

[15] Muhammad Yunus, *Creating a World without Poverty: Social Business and the Future of Capitalism* (New York: Public Affairs, 2007), pp. 56–66.

providing credit to communities, or what we could call practicing an economics of provision rather than property.

THE INTERNATIONAL FRONT

On the international scene, credit and debt relationships are complicated because of the existence of different monetary units, such as the European euro, the Japanese yen, the Brazilian real, and the Chinese yuan. After World War Two and until recently, the dollar dominated these other currencies. Some would say that what kept the dollar dominant was the agreement of the oil-producing nations to sell oil in dollars, an agreement the United States made with Saudi Arabia in 1974. For years, the oil states poured their enormous oil revenues into US banks, which the banks then used to provide loans for developing nations. Just as homebuyers were given more credit than they could handle in the 1990s, developing nations were given more credit than they could reasonably manage in the 1970s and 1980s. This resulted in developing countries having to restructure their financial and social programs – to the detriment of their people – to repay these debts. Once again, the function of money to provide credit for economic development was overturned so it provided profit for the issuers of credit.

More recently, the US government has become a major debtor in the global financial market. Because we import much more than we export, especially from China, we have issued treasury notes that China has bought. Our continued consumption of imports made in China, in other words, depends on China's continued buying of US notes and bonds. China is not the only developing nation extending this kind of credit to the United States. As Joseph Stiglitz has remarked, "There is something peculiar about poor countries desperately in need of capital lending hundreds of billions of dollars to the world's richest country."[16] The peculiarity is quite striking. The challenges China faces are stark, and yet it is holding in reserve, according

---

[16] Joseph E. Stiglitz, *Making Globalization Work* (New York: W. W. Norton & Company, 2006), p. 245.

to Stiglitz, approximately $900 billion. The reserves of all developing countries of US notes were estimated at $3.35 trillion at the end of 2006.[17]

What a reversal from the 1980s! Then, developing nations were burdened by debts they owed to the US banks. Now they are burdened by holding debts that the United States owes them. Instead of using their reserves for economic development, they keep them to allow the US consumer to continue shopping. As long as US consumers do not have to pay their government's expenses, and let China and other countries buy US government notes, they can continue to shop. As long as they continue to shop, China and other countries can continue to export products to the United States. This, of course, prevents developing nations from providing for their own people, while it perpetuates unsustainable consumption. In this case, the burden of debt has prevented money from performing its primary function – providing credit for economic development. As long as the dollar remains the dominant global currency and the global economy remains dependent on US consumption, this global credit/debt relationship seems both impossible to continue (it is not sustainable) and impossible to change. On the other hand, the situation may change if the status of the dollar changes.

In the global market, it turns out we can haggle about the value of the dollar as well as the price of the guitar. Given that banks and the US government have been influenced more by an economics of property than an economics of provision, the decline of the dollar's value is viewed in terms of its value as one commodity among other commodities. Phillips even suggests that since 1974, when Saudi Arabia agreed to sell oil in dollars, oil replaced gold as the standard for measuring the dollar.[18] This makes sense from an economics of property. It also makes sense that property must be protected. Some would argue that the reason we invaded Iraq was that Saddam Hussein was talking of changing the currency of oil trade from the dollar to the euro. Today,

---

[17] *Ibid.*, p. 249. [18] Phillips, *Bad Money*, p. 143.

more than one nation is making similar calculations. The dollar may become one among other currencies. If the United States remains trapped in an economics of property, it is difficult to imagine what it might do to protect its property. After all, the legacy of the Smithian tradition is that the purpose of government is to protect property. On the other hand, if we could move to an economics of provision and recognize that the function of money is to provide credit for economic development, then the United States, instead of striving to be above all other nations, could become one among other nations, as its currency has become one among other currencies.

Is this possible? The model to watch is the European Union. Not a perfect model, but still. The euro is not possessed by any one nation, which means it cannot be treated only as a commodity. The euro provides credit, a means for evaluating and exchanging goods and services, and a "promise to pay." The unknown is whether the European Union has the political will to protect the euro from speculators, who treat money as a commodity.

The legacy of large banks in the Anglo-American tradition is to pretend that money is a commodity that they manage for property owners. An economics of provision, on the other hand, sees money as a provider. It provides credit. It exists in social relationships of credit and debt. How we organize those relationships is part of the larger question of how we want to live together – which is finally a civic question that should be answered in civic conversations. Money does make the world go around. How it goes around will largely depend on our government's selection of what communities within the economy it wishes to develop. Actually, how we view the function of money will depend on our understanding of its role in economic systems. This brings us to the new set of questions about the economy as a system, which is the theme of the following chapters.

Part IV **Civilizing economic systems**

A civic economics of provision has three goals: making provisions, protecting providers, and creating a worthwhile purpose. The three traditional sources of wealth – labor, land, and money – are key providers that should be protected from exploitation and misuse and enlisted in achieving the goals of human communities. Most of this work occurs in various systems. To meet the expectations of an economics of provision, we will need to think of the economy as a system and then figure out how to move the system toward fulfilling its purposes with justice and in a sustainable manner.

If we define a system as a set of interdependent and interconnected parts that constitute some whole, then it is clear that most of our everyday life occurs in some system. We go shopping for dinner in the food system. We discard our leftovers in the ecological system. We breathe in the atmospheric system. The quality of our life depends on the quality of our body's immune, digestive, and circulatory systems. Our life, in other words, is a life in a global system that is comprised of a series of large and small sub-systems. In this chapter, we will explore the nature of economic systems. Following chapters will provide strategies for reframing, evaluating and changing these systems.

In a sense Adam Smith's idea of the market's "invisible hand" was an early system concept. The dynamics of the market – supply and demand – produced results that were intended or caused not by individuals, but by the miracle of the system itself. Even today, some scholars studying what are called complex adaptive systems see the notion of the invisible hand as an early contribution to their field, as evidenced by the following quote:

Writings on complexity in the social sciences go back hundreds of years, with Adam Smith's *The Wealth of Nations* (1776) representing one of the earliest and most cohesive discussions of the topic. One of the prime drivers of economic theory over the past two centuries has been Smith's concept of an "invisible hand" leading collections of self-interested agents into well-formed structures that are no part of any single agent's intention. Although much theoretical progress has been made on this idea, for example, the elegant proofs of existence given by Arrow and Debreu or the various contributions based on fanciful mechanisms like Walrasian auctioneers, the actual mechanisms behind the invisible hand still remain largely, dare we say, invisible.[1]

This seems quite astounding, especially since we know that behind the "invisible hand" of Scottish commerce were governmental and commercial decisions to enslave Africans, to privatize the land of the Americas, and to create a police force that protected property (slaves and land). The Scottish economy was not self-organizing; merchants, governments, and plantation owners organized it. Human actors, in other words, not system dynamics, organized early capitalism. That does not mean, however, that economics is not systematic. It does mean that we must find out what kind of system it is. We can begin our investigation with the portrayal of Smithian economics shown in Figure 12.1.

If one stands in the center of this picture, looking at the planet, one sees land as a commodity. The rest of the planet, for the most part, is invisible. Looking at society, one sees the commodity of labor; at government, the laws protecting property. Civic society appears as sets of organizations that do good and deserve the support of corporations. Such charitable activities are known today as the contributions of "corporate citizens." Money in this picture is seen as an economic institution.

---

[1] John H. Miller and Scott E. Page, *Complex Adaptive Systems: An Introduction to Computational Models of Social Life* (Princeton, NJ and Oxford: Princeton University Press, 2007), p. 4.

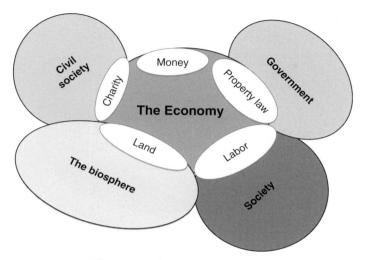

FIGURE 12.1 The system of an economics of property

Although this picture does not depict exactly why we are in trouble today, we do get some indications. This model pictures society as labor, ignoring the social inequalities of class, gender, race, religion, and ethnicity. It sees the biosphere as a commodity – land – oblivious to the planet as a living interconnected system. It views government only as a protector of property, and it sees civil society as charitable organizations that assist those who fall through its cracks. Finally, it assumes that all would be fine if everyone just let the market do its thing. The misery of the providers of wealth is nowhere in the picture, of course. That has been split off and hidden from everyday consciousness.

So, what kind of picture would depict a civic economics of provision? First of all, it would not present the economy as an isolated system. It would show the economy as it really is: a sub-system inter-twined with other sub-systems, including the social system, the eco-logical system of the planet, and the discursive system of civil society. Furthermore, money would be tied to the government and government would not be separated from civil society; government represents the members of civil society – global citizens. If we portrayed just the

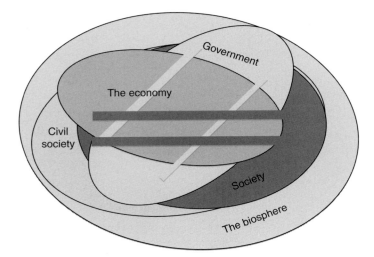

FIGURE 12.2 The system of an economics of provision

systematic aspects of the world in which the economy exists, it might look something like Figure 12.2.

This picture allows us to recognize that the economy belongs to three distinct sub-systems: the ecological system of the biosphere, the social system of human societies, and the civic system of discourse. (Government, for the most part, belongs to the civic system.) These three systems create and maintain much of the world in which we provide, protect, and give purpose to our lives. The ecological system sustains us and other living things. We belong to it. Social systems comprise sets of relationships that unite and separate us. And the civic system of discourse gives us the possibilities to say what needs to be said. Since the motivation for writing this book has been to offer a more complete and integrative way of talking about our economic life, we first explore the civic system of discourse, or the system of civic conversations.

THE SYSTEM OF CIVIC CONVERSATIONS

The civic sphere becomes a civil society because people divided by social differences join together in civic conversations about issues that concern them. These civic conversations can take place in a variety of forums, from neighborhood meetings and workplace sessions to mass media events and city council meetings. They create and maintain the civic relationships that serve as the foundation for an economics of provision. Furthermore, these conversations belong to systems of discourse that give participants things to think about. As we engage in such conversations, they can become truly thought-provoking. We need to understand the various elements that constitute the system of civic conversations, if we are to replace property relations with civic relations.

One way to begin thinking about this civic system of discourse is to reflect on this book. Where did it come from? Well, it came mostly from other books and conversations, from observations, and from reflecting on ideas. What is available to me and to others who have participated in similar work emerges out of our interpretations of our current situation. Why do we interpret things one way rather than another? Perhaps there are multiple reasons, of some of which I am unaware, but I know that anyone's interpretation of situations will be strongly influenced by the images of reality and the narratives or stories that constitute the world in which they live. These stories, in turn, are interpretations of events that have been recorded in one's communities. Some of these events were caused by the actions of previous individuals and groups who chose one course of action rather than another. These elements and their relationships can be drawn as a cycle, such as that in Figure 12.3.

When we engage in conversations with others, we participate in this system. Although one can enter the cycle at any point, we usually enter at the point of disagreements – the place of reflections and deliberations. Disagreements arise because we have different ideas about what to do (action), which have their immediate source in differing interpretations of our situation. These differences have their source, for the most part, in the different images and stories in which they live. Stories and images provide the framework for interpreting one's world. As the picture in Figure 12.3 shows, stories emerge from making sense of past events that are the result of human actions. They also provide the framework for interpreting current situations,

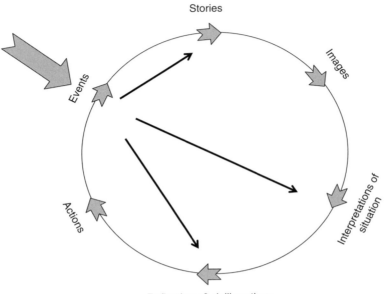

FIGURE 12.3 Cycle of civic conversations

especially situations that call for action. All the parts of the cycle, in other words, are interconnected. Humans must engage in this system, of course, for it to exist, but their capacity to say what needs to be said depends on what the whole system provides to them.

This cycle can be used to understand the purpose of this book, which aims at changing the stories and images of economic life, which in turn will change what we deliberate about and what actions we take. As an alternative to the Enlightenment story of four stages of history, the book offers the framework of making provisions that included provisioning, protecting, and creating a worthwhile purpose. Instead of the image of the economic man the book suggests the image of the parent-child relationship. It argues that we should replace property relations with civic relations as the foundation for economic trans-actions. Finally, instead of seeing labor, land, and money as commod-ities, the book proposes that we should treat these sources of wealth as provisions. All these changes in perspective and terminology provide us, as citizens, new ways to formulate issues that need our attention and to develop appropriate actions and policies.

In Part Five, we will return to the key element of this cycle – reflection and deliberation – to examine what circumstances are necessary for such deliberations to occur in our everyday lives. Most of the time, this system of civic discourse does not demand our attention, but it gives us the language and perceptions for approaches to issues that do. Since the late 1970s, no issue has demanded more attention than the deteriorating state of the planet. In large part, the failure to respond adequately to this deterioration has stemmed from an economic discourse that sees the planet as property rather than as a living system. As long as we treat the land as property, we further decrease the chances that our children and grandchildren will have a good life. Actually, we must go beyond simply recognizing the biosphere as a provider for us. We need to recognize and maintain its integrity as a self-organizing, living system. This brings us to the second system that makes and keeps human life human – the biosphere.[2]

THE BIOSPHERE AS A LIVING SYSTEM

The biosphere is the sphere of life on earth. It is an autopoietic system, meaning that it is self-organizing or self-making. Fritjof Capra describes autopoietic systems as follows:

> Since all components of an autopoietic network are produced by other components of the network, the entire system is organizationally closed, even though it is open with regard to the flow of energy and matter. This organizational closure implies that a living system is self-organizing in the sense that its order and behavior are not imposed by the environment but are established by the system itself. In other words, living systems are autonomous. This does not mean they are isolated from their environment. On the contrary, they interact with the environment through a

[2] Paul Lehmann, *Ethics in a Christian Context* (New York: Harper and Row, 1963).

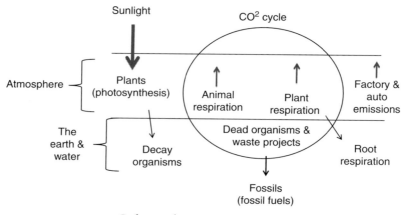

FIGURE 12.4 Carbon cycle

continual exchange of energy and matter. But this interaction does not determine their organization – they are self-organizing.[3]

Self-organizing systems, in other words, do not need to be managed or organized by us. This is obviously true of the biosphere, since it did quite well before human beings appeared. The cyclical movement of the biosphere is maintained by photosynthesis, as the graph of the carbon cycle in Figure 12.4 demonstrates.[4]

With the sun providing the energy for the whole system, photosynthesis absorbs carbon dioxide from the atmosphere and emits oxygen, which is necessary for animal life. Decayed organisms become food for future plant growth. This process balances carbon and oxygen and maintains the planet's living system. For most of the planet's lifespan, the balance among carbon and oxygen and other gases maintained itself. Today, the burning of fossil fuels, as well as other human activities, has disrupted this cycle.

The environmental crisis we face today is partly due to over-loading the natural cycles of the biosphere so they can no longer absorb

---

[3] Fritjof Capra, *The Web of Life: A New Scientific Understanding of Living Systems* (New York: Anchor Books, 1997), p. 167.
[4] www.windows.ucar.edu/tour/link=/earth/Water/co2_cycle.html

the amount of carbon we emit. One way of framing this conflict is in terms of the relationship between economics and ecology.

ECONOMICS AND ECOLOGY

The words economics and ecology do have a thought-provoking similarity. They both come from the Greek root word *oikos*, which means house or household. Ecology is the logic or the study (*logos*) of the household. Economics is the management (*nomos*) of the household. Although one would assume that we try to understand something (ecology) before managing it (economics), it seems that modern economics has ignored the logic or patterns of ecosystems. In fact, the "logic" of a property-based economy has apparently been in direct contradiction with ecological logic, as the increases in global warming demonstrate. Today, economics and ecology continually conflict with one another. Fritjof Capra wrote of the relationship between the two in his book *The Web of Life*:

> A major clash between economics and ecology derives from the fact that nature is cyclical, whereas our industrial systems are linear. Our businesses take resources, transform them into products plus waste, and sell the products to consumers, who discard more waste when they have consumed the products. Sustainable patterns of production and consumption need to be cyclical, imitating the cyclical processes in nature.[5]

If our economic patterns are linear as Capra suggests, then they are really quite different from the cyclical patterns of the biosphere. As we shall see later, it is possible to redesign economic systems so that they mimic ecological systems – so that they are allies, not enemies, of nature.

These two systems – represented by the cycle of civic discourse and the carbon cycle – provide the foundation for human communities. We are speaking animals. We belong to the world of language and to

---

[5] Capra, *The Web of Life*, p. 299.

the world of nature. These two worlds unite us in our everyday associations with each other – our social life. Economics, like society, relies on both the civic and biospheric systems. It is composed of both but does not follow the pattern of either. Social and economic systems, in other words, have their own dynamics. Perhaps the most significant aspect of social systems is the phenomenon of social trends.

THE SYSTEM OF SOCIAL TRENDS

As social beings, we live in interdependent relational systems with others. Remember the diversity wheel presented in Chapter 6? All of us belong to several of these categories and most of them influence our expectations of our selves and of others. Social interactions, in the family, among friends, or in the workplace, can be quite complex, and in many cases individual behavior will be largely determined by the expectations of these settings.

Sometimes, social expectations seem to take on a life of their own. We are expected to do well in school, so we strive to excel, which only increases the expectation that we will do well. As we continue to do well, and find support for doing well, we can see the emergence of a social trend – things are moving in a specific direction. If social expectations are for failure, and we do fail, then the trend could move in the opposite direction. The relationship between social expectations and trends can actually work both ways. Fulfilled expectations can create trends. But also existing trends can create expectations. A new trend of three-button sports jackets, instead of the old two-button, can create an expectation that one will get the new jacket style. In general, the fashion industry lives on this relationship between trends and social expectations. Many other industries in our current consumer economy do as well. Much of our consumption, at least in rich countries, is guided not by our basic needs, but by the social expectations of what we should have. Do you have the latest cell phone? The latest style of sneakers? The latest "green" automobile? Are you "with it" or not?

Most of us have probably noticed how social trends tend to gain momentum, and achieve dominance, then slow, eventually being superseded by something else. The discipline of cybernetics has provided us with a set of terms to understand this process – positive and negative feedback loops. When people draw these loops, they sometimes look something like the cyclical patterns of natural processes or even the cycle of public discourse, but they are quite different. Feedback loops can be understood as information about the result of one's action or motion. If the information is positive, then it reinforces the trend that the action initiated; with enough reinforcement, it seems to develop its own momentum. As they say, "Nothing succeeds like success." If the information is negative then there exists some resistance to the motion or action. Continued negative feedback will eventually grind a movement to a halt. We often see this in political campaigns where a defeat in one primary stalls the momentum in subsequent primaries.

The social movements during the second half of the twentieth century provide a good example of the role of feedback loops. In the 1950s, 1960s, and early 1970s, there was a growing emphasis on extending civil rights, getting out of Vietnam, and protecting the environment. Public awareness and small successes spurred more people to "get on the bandwagon," as they say, and the movements developed momentum. The momentum increased with the advent of affirmative-action policies and more environmental regulation. Then, in the 1980s and 1990s, these trends created a growing resistance to change and to what was seen as an assault on individual choice. This resistance increased, especially during the administration of Ronald Reagan, as a reaction against both social and environmental protections, and we entered a trend with an emphasis on the self instead of on the community or the planet. This momentum continued, leading to our current environmental and financial crises. These trends, of course, did not solely happen by themselves, but were influenced by individual and collective decisions. At the same time, some of these decisions seemed reasonable in light of the social trends in which they were made.

Today, we see a myriad of trends that are creating expectations for how we should live together. There is momentum building for living a more sustainable lifestyle. More people are recycling. More people are moving back to cities to decrease their environmental footprint. There are actually a multitude of trends that are moving us toward a more sustainable economy. But there are opposite trends as well. Global population increases. Global resources decrease. The gap between the richest few and the poorest many increases. All these trends are social and economic. It is impossible to somehow isolate a global market from these social realities, just as it is impossible to address the challenges of these trends apart from market realities. All these trends are systemic, and our responses to them must be systemic as well.

Even though we know that most social trends will eventually bring about resistance to their expansion, we often choose not to take them seriously, especially when there is a long time delay between actions and feedback. Sometimes, business trends gain so much momentum that their negative feedback loops never become strong enough to prevent unwanted consequences. A stronger company, for example, may be able to offer lower prices for its goods than smaller companies, with the result that smaller companies cannot survive. As this trend continues, soon the large company has a monopoly in the market, and then can set prices at will. Since there is no resistance to this trend within the system itself, some governments have passed antimonopoly laws to stop the trend before it destroys the competitiveness of the market. This is just another indication that market economies do not have internal constraint; they are not self-organizing like the biosphere. If we hope to bring our economy in line with the logic of ecology, we will need to have a firm grasp of how the economy should fit with the natural systems in which we live. If we create civic conversations from a language of making provisions instead of accumulating property, and relate to one another as citizens instead of as property owners, then we can both imagine and organize the economy as a series of systems of provision.

THE ECONOMY AS A SYSTEM OF PROVISION

Economic systems today bring the planet's resources – its provisions – to the global population. The economic system itself has no self-organizing

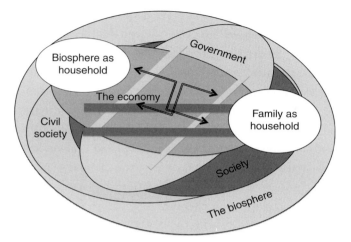

FIGURE 12.5 Economy as a system of provision

principles that push it to align itself with the planet as a living system or to ensure that the men and women who provide us with what we need are given their due. To look at global markets from an economics of provision perspective, in other words, is to see markets in the context of civic and natural systems, and to recognize our responsibility to manage their trends so they will they move toward a just and sustainable world.

Remember that the idea of the household has been used to refer both to the biosphere and to a family's household. This double meaning would allow us to understand economics as the process of making provisions between these two households. That gives us the picture of the economy as a system shown in Figure 12.5.

For our earliest ancestors, the economy would have been totally embedded in the daily activity of gathering provisions from the planet to provide for one's family and clan. Today, of course, a myriad of institutions and organizations mediate these transactions between the two households – between the ecological household and the family household – from the companies that drill oil out of the earth to the brokerages that trade oil in commodity exchanges to the gas stations that sell us fuel for our vehicles.

This view of the economy as systems of provision has the advantage of looking at the whole "lifecycle" of a product, beginning with its extraction from the earth as a raw material and ending with its return to the earth as waste. As we outline the transformation from the ecological to the family household, we can pay attention to the human providers who contribute to the process and to the impact on the ecological systems in which it occurs. In order to create a framework for this understanding of economic systems, however, we will need to move from the current notion of the economy as economic sectors to the notion of the economy as different systems of provision, which is the topic of the next chapter.

13 Imagining a stakeholder economy

In the previous chapter we defined the economy as the transformation by human providers of nature's provisions into provisions for human households. This transformation, of course, involves various organizations working together in interrelated systems of provision, such as the food system or the housing system. This chapter will clarify the nature of these systems and provide a model for organizing them.

As we have said before, we know what we want. We want a just and sustainable economy. What we need to know is how we can get there from here. Our first step will be to review the current typology of economic systems and see how we might change it to move us in the right direction. One economic typology that is currently used – and that frankly hinders our imagining of systems of provision – is the typology of economic sectors.

THE WORLD OF ECONOMIC SECTORS

Although there are different lists of economic sectors, that given in Figure 13.1 is a good example. Developed recently by the United States, Canada, and Mexico to provide a way of comparing business activity across North America, it is known as the North American Industry Classification System (NAICS).[1]

Note that the industries listed move in a sequence from sectors that extract resources from the earth and biosphere such as fishing and mining, to sectors that transform resources into products, such as construction and manufacturing, to those that distribute products, such as retail trade and transportation. The list continues with

[1] www.census.gov/cgi-bin/sssd/naics/naicsrch?chart=2007

Agriculture, forestry, fishing and hunting	Professional, scientific, and technical services
Mining, quarrying, and oil and gas extraction	Management of companies and enterprises
Utilities	Administrative and support, and waste management and remediation services
Construction	
Manufacturing	Educational services
Wholesale trade	Health care and social assistance
Retail trade	Arts, entertainment, and recreation
Transportation and warehousing	Accommodation and food services
Information	Other services (except public administration)
Finance and insurance	Public administration
Real estate, and rental and leasing	

FIGURE 13.1 Economic sectors

various services, from finance to health care, and ends with public administration.

Economists group these industries into three sectors: the primary (extraction of materials), the secondary (transformation into products), and the tertiary (service industries). A common view holds that a nation's economic development normally progresses from a heavy dependence on the extraction industries to a dependence on manufacturing and finally to services. One could thus chart economic growth by examining the ebb and flow of the different sectors and, in some cases, develop policies that would favor one sector over another – such as favoring the entertainment sector over the agricultural by building sports centers on prime farmland.

This division of the economy into sectors has, of course, had other significant consequences as well. In general, it has kept the right hand from knowing what the left hand is doing. One could take pride in the increased productivity of the manufacturing sector, for example, without being aware of the depletion of resources in the primary sector.

Or one could invest in the entertainment sector without being concerned about its impact on transportation. In fact, dividing the economy into sectors makes "invisible" the many connections and interdependencies between different aspects of the system.

To understand the need for an alternative to sector analysis, consider the following description by Jeremy Rifkin of the energy used in providing someone with a typical English muffin:

> Here are just some of the energy steps that go into making your English muffin. (1) The wheat is taken by a fossil-fuel-driven truck made of nonrenewable resources to (2) a large, centralized bakery housing numerous machines that very inefficiently refine, enrich, bake, and package English muffins. At the bakery, the wheat is (3) refined and often (4) bleached. These processes make for nice white bread, but rob the wheat of vital nutrients, so (5) the flour is then enriched with niacin, iron, thiamine, and riboflavin. Next, to insure that the English muffins will be able to withstand long truck journeys to stores where they will be kept on shelves for many days, or even weeks, preservative (6) calcium propionate is added, along with (7) dough conditioners such as calcium sulfate, monocalcium phosphate, ammonium sulfate, fungal enzyme, potassium bromate, and potassium iodate. Then the bread is (8) baked and placed in (9) a cardboard box, which has been (10) printed in several colors to catch your eye on the shelf. The box and muffins are placed within (11) a plastic bag (made of petrochemicals), which is then sealed with (12) a plastic tie (made of more petrochemicals). The packages of English muffins are then loaded into (13) a truck, which hauls them to the (14) air-conditioned, fluorescent-lit, Muzak-filled grocery store. Finally, you (15) drive two tons of metal to the store and back and then (16) pop the muffins in the toaster. Eventually, you will throw away the cardboard and plastic packaging, which will then have to be disposed of as (17) solid waste. All of this for just 130 calories per serving of muffin.[2]

---

[2] Jeremy Rifkin, *Entropy: A New World View* (New York, Viking, 1980), p. 131.

Rifkin's description allows us to see all the providers, both human and non-human, the impact of making the provision, and what is provided – 130 calories. This is the kind of talk an economics of provision would encourage. The talk that economic sector analysis generates is quite different: "Wheat production has increased." "Transportation has suffered from higher oil costs." "Retail sales will improve in the coming months." "Advertising has been moving away from television and onto the Internet." If you listen to the conversations emanating from the world of economic sectors, you will never know the whole story of the English muffin – or that of any commodity that provides us with what we need. An economics of provision, on the other hand, informs us about the actual costs of providing the muffin. Furthermore, it raises the question whether a muffin that takes all these resources is really the best way of providing us with the nutrition we need. The many ways that we could provide nutrition would only be known once we know the *whole process* of making provisions, beginning in the wheat field and ending at the breakfast table.

Economic sectors are not designed to follow the lifecycle of any product, nor are they designed to include the different agencies, contextual elements, or environmental impacts inherent in making provisions. A sector framework prevents us from seeing these relationships. A sector analysis also prevents us from having easy access to knowledge about how our use of products impacts the earth and biosphere, from which the products originated.

If we think of the economy as a system of provision, we can broaden our field of inquiry to look at how production impacts labor and land – the two key living providers. This would promote the sort of way of thinking advocated by many who are working for sustainable business practices. It is called "closing the loop." In Figure 13.2, the first line shows one view of productivity: Resources are taken from the earth, transformed into products used and then thrown away. This is traditional linear thinking. In nonlinear systems, "away" does not exist. The waste of the production process and the waste created by discarding the used product are returned to become part of the earth and biosphere.

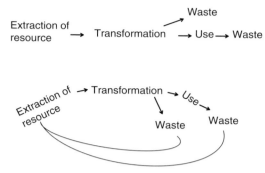

FIGURE 13.2 Linear versus cyclical thinking

This cyclical method of production mirrors nature's process of treating "waste." As William McDonough and Michael Braungart have said: Waste equals food.[3] In nature, everything is reused. More correctly, everything is part of the system.

Another advantage of moving away from dividing the economy into economic sectors and toward an integrated economy of systems of provision is that it would allow us to restore money to its rightful function of providing credit for economic development and human welfare. Financial services, in other words, would become part of various systems of provision, instead of being isolated from them.

MONEY AND SYSTEMS OF PROVISION

Perhaps the most daunting challenge to moving from the economics of sectors to integrated systems of provision is the power and prestige of the financial sector. As the former Federal Reserve Governor Frederic Mishkin said, the financial system is "the brain of the economy." Niall Ferguson shares this quote from Mishkin in his recent book on the history of money, as well as the following from Mishkin:

> It [the financial system] acts as a coordinating mechanism that allocates capital, the lifeblood of economic activity, to its most

[3] William McDonough and Michael Braungart, *Cradle to Cradle: Remaking the Way We Make Things* (New York: North Point Press, 2002), p. 92.

productive uses by businesses and households. If capital goes to the wrong uses or does not flow at all, the economy will operate inefficiently, and ultimately economic growth will be low.[4]

Given the millions who lost their homes, the millions who lost much of their retirement savings, and the overall misery caused by the financial sector in the past years, one wonders if Mishkin would still see the financial system as the brain of the economy.

Money is certainly necessary for a market economy, but it does not provide food or housing or health care. A dollar in the desert will not provide water if the well is dry. You need a shovel to dig the well deeper. When the lifeblood of an economy is not those who provide us with what we need, then we have lost sight of what the economy is all about. As Julie Nelson has reminded us, the economy is essentially a human economy.[5]

The men and women who have made millions controlling the economy's finances have done so primarily because they have treated money as property – as a commodity. As we demonstrated earlier, this violates the actual function of money in a capitalistic economic system. Its function is to provide credit. Furthermore, to let the financial system be the "coordinating mechanism" of the economy is to turn the economy over to those who coordinate the financial system. Once again, there is no "invisible hand" here, but the hands of financiers.

It is common knowledge that speculators have raked in millions, even billions, by treating national currencies as commodities and cashing in on changes in their relative value. Does this practice provide anyone with anything, or is it simply a case of taking things out of the pot without putting anything back? Furthermore, does such speculation damage the capacity of money to perform its appropriate function of providing credit? The fact is that such transactions can devalue a

---

[4] Niall Ferguson, *The Ascent of Money: A Financial History of the World* (New York: The Penguin Press, 2008), p. 342.

[5] Julie Nelson, *Economics for Humans* (Chicago, IL: The University of Chicago Press, 2006).

Economic sectors	Systems of provision
• Divides economy into investment opportunities	• Divides economy into cycles of making provisions
• Ignores providers (land and labor) when trading provisions	• Recognizes providers (land and labor) when trading provisions
• Separates financial services from providing goods and services	• Integrates financial services with provision of goods and services

FIGURE 13.3 Economic sectors versus systems of provision

currency and thereby decrease its reliability as a secure and knowable monetary unit. The solution to this problem is obvious: Ensure that money retains its character as a provider of credit in systems of provision. The resistance to this solution is just as obvious, but this is merely the resistance of those who would treat money as a commodity or as property. If we can agree that money is not a commodity, as we suggest here, then banks – the controllers of money – will find themselves in relationships of debt and credit, rather than property and power. This also means, of course, that banks will not belong primarily to the system of finance, but to those systems of provision that rely on credit for economic growth.

This may appear to be a radical change in current economic policy, but it is not unreasonable. If we can stay focused on the purpose of the economy, which is to make provisions, then those activities that damage the providers (labor, land, or money) should be corrected. Government, in this system, has an obligation to protect providers, not property – and certainly not property speculators.

It is unlikely that we will eliminate all talk about economic sectors, and there is little reason to do so. But we should not allow this method of dividing the economy to determine how we organize it. If we are to understand the purpose of the economy – to make provisions – then we need to think in terms of systems of provision as well. Figure 13.3 summarizes the basic differences between the two ways of thinking about the economy.

To translate economic processes into a language of systems of provision, we will need to develop a different vocabulary and set of themes for everyday conversations. When we sit at the dinner table, for example, we can ask such questions as: "Who provided this food?" "Where did it come from?" "How are the providers doing?" or "What are the environmental impacts of its production?" At a neighborhood or city council meeting, we might ask: "Where is the source of our water?" "How do we ensure its quality?" "How can we live as a part of nature rather than apart from it?" and "How do we organize our communities to provide water for agriculture, people, and the living planet?" In meetings in corporations and public policy agencies, we can ask: "Are all providers receiving their due?" "Is the current set of products or commodities the best way of providing people with what they need?"

We can modify and enrich these questions, of course, as we move from one system of provision to another, such as, say, from the systems that provide food to the systems that provide health care. Once we make these questions a part of our everyday conversations, we can begin to imagine a stakeholder economy that includes all those who should be represented in the organization of any system of provision. We really need to answer two questions: "Who should be involved in organizing the economy?" and "How should they do it?" To answer the first question, we need to look at the stakeholders that would constitute any system of provision.

THE STAKEHOLDERS OF SYSTEMS OF PROVISION

The concept of stakeholder has been an important term in the area of management theory and business ethics for several decades. Although the concept has been used in different ways during this time, its basic meaning has more or less remained the same. In a recent study of the twenty-five-year history of this concept, R. Edward Freeman and others have diligently traced the different uses of the notion, and I think they have persuasively shown that its primary use has been as

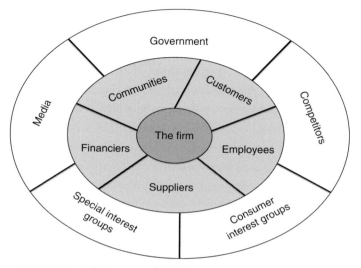

FIGURE 13.4 Corporate stakeholders

a tool for strategic management.[6] The idea is that managers of businesses need to consider all the groups affected by corporate decisions. Figure 13.4, from an essay by Freeman on stakeholder theory, shows all the groups that should be considered.[7]

The business of the firm, in this stakeholder perspective, is to balance the claims of the different stakeholders – all those who have a stake in corporate decisions.[8] Since we are not concerned with the management of the firm, but with the economy, we will need to make several changes to develop the notion of the stakeholders of systems of provision. We would need to do the following:

1. Remove the firm from the center of the picture and replace it with civic conversations – conversations among citizens that are based on civic

---

[6] R. Edward Freeman, Jeffrey Harrison, Andrew Wicks, Bidhan Parmar, and Simone de Colle, *Stakeholder Theory: The State of the Art* (Cambridge: Cambridge University Press, 2009).

[7] R. Edward Freeman, "Managing for Stakeholders," in *Ethical Theory and Business*, eighth edition, ed. Tom Beauchamp, Norman Bowie, and Denis Arnold (Upper Saddle River, NJ: Prentice Hall, 2009), p. 6.

[8] See Muel Kaptein and John Wempe, *The Balanced Company: A Theory of Corporate Integrity* (Oxford: Oxford University Press, 2002).

norms. These conversations could certainly occur in a firm, but they will occur elsewhere as well. It is not the location but the relationships that determine whether or not a civic conversation occurs. One can imagine that these civic conversations would usually begin with deliberation about possible action, but they could also expand to consider any or all the aspects of the cycle of civic conversations that we previously detailed: stories about events, images, and interpretation of situations. The search for the best course of action would direct the conversation, and the various aspects of the cycle could be drawn on to the degree that they help in discovering what that action might be.

2. Place in the second circle, as "primary stakeholders," those groups that would be involved in all systems of provision; natural provisions that provide what we need, human providers that transform these provisions into human provisions, and the families and communities that need provisions. We should think of this as the circle of social life. It contains all the social divisions and inequalities that a civic identity seeks to mitigate.

3. Place corporations into the third and outer circle. This circle would also contain all the agencies and organizations (public and private) that belong to any particular systems.

Given these changes, the revised model would now show the key stakeholders as members of an economics of provision, which would look like Figure 13.5.

Perhaps the most significant difference between the corporate stakeholder view and the economics of provision view is that civic conversations now occupy the center. These conversations would occur at the neighborhood, local, regional, national, and international level. They could also occur in any of the organizations in the outer ring or among any of them.

The middle circle contains the basic elements of an economics of provision, which would be the same for all systems of provision. This middle circle is grounded in the civic sphere (civic conversations) and fulfills the basic civic purpose of the economy: for human providers to

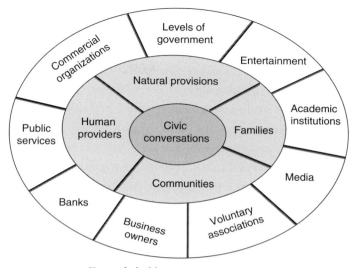

FIGURE 13.5 Key stakeholders in an economics of provision

transform the provisions of nature to provisions for our families and communities. These processes today occur through a variety of organizations, which comprise modern systems of provision. How we organize these transformation processes are the questions that civic conversations would address, investigate, and answer. These conversations create and maintain the civic relationships that provide the foundation for organizing systems of provision. The systems of provision include all or at least most of the organizations in the third circle.

The organizations in the outer circle are quite varied. Some are designed to represent citizens, at least in democratic countries. Some, such as public services and to some extent academic institutions, carry out the will of government. Others have a mix of civic and commercial interests, such as voluntary associations and even the media. Others, such as voluntary organizations, may not belong to either government or commercial organizations – such as religious institutions – but may significantly influence the overall system. In fact, entertainment, media, voluntary associations, and even academic institutions all play a role in creating and maintaining the social expectations and trends that must be taken into account when trying to improve any systems of provision. Finally, there are commercial organizations, such as corporations, and owners of small businesses, farms, or large enterprises. Any of these organizations could be candidates for change and renewal if that would be the conclusion from deliberations in civic conversations. Furthermore, the civic conversations that would require such changes may well take place in these outer-circle organizations. The key criterion for a "civic" conversation is not that it occurs in some particular place or organization, but rather that it is grounded in civic identity and guided by civic norms. In all such situations, however, the second circle would influence the conversation so that the system stays true to its purpose: making provision for families and communities and protecting providers. So, how would the various stakeholders organize systems of provision?

THE PROCESS OF ORGANIZING SYSTEMS OF PROVISION

According to the notion of reciprocity of participation we developed earlier, all who participate in a process should be represented in organizing it. So this would mean that all the agencies and organizations in the third circle of our model should have a voice in determining the direction of the overall system. How much voice? That depends on how we understand the relationships among different stakeholders, especially the relationship between government and non-government agents. The question we need to ask is: "What are the appropriate roles for government and non-government stakeholders in systems of provision?"

Government organizations have three characteristics that are important in this context: They represent the will of the people, they pass laws and regulations, and they have the law enforcement capacity to ensure that their laws are obeyed. One could argue that non-government organizations also represent the people's will or preferences, but they do not pass laws and regulations nor do they have a capacity for law enforcement.

Consequently, non-government organizations – nonprofits and for-profits – are limited to persuasion – as well as to financial reward and punishments – to influence other stakeholders.

The problem, at least in the current situation in the United States, is that corporations have used their vast sums of money to largely control political elections, congressional legislation, and even public opinion. Because of the dominance of money in politics, those with the most money have the most control, and it turns out these are rarely elected officials. As Robert Reich has argued in his recent book on the relationship between government and corporations:

> The most effective thing reformers can do is to reduce the effects of corporate money on politics, and enhance the voices of citizens. No other avenue of reform is as important. Corporate executives who sincerely wish to do good can make no better contribution than keeping their company out of politics. If corporate social responsibility has any meaning at all, it is to refrain from corrupting democracy.[9]

A retreat of corporate lobbyists from the halls of government would allow government representatives to have time and space to listen to their real constituency – the citizens they represent. This would also mean that their decisions could reflect the will of the people rather than the will of corporations. Remember the earlier discussion about the relationship between the commercial and the civic. In many ways, we still live in the Smithian tradition where the commercial trumps the civic. If we are to develop an economics of provision, we will need to end this legacy and restore a civic foundation for governing.

Current relationships between the major pharmaceutical companies and government organizations provide a good example of the challenges we face today in switching from an economics of property to an economics of provision. An in-depth investigation by the consumer watchdog group Public Citizen reveals that in 2002 the drug industry:

---

[9] Robert Reich, *Supercapitalism: The Transformation of Business, Democracy, and Everyday Life* (New York: Alfred A. Knopf, 2007), p. 216.

- Reported a profit of 17 cents for every dollar of revenue, compared with a Fortune 500 median of 3.1 cents per dollar of revenue.
- Devoted 30.8 percent of their revenues to marketing and administration, compared with the 14.1 percent of revenues spent on research and development.
- Spent $91.4 million on lobbying Congress and $20 million on campaign contributions in 1999–2000, in sum more than any other industry.
- Employed 675 lobbyists in 2000 – more than one for each member of Congress.[10]

Where does all this profit come from that allows such activities? It comes from selling products. These products – medications – are the result of years of research, much of it done in universities and medical schools largely funded by tax dollars. Furthermore, the biggest customer of medications, at least in the United States, is the government-funded programs of Medicare and Medicaid. Taxpayers, in other words, are paying part of the bill for corporate lobbyists to influence their elected representatives, corporate contributions to finance their candidates for public office, and for corporate advertising to sponsor their prime-time television programming. On top of all of this, pharmaceutical corporations do not even pay taxes on most of their profits, because they have moved their headquarters to oversea tax shelters such as the Cayman Islands and Bermuda.

If we see pharmaceutical companies as part of the system that provides health care, then these practices become highly questionable. In an economics of provision, pharmaceutical companies would no longer be treated as profit-centers, producing and selling commodities, but rather as centers of provision, providing medications for relieving pain and suffering. Their research would not be directed by what products would have the highest return on investment, but on medications that would meet people's basic health needs. They would

---

[10] Neal Pattison and Luke Warren, *2002 Drug Industry Profits: Hefty Pharmaceutical Company Margins Dwarf Other Industries* (Washington, DC: Public Citizen's Congress Watch, June 2003).

become partners with government agencies, such as public health agencies, in creating healthy communities. As long as we treat medication as a commodity, these changes are unlikely to happen. If we see medications as part of a health care system of provision, we could imagine civic conversations taking place in pharmaceutical companies as well as in the other organizations that belong to the system. If the conversations are based on civic norms and address participants as citizens, the results of the conversations could certainly influence the direction of the health care system. Still, different organizations have different means at their disposal to influence the decisions that determine the direction of the system. In fact, analyzing the differences in how various agents in a system can change or prevent change of the system is a good way of assessing their relationship with each other and their appropriate role in the system. There are essentially three ways to change systems: by incentives, regulation, and persuasion.

THREE STRATEGIES FOR CHANGE: INCENTIVES, REGULATION, AND PERSUASION

Just as there are three basic activities of human communities (providing, protecting, and creating a worthwhile purpose), so there are three basic strategies (incentives, regulation, and persuasion) for changing systems of provision – each one appropriate to one of those activities. We can change how a system exchanges goods and services through changing incentives, how it protects providers through regulation, and how it understands its purpose and beliefs through persuasion. Table 13.1 shows how the strategies match the human activities.

Table 13.1 *Strategies for change*

Basic human activities	*Strategies for change*
Provisioning	Changing incentives
Protecting	Changing regulations
Creating a worthwhile purpose	Changing beliefs through persuasion

Given the clear evidence that all of the systems of provision in which we live today are unsustainable, we need to make changes in the rewards that support them, the regulations that constrain them, and the beliefs that legitimize them. Incentives in the market can promote technological innovations to create more sustainable products and processes. New government regulations can improve the protection of the key providers of wealth – the natural environment and human providers. And education by school systems, advocacy groups, and the media can change public opinion. All three strategies belong to any competent plan for change, and the correct balance among them will depend on the particular system of provision. The city is the one system of provision that includes most of the others. Once we understand how it functions, we can more easily understand some of the challenges and changes that are necessary in other systems.

THE CITY AS A SYSTEM OF PROVISION

For a large majority of the world's population, the provisions they need are available in the cities in which they live. From the perspective of an economics of property, cities represent vast holdings by owners of office buildings, businesses, apartment houses, and residences. From the perspective of an economics of provision, cities are places where citizens – members of cities – make provisions together. A picture of the civic systems of provision would look something like Figure 13.6.

All of the provisions listed are important for a good life, but perhaps some are more necessary than others. Water, food, housing, and security perhaps are more necessary than entertainment, for example. Still, a life without time for entertainment, whether in terms of theatre, sports, games, or storytelling, would not be a life with much meaning.

Does the third circle include all the key providers for city dwellers? What about finances, or communication? After all, our economy depends on financial services and communication technology. As we have said earlier, the separation of finances from what is being financed easily leads to the treatment of money as a commodity instead of a

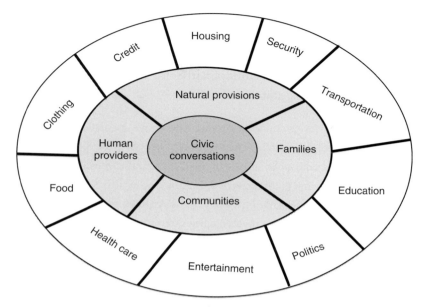

FIGURE 13.6 Civic systems of provision

provision. Money certainly is important in all the systems of provision, but it is not a separate system of provision. In fact, money is useless unless it can be used in some system of provision.

Not seeing communication systems as a separate system of provision may seem even more odd. After all, we speak of communication systems, IT systems, and so on. But what do these "systems" provide? They only provide information or communication about something and the "something" constitutes some system of provision. They belong, in other words, to systems of provision as services to facilitate the production and distribution of provisions. When we use communication technology, we just need to ask, "What do I want to accomplish in using this device?" Is it for entertainment, political education, or information about any number of provisions? Communication systems, in other words, are a means for making provisions, but not a provision in and of themselves.

Since citizens (members of cities) constitute civic communities, it seems quite natural to apply to cities the civic norms of reciprocity and moral equality. These norms support not only the obligation for a representative civic government, but also the right to the city itself. This "right to the city" is slowly becoming recognized as a human right for all people. The World Charter for the Right to the City includes the following statement:

> Urban territories and their rural surroundings are also spaces and locations of the exercise and fulfillment of collective rights as a way of assuring equitable, universal, just, democratic, and sustainable distribution and enjoyment of the resources, wealth, services, goods, and opportunities that cities offer. The Right to the City therefore also includes the right to development, to a healthy environment, to the enjoyment and preservation of natural resources, to participation in urban planning and management, and to historical and cultural heritage.[11]

We would be hard-pressed, of course, to find any global city designed so all members have the capacity to make provisions for themselves and their families. In part, that is because the providers in the city – from the migrant worker to the housecleaner – have not been protected, and in part because those who depend on the city for provisions – the sick and the homeless – have not been recognized.

Our challenge is not just to include all members of cities in the organization of the city, but it is also to recognize the dependency of cities on the land and human providers that bring the city its daily provisions. One can easily overlook the complex systems that grant many city dwellers access to all they need for a good life. Most of these systems of provision are not sustainable and must be radically changed if we are to have vibrant cities and communities.

So how will these changes come about? They must emerge from civic conversations, in which all the groups, whatever their social status in the city, are represented. Sure, there are experts who have more knowledge than laypersons, and in many cases their knowledge

---

[11] www.hic-net.org/foundingdocs.asp#

should strongly influence civic conversations. At the same time, family and community representatives have an expertise as well, especially about the provisions they value for themselves and for future generations. So we should not exclude anyone from civic conversations, nor should we ignore the suggestions of any organization, whether private or public.

The strategies for change – incentives, and regulation and persuasion – need to be carefully and yet boldly implemented. Some of the changes will be quite obvious once we begin treating labor, land, and money as provisions. Workers should be treated as citizens. Justice and reciprocity should guide relationships at work. Land should be treated as part of a living system. The management of money should be limited to its function in relationships of credit and debt, and governments should prevent speculators from exploiting shifts in its relative value as a commodity.

How we organize these systems depends on our values. That does not mean, however, that we should act from whatever values we happen to have right now. At present, for example, our economy lives off a set of values that support social alienation and unsustainable consumption. Sticking to these values will certainly not lead us to a brighter future. The next chapter explores the issue of values in terms of an ethics of systems.

14 The ethics of economic systems

Once we have included the various organizations and groups that should be represented in the civic conversations of any system of provision, we need to agree on the guidelines for making good decisions, which brings us to the ethics of economic systems.

For our purposes, ethics concerns working through how things "should be." There are really two basic questions: "What should I (or we) become?" and "What should I (or we) do?" In the organizing of systems of provision, the questions are "we" questions and the answers should represent the best courses of action when different groups have differing views about the right course of action. The ethical analysis of systems usually occurs in conversations where participants disagree and each party thinks they are right. Their conflicts, in other words, are not between right and wrong, but between different versions of what is right. Ethics, in this context, explores the reasons for the different positions and weighs the merits of these reasons by shared values and principles.[1]

Already, in the introductory chapter, we presented justice and sustainability as the two primary aspirations of our global economy and as the basic guidelines for an economics of provision. To use these aspirations in making good decisions, we simply examine different courses of action in terms of whether they bring us closer or take us further away from a just and sustainable economy. In fact, these aspirations have guided many of the arguments in this book. The ethical norms of justice and sustainability, for example, have played just as much of a role in our assessment of labor and land as our descriptions of

[1] See my *The Ethical Process: An Approach to Disagreements and Controversial Issues*, third edition (Upper Saddle River, NJ, Prentice Hall, 2003).

them as providers. Justice and sustainability, of course, need to be more concretely related to the actual decisions that people will face in organizing systems of provisions, which is the theme of this chapter. We will examine three ethical challenges: the distribution of provisions, the protection of providers, and the creation of purpose.

THE ETHICS OF THE DISTRIBUTION OF PROVISIONS

Because the civic sphere serves as the foundation for the economics of provision, we already know that the civic norm of reciprocity will guide the distribution of provisions. As we argued in Chapter 7, the reciprocity of exchange creates the moral obligation that good is returned for good, and the reciprocity of participation and deliberation means that participation will never be to one's disadvantage, and that representation of all groups will be taken seriously. At the core of the principle of reciprocity is the idea that membership comes prior to ownership, which has important consequences for the issue of distribution.

Some might take reciprocity to mean that if one has not contributed anything, they should not receive anything in return. A person should provide for himself or herself. But this belief comes from a mistaken view of the relationship between reciprocity and membership. Membership comes first. Membership is the basis for reciprocity; reciprocity is not the basis for membership. There are many – children, the disabled, the sick, the aged, and so on – who may not contribute directly to the economic pot, so to speak, and yet they still deserve what is necessary for a good life. Why? Because reciprocity means not only that we receive as we have given, but also that we should give as we would want to receive. Any one of us could have been – or perhaps will be – unable to contribute directly to the economic pot. But we would still deserve the same basic provisions as those who can contribute. One can see this as a variation on the Golden Rule – "Do unto others as you would want them to do to you" – the basic tenet of moral communities. If we remember that reciprocity is a means of sharing provisions among all persons, not a means of inclusion and exclusion, then it can be used to care for those citizens who need more than they can give. How this works in particular cases, of course, must be decided. What we can do here is to provide some guidelines for how a community would make such decisions.

In his book *Spheres of Justice: A Defense of Pluralism and Equality*, Michael Walzer provides an effective way to think about issues of distribution. He suggests that we examine the social meaning of the things a system is distributing, and then use that meaning to determine how it should be distributed.[2] The idea of "social meaning" refers to the significance or value that something has in a particular society. Some things are fairly universal – everyone requires them. Water, for example, is necessary for survival, so a system that does not provide water to some would be unjust. Other things are more contingent, and different societies may give them different meanings, which means they could be distributed by different types of justice. In his book on human development, Des Gasper presents a fairly comprehensive list of different views of how things should be distributed that was developed by William Blanchard. The list is followed by brief explanations.

A. Equality
B. Need
C. Effort expended
D. Money invested
E. Results
F. Ascription
G. Fair procedure
H. Demand and preferences[3]

View A, equality, is that each would receive the same. In some cases, such as police protection, we would say that a city distributes it equally to all citizens, but only those who need it actually use it. Need (view B),

---

[2] Michael Walzer, *Spheres of Justice: A Defense of Pluralism and Equality* (New York: Basic Books, 1983), p. 19.
[3] Gasper, *The Ethics of Development*, p. 90.

on the other hand, would be a distribution system that would give more to those who needed more, such as providing extra educational resources to those with learning disabilities. Views C and D have more to do with one's contribution to some project. This fits well with the reciprocity of exchange. View E allocates resources in terms of those who would make the best use of them. This takes into account the element of efficiency or stewardship of resources, and could be used for granting ownership concession to those who have the interest and talent to create business operations. This would be quite different than allocating resources by ascription (view F), which refers to one's status or character. In a family business, for example, family members might be promoted not because they are the most qualified (results), but because they belong to the family. Both of these views of distribution differ from G, fair procedure, which does not take persons into account but rather processes. The final view (demand and preferences) would allow people's interests to determine who gets what. Those who wanted something would be able to get it.

When we review these different forms of allocation or distribution, we can easily understand that no one form of justice will fit all occasions. It depends on the social meaning of the things that are distributed.

In many cases, citizens will opt for multiple means of distribution, such as we have today in education. Education is distributed though both public and private schools, with government agencies setting standards for both. In any system of provision, there are multiple stakeholders – both public and private – and all of these stakeholders could play a role in the distribution of provisions. What role they play would depend on the choices made in civic conversations. In these conversations, participants will need to determine the social meaning of different provisions and the appropriate form of justice to distribute them. Distributing provisions, of course, assumes that someone has provided them, which brings us to our second aspect of an ethics of economic systems: the ethics of protecting the providers.

THE ETHICS OF PROTECTING THE PROVIDERS

Perhaps there is no greater moral failure in the Smithian tradition of economics than its failure to protect providers. The economics of dissociation that Smith allowed by his silence about the role of the slave-based tobacco trade has continued to blind many to the misery of human workers and the degradation of the planet. This suspension of the ethical within the core of market transactions has given us a world that is in dire need of reconciliation and repair.

In most ethical traditions, the first principle is to do no harm. Human systems are much too complicated to obey this principle completely. The world is simply an imperfect place. What we can do, however, is to protect providers from harm as best we can. In the real world, just as we have laws that protect citizens from crime, we also need ways to protect all providers – labor, land, and money – from exploitation and degradation. We begin with labor.

Protecting labor

A fundamental notion in ethics is the distinction between ought and is, or between normative and descriptive thinking – between what is and what should be. In protecting labor, however, this distinction seems to miss the main point, which is how we should describe workers. In the master-servant tradition, they are seen as servants who are under the control of the master. If we describe workers first of all as citizens, however, then we find ourselves in a different world. It all depends on the story we decide to tell. The story supporting an economics of provision is the story of the emergence of the civic sphere as the foundation of trade and the development of civic relationships so that today we recognize workers as citizens. If we choose this option as a way of understanding labor, then the civic norms of reciprocity and moral equality would be the first things that we should protect. We should protect, in other words, the moral agency of workers. In the Western tradition of ethics, the one philosopher usually recognized as the clearest and most emphatic protector of moral agency is the nineteenth-century German philosopher Immanuel Kant.

Kant and worker protection

Kant begins his ethical reflections with the desire to protect human freedom, which he believes is most fully protected by recognizing the autonomy of persons as moral agents. He states as much in his second formulation of his Categorical Imperative – which simply means that one should obey this principle regardless of consequences: "Act in such a way that you always treat humanity, whether in your own person or in the person of any other, never simply as a means, but always at the same time as an end."[4] To treat someone as an end, for Kant, is to recognize his or her autonomy or capacity for engaging in moral action, which would certainly include what we have called the civic rights of participation and representation in the workplace. This would seem to require that laborers be treated as citizens rather than servants, since servants submit their will to others while citizens maintain their civic rights of representation. But is that what Kant really had in mind?

In another section of the *Groundwork*, Kant picks up this theme of treating people as ends in terms of price and dignity:

> Therefore morality, and humanity so far as it is capable of morality, is the only thing which has dignity. Skill and diligence in work have a market price; wit, lively imagination, and humour have a fancy price; but fidelity to promises and kindness based on principle (not on instinct) have an intrinsic worth.[5]

Kant's distinction between what has a market price – skill and diligence – and what does not have a price – fidelity to promises and kindness – seems to mirror the distinction we observed earlier in Adam Smith's distinction between laboring and the laborer. In fact, one finds a similar separation of the worker from his or her work. It turns out that Kant did not see the laborer as an active citizen because, as Allen Rosen points out, for Kant the laborer was under the "will" of another, rather than his own will.[6]

---

[4] Immanuel Kant, *Groundwork of the Metaphysic of Morals*, trans. H. J. Paton (New York: Harper Torchbooks, 1964), p. 96.

[5] *Ibid.*, p. 102.

[6] Allen Rosen, *Kant's Theory of Justice* (Ithaca, NY and London: Cornell University Press, 1993), p. 39.

So we find some of the same difficulties in Kant's ideas that we found in Smith's: The worker is fragmented and sells his skills without affecting his dignity. According to Kant's view, it would be impossible to receive an "undignified wage," since one's work has been separated from one's self. Kant failed to recognize that human dignity is an issue at work. If we are to protect workers as providers, then we must design workplace relationships that protect their dignity. Protecting human dignity is quite different from protecting property. One can protect property by hiding it so no one will take it. With human dignity, it is protected when it is allowed to flourish – to become engaged in creating a good life.

As we have seen, the economics of property assumes that only property owners have control over the workplace. Within this framework of property management, attempts to protect the civic rights of workers have been supported only when such support improves employee behavior. This all seemed very reasonable, because the owners owned the company.

An economics of provision opens up another line of thought and another description of the workplace:

> The workers do the work. They grow the wheat. They run the mills. They deliver the bread. They stack the shelves. In large businesses and corporations, workers need coordination to ensure that their work is productive and successful. That is the job of their supervisors and managers. Supervisors work for the workers, rather than workers working for the supervisors. Managers develop the organizational structure that facilitates getting the work done. Senior managers and even CEOs coordinate these folks so they can coordinate the work of the workers. In this framework, the senior management and even the CEO can be seen as community organizers, paid to organize the work community so it can make the provisions that people value. If we see the business or corporation as a community of workers designed to provide something of value for consumers, then it makes sense that managers support the workers in accomplishing their task.

This description may sound a bit strange. Its power resides in its recognition of the dignity of workers and the ethical character of relationships among citizens at work. As citizens, what should be the relationship between an employer and an employee? They have equal moral rights. One is doing the work and the other is watching, monitoring, perhaps advising, but in many cases the worker knows more about the work than the employer watching the work being done. Who should work for whom? The issue here is one of degree. If I am more engaged in getting the work done, then I should have a greater say in organizing the work. The ethical challenge is to protect this right to co-organize the work with other workers as well as managers. As Walzer points out, the right to participate in conversations at work is essential to being a citizen.

> The citizen must be ready and able, when his time comes, to deliberate with his fellows, listen and be listened to, take responsibility for what he says and does. Ready and able: not only in states, cities, and towns, but wherever power is exercised in companies and factories, too, and in unions, faculties, and professions.[7]

If the right to participate were protected, which means that we were serious about switching to an economics of provision and civic relationships, this right would include the right to have a say in executive salaries. Who knows better an executive's contribution to the workplace than the workers? Instead of property owners basically determining salaries for themselves by sitting on each other's boards, an economics of provision would place worker representatives on the boards to speak of the contribution of executives in improving the productivity of the workplace. This is not impossible. Germany now requires that large companies have union representatives on their board of directors. Other countries and companies could expand on this example so the real providers in the workplace could be included

[7] Walzer, *Spheres of Justice*, p. 310.

in the organization of their work. Recognizing and protecting the civic and human rights of workers could also promote the recognition that land, another living being, must also be protected from abuse and exploitation.

Protecting land

We have already referred to Leopold's land ethic in Chapter 10, which helped us distinguish between seeing land as a commodity and seeing land as part of a living system. And we now know that the entire biosphere is threatened, not just some forests or a few waterways. The current trends of global warming, death of species, and declining resources have not yet been contained. We are continuing to fail at what future generations will see as our biggest test.

In his most recent book, James Gustave Speth argues that current trends portend disasters for future generations unless we make radical changes immediately. He shares the following findings of the Intergovernmental Panel on Climate Change (IPCC):

- Warming of the climate system is unequivocal, as is now evident from observations of increases in global average air and ocean temperature, widespread melting of snow and ice, and rising global average sea level.
- Eleven of the last twelve years (1995–2006) rank among the twelve warmest years in the instrumental record of global surface temperature (since 1850). Most of the observed increase in global average temperatures since the mid-twentieth century is very likely due to the observed increase in anthropogenic greenhouse gas concentrations. Discernible human influences now extend to other aspects of climate, including ocean warming, continental-average temperatures, temperature extremes and wind patterns.
- Mountain glaciers and snow cover have declined on average in both hemispheres. Widespread decreases in glaciers and ice caps have contributed to sea level rise. New data ... now show that losses from the ice sheets of Greenland and Antarctica have very likely contributed to sea level rise over 1993 to 2003.

- More intense and longer droughts have been observed over wider areas since the 1970s, particularly in the tropics and subtropics. Increased drying linked with higher temperatures and decreased precipitation has contributed to changes in drought.
- The frequency of heavy precipitation events has increased over most land areas, consistent with warming and observed increases of atmospheric water vapor.[8]

Given these trends, the biosphere no longer exists independently of human decisions. Its fate and the fate of human communities are inextricably bound together. If we do not protect its capacity for maintaining itself, then both human and non-human communities will suffer. One principle that has been proposed to address this issue is what has been called the precautionary principle.

The simple basis of the precautionary principle is that actions have consequences. On a deeper level, Kerry Whiteside says, it is a signal that humans are not the masters of the universe.[9] Whiteside states the essence of the principle as follows:

> The fundamental logic for precaution is this: the fear of serious consequences, combined with uncertainty about the conditions under which they might materialize, creates a moral obligation to take precautions.[10]

Advances in science and technology have made many things possible but they have not made them trustworthy. The idea of precaution requires that agents who propose something new must also bear the burden of proof. To halt a new scientific or industrial development, critics do not have to prove it will cause harm. Rather, those who are introducing it most show that there is only light risk of doing

---

[8] James Gustave Speth, *The Bridge at the Edge of the World: Capitalism, the Environment, and Crossing from Crisis to Sustainability* (New Haven, CT and London: Yale University Press, 2008), pp. 21–22.

[9] Kerry Whiteside, *Precautionary Politics: Principle and Practice in Confronting Environmental Risk* (Cambridge, MA: MIT Press, 2006), p. xiii.

[10] *Ibid.*, p. 111.

harm. The widely quoted Wingspread Statement on the precautionary principle puts it this way:

> When an activity raises threats of harm to human health or the environment, precautionary measures should be taken even if some cause-and-effect relationships are not fully established scientifically.[11]

If we recognize the biosphere as a living system that self-organizes and self-regulates, then we have a moral obligation to exercise caution and to mitigate the effects of our actions when we do intervene. Furthermore, since the planet's health is finally the source of our health, precaution is a clear obligation when the consequences of proposed interventions are largely unknown. If we destroy our natural providers, then an economics of provision will also fail. If we learn to protect our planet, we can provide for ourselves and give future generations a chance to provide for themselves. Some would say it depends on whether we have the money, which also needs protection from exploitation.

Protecting money
As we know from Chapter 11, money has various functions in our economy. It provides credit, serves as a medium of exchange, and stores value. We can also treat it as a commodity and use it to make more money without regard to who bears the risk of future events. At the center of the ethics of money is the act of promise-making. When someone issues credit, a promise is made between the creditor and the user. The creditor promises to have provided good credit. The user promises to use the credit for its stated purpose and to repay the debt. In some cases, the two represent different classes – the haves and the have-nots: the banker who has some expertise in the management of money and a homeowner who does not. When this inequality exists – as it did in the sub-prime mortgage fiasco – it imposes an added burden

[11] www.gdrc.org/u-gov/precaution-3.html

on the creditor to ensure the security and safety of the credit. The user needs to be creditworthy and the debt repayable. Otherwise, the relationship violates the implicit promises made between the two.

This does not prevent the creditor, such as a bank, from using the debt as a form of credit for other users. Such leverage is not a violation of the original agreement as long as the money retains its strings, so to speak, to its origin. In the financial crisis of 2008, banks bundled sub-prime loans together as securities – that is, as a commodity – giving them a rating they did not deserve and treating them as property. This was a violation not only of the original promise, but also of the function of money. Protecting the credit function of money requires that banks not be permitted to change their assets from loans into investment securities.

Protecting what people have saved for retirement is another aspect of the ethics of protecting providers. Some corporations and public institutions have speculated with workers' retirement funds, and many retired workers find themselves caught between high living costs and reduced retirement payments. If the companies had kept the workers' funds as a reserve, retired workers would not be at such risk today. In a sense, this aspect of money is also a social relationship based on promise-keeping, and these promises should be kept. Laws can protect such promises to a degree, but we need to protect them further by creating a culture of trust and reciprocity. Which bring us to our third ethical challenge – the ethics of purpose.

The ethics of creating purpose

An economics of property and property relations promotes the idea of finding pleasure in identifying with things, with the brands of products. Also, new things are better than old things, and bigger things are better than smaller things. In an economics of provision, meaning resides in making provisions and enjoying them. Instead of being alienated from one's work, one becomes involved in it. This can also happen on the organizational level. Business people can find meaning in what they provide for their customers or clients rather than in what they accumulate. The ethical challenge here is to discern whether or not one is involved in an enterprise that is up to some good.

Charles Handy, the British writer on business and society, posed the intriguing question "What's a Business For?" in an article with that name for the December 2002 issue of the *Harvard Business Review*.

> By creating new products, spreading technology and raising productivity, enhancing quality and improving service, business has always been the active agent of progress. It helps make the good things of life available and affordable to ever more people. This process is driven by competition and spurred on by the need to provide adequate returns to those who risk their money and their careers, but it is, in itself, a noble cause.[12]

Implicit in Handy's answer is that businesses are not only *for something*, but that they are also *good for something*. Still, it is a different question to ask, "What are businesses *good* for?" Businesses are good for making provisions that people value. They are an important player in any system of provision, though not the only player. There are also government agencies, civic organizations, voluntary organizations, and so on. Still, business can make a contribution to a system's purpose, and if the contribution is a good one, people in the organization will identify with it. They will be able to find a worthwhile purpose in their work.

It makes a difference if I am helping to build an energy-efficient, non-polluting vehicle rather than an SUV that pollutes more than it should and promotes unnecessary consumption. Likewise, it makes a difference if I work in a shirt factory where our products are well made and I am part of a community that ensures our safety and protects our civic rights, rather than in a shirt factory where I must treat myself as a commodity in order for my family to survive. If I work in an advertising company, striving to imagine ways to increase

---

[12] Charles Handy, "What's a Business For?" *Harvard Business Review* (December, 2002), p. 54.

unsustainable consumption, I doubt that I would want to identify with my work. If we are to invite people to identify themselves with the economics of provision, then we must create products, services, and processes that are themselves meaningful.

Many businesses and corporations have developed mission and value statements to say what they are good for. Fetzer Vineyards, one of the largest suppliers of wine in the United States, has the following mission statement:

> We are an environmentally and socially conscious grower, producer and marketer of wines of the highest quality and value.
>
> Working in harmony and with respect for the human spirit, we are committed to sharing information about the enjoyment of food and wine in a lifestyle of moderation and responsibility.
>
> We are dedicated to the continuous growth and development of our people and our business.[13]

Paul Dolan, the guiding spirit and retired president of Fetzer Vineyards, sees this mission statement as a set of talking points for creating the winery's context and culture. This statement, in other words, serves as a guideline for determining the company's actions and policies. Making a provision that people enjoy can become a source of meaning for one's work. The ethical challenge of every organization in a particular system of provision is to find its contribution to the overall system and to make that a good contribution.

When we place businesses and corporations in the systems of provision to which they belong, the language of corporate purpose automatically changes. Instead of talking about how to maximize profit, the language is about how to fulfill one's function in the larger system. This all makes sense if we take a civic perspective on systems of provision. As citizens, we want economic systems that provide citizens with what they value.

---

[13] Paul Dolan, *True to our Roots: Fermenting a Business Revolution* (Princeton, NJ: Bloomberg Press, 2003), p. 61.

Basic human values arise out of and also shape the practices that create and maintain human communities: making provisions, giving protection, and creating a worthwhile purpose. How we should accomplish these tasks today remains a matter of debate and dissention. Civic conversations do not require agreements. In fact, they become vital with disagreements. Disagreements allow us to deliberate. The function of ethics in these deliberations is to provide some general principles and norms that could guide the deliberations. In general, the deliberations should aim for a just and sustainable economy. More specially, they should aim for policies and actions that distribute goods and services in terms of their social meaning for the receivers, protect the providers of these goods and services from harm, and create purposes that allow us to aim for a life worth living.

15 Changing systems of provision

When we sit down to dinner at home or in a café, it is easy to ignore the source of the food we eat, how it got to the table, or the providers that grew, harvested, prepared, and served it. Still, the food on our plate has a history, perhaps like Rifkin's tale of the English muffin discussed in Chapter 13. If we are to understand how to evaluate and to improve systems of provision, sometimes we need to think about the subsystems within them and the other systems with which they interact. In this chapter, we will look at three systems of provision: food, transportation, and housing. Our purpose here is not to definitively answer the many questions we face about how to organize our economic life, but rather to demonstrate how an economics of provision adds to the conversations about the changes we need to make for a more just and sustainable economy.

The systems of food, transportation, and housing provide basic human needs – nutrition, access, and shelter. Others may be equally important, but these three are central to any civic economy, and today they must function in a world that is suffering from the impoverishment of natural and human providers. To begin thinking about how to change these conditions, we can return to the picture of the stakeholders of systems of provision that we developed in the previous chapter. In Figure 15.1, the primary stakeholders are given; the secondary stakeholder ring is left empty, because different systems of provision will have different stakeholders.

The inner circles illustrate the basic economic task of any system: Human providers transform natural provisions into provisions for their communities and families. The outer circle is open to be filled with those stakeholders that belong to particular systems of provision. All systems should aim for a more just and sustainable economy. The

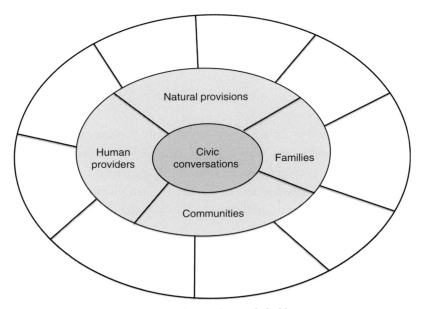

FIGURE 15.1 Primary and secondary stakeholders

current systems that provide us food, transportation, and housing fail to meet these standards, so they are good candidates to illustrate how a civic economy of provision would tackle them. We begin with the provision of food.

THE SYSTEM OF PROVIDING FOOD

"Give us our daily bread" has never been so complicated as it has become in the past century. Today, our bread – like the muffin – comes to us from the collaboration of multiple organizations and agencies that constitute the system that provides food. What elements or stakeholders one would include in the systems of providing food will probably depend on one's position in the system, but it seems the items suggested in Figure 15.2 could be found on most people's list.

If we review the stakeholders in the outer ring, we get some idea of who participates in preparing our dinner at the restaurant or at home. It is a mixture of public and private organizations, of people on the land, in

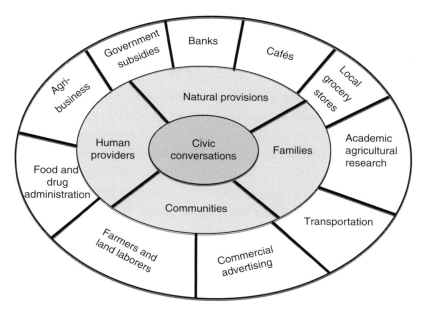

FIGURE 15.2 Stakeholders of the food system

the lab, on the slaughterhouse floor, in government and corporate offices, and in trucks. Although people may view particular characteristics of this system differently, the system itself clearly needs improvement, in terms of justice, sustainability, and human health. Looking at the impact of the current systems of providing food, we can see people in some rich countries struggling with obesity and diets while people in some poor countries struggle with hunger and malnutrition. Plus, our agricultural practices have created trends that deplete our natural resources, endanger the food supply, and limit the diversity of crops for future use. Perhaps the most serious trend is the depletion of water resources, not only for agriculture, but also for cities.

Take the Great Plains region, the breadbasket of the United States, for example. It owes much of its productivity to the water pumped from the underground Ogallala aquifer, which stretches from the Dakotas to Texas and supports nearly one-fifth of the wheat, corn, cotton, and cattle produced in the United States. Since the 1960s, this aquifer has been so depleted that the water table has dropped by more than 100 feet.[1]

There are actually two kinds of aquifers: renewable and non-renewable. Renewable or replenishable aquifers provide limited amounts of water, but whatever the amounts, they will be available in the future, as long as the surface water systems do not drastically change. Nonrenewable aquifers – also called fossil aquifers – are another story. They were formed thousands or even millions of years ago, and the water they contain will not be naturally replaced. These aquifers are now the source of water for extensive irrigation in such regions as the North China Plain, Saudi Arabia, and the Great Plains states of the United States (the Ogallala), and they will be depleted in the next decades if the current rate of withdrawal continues.[2]

We simply cannot sustain our current water use for food production. According to the World Watch 2003 report, more than a half-billion people live in regions prone to chronic drought. By 2025, taking projected population increase into account, that number will likely have increased at least fivefold, to between 2.4 billion and 3.4 billion.[3] These communities will be struggling to get safe drinking water as well as enough food. Some countries that used to produce enough rice for their people – China, for one – have already begun to import rice, because of the shortage of water. Lester Brown cites the following prediction from the International Water Management Institute:

> Many of the most populous countries of the world – China, India, Pakistan, Mexico, and nearly all the countries of the Middle East and North Africa – have literally been having a free ride over the past two or three decades by depleting their groundwater resources. The penalty for mismanagement of this valuable resource is now becoming due and it is no exaggeration to say the results could be

---

[1] Lester R. Brown, *Plan B 2.0: Rescuing a Planet under Stress and a Civilization in Trouble* (New York: Norton, 2006), p. 46.

[2] www.waterencyclopedia.com/Oc-Po/Ogallala-Aquifer.html

[3] Chris Bright, "A History of Our Future," in *State of the World 2003* (New York: Norton, 2003), p. 5.

catastrophic for these countries and, given their importance, for the world as a whole.[4]

It turns out that the amount and kind of food we consume makes a big difference in the conservation of water. While we drink only about 4 liters of water a day per capita, producing our food requires around 2,000 liters – 500 times as much.[5] Furthermore it takes much more water to produce a diet of meat than a diet without meat. The increasing consumption of meat throughout the world is another trend that needs attention. It places ever more stress on water supplies and on the land, as forests are cleared for the more profitable business of raising livestock.

The amount of food the earth can produce is finite; the planet can support only a limited number of people. How many? Lester Brown offers the following answer:

> One of the questions I am most often asked on a speaking tour is, "How many people can the earth support?" I answer with another question: "At what level of food consumption?" At the U.S. level of 800 kilograms per person per year for food and feed, the 2-billion-top annual world harvest of grain would support 2.5 billion people. At the Italian level of consumption of close to 400 kilograms per year, the current harvest would support 5 billion people. At the nearly 200 kilograms of grain consumed per year by the average Indian, it would support a population of 10 billion.[6]

Things can improve, of course, but if we have an ideal image where everyone has the water and food they need to live a good life, then the projection that our global population will probably increase from the current 6.7 billion to around 9.3 billion by 2050 is simply forecasting a disaster.[7]

As many have pointed out, our current food industry practices are clearly unsustainable. Commercial advertising, agricultural research, and government subsidies continue to support these unsustainable

---

[4] Brown, *Plan B 2.0*, pp. 57–58.   [5] *Ibid.*, p. 42.   [6] *Ibid.*, p. 177.
[7] www.prb.org/Publications/Datasheets/2007/2007WorldPopulationDataSheet.aspx

practices. But we could turn these institutions around to support sustainable food production and consumption. How? With the strategies of persuasion, incentives, and regulation. In civic conversations, we can resolve to diminish advertising of fast foods, either through persuasion or regulation. We can decide to buy locally and curtail transportation costs, either through incentives or regulations. We can use persuasion to show that it is not your size, but your health that matters. Health professionals, restaurateurs, grocery shoppers, and government agencies can campaign for a diet that is both healthy and friendly to the earth. We should marshal all three strategies – persuasion, incentives, and regulation – to bring about the changes we need to move the system toward providing healthy, sustainable nutrition. Many organizations, of course, have been involved in such conversations for several decades. In fact, one can see a trend toward sustainability that is changing what we expect from the food industry and what it expects of itself. There is no better example of this trend than the overview statement for the 2009 sustainability conference of the Food Marketing Institute:

> Sustainability opportunities focus on people, planet and profits and are woven throughout every inch of our supply chain, from the farm to the fork. The food industry has a landmark opportunity to lead, innovate and drive faster, more effective adoption and integration of sustainability throughout our supply chain. A "triple bottom-line" [paying attention to financial, environmental, and social performance] approach enables the program's focus on proactive responses to emerging green consumers, skyrocketing global population demands, increased government regulations, energy and resource depletion.
>
> From agricultural practices to sourcing, operations, packaging, design, energy, distribution, marketing, human resources, government policies, community relations – there are new ways of thinking and working that will help us reap "triple bottom-line" rewards.[8]

[8] www.fmi.org/forms/meeting/MeetingFormPublic/view?id=4325F00000097

One can expect many more such conferences in the future – conferences where all stakeholders are represented as we work together to create a just and sustainable food system. Another aspect of moving the food systems toward sustainability, of course, is to address the use of transportation, which is the second system of provision that needs reorganizing.

THE SYSTEM OF PROVIDING TRANSPORTATION

The transportation system is really a set of sub-systems that move people and goods by way of everything from bikes to airplanes. Walking, of course, is the most sustainable means of transportation we know. In the past decades, the roads for automobiles have largely replaced the sidewalks for walking, and until quite recently driving instead of walking was the expected way to move from one place to another. Although the automobile industry is only one sub-system in a much larger transportation system, we will focus on it here because it is currently so unsustainable. Figure 15.3 highlights its key stakeholders.

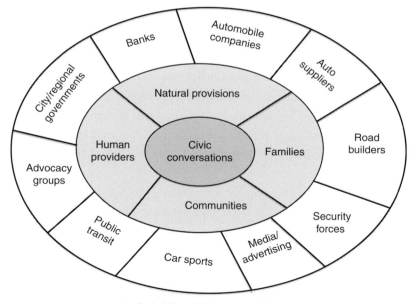

FIGURE 15.3 Stakeholders of the automobile system

If we were to ask who organized the transportation system in the United States so that we are saddled today with an unsustainable automobile system, we could point to most of the system's stakeholders. Families wanted large affordable homes out in the suburbs and large automobiles like their neighbors'. The government refused to place strict fuel-consumption requirements on trucks. Public agencies spent billions of tax dollars building an automobile infrastructure instead of investing in public transit. Media and advertising helped glorify the romance of the road and create a car culture. Banks offered easy credit so people could buy the latest model simply by increasing their debt. Corporations sponsored auto sports and spent billions of dollars to develop and bring out new models annually to spur sales. The result: oil wars, planetary destruction, and, until we change, a dismal future for our children and grandchildren.

So how do we begin to change this system? We could begin by using the ethical guidelines of the previous chapter to ask specific questions: What is the purpose of the system? How does it promote civic equality? How can we make it more sustainable? The purpose of any transportation is to provide access to what people value. And access requires mobility in most cases. But urban design can also provide access – and more efficiently. One can design cities so that cars are not necessary, or at least not necessary for access to most things we value. This would require that the government change its current spending of billions of dollars on the automobile infrastructure and shift to supporting urban transit and urban housing projects.

Another project currently under way is to build more efficient autos, such as electric cars. This plan would not decrease the government spending on roads and highways; nor would it promote the redesign of communities so all members have access to what they value. The project of electric cars, while certainly more attractive than cars dependent on the earth's oil reserves, still assumes the perspective of an economics of property. We should be asking how we can ensure that citizens have access to what they need and value instead of asking how we can make private property (autos) sustainable. This would not mean the demise of the automobile industry, but it would mean that it does not dominate our transportation systems as it has in the past.

As we move toward a sustainable transportation system, civic conversations would determine the general direction of transportation development, instead of corporations and advertisers. Businesses would produce vehicles (automobiles and buses, for example) that would fit with a system of access and distribute them through markets. Advertisers would highlight the advantages of different forms of transportation. As a civic system, the system would have obligations to respect the contribution of the providers of access – both human and environmental – and promote the basic principles of reciprocity and moral equality. The system as a whole would be evaluated in terms of how well it provides access for all its participants and how well it treats its providers.

All our system strategies – persuasion, incentives, and regulation – would play a part in this change. Educational organizations and the media in general would need to transform the current car culture into a more realistic view of what a car is – a way of moving from point A to point B. For the sake of sustainability, we will have to find more suitable objects for romantic notions.

There must also be incentives to encourage people to sacrifice the convenience of having a car to go when and where they want. This may take the form of higher gas taxes and lower prices on public transit. One could also imagine designing urban areas where owning a car would be more of a nuisance than a contributor to one's well-being.

Regulations will also prove helpful. Governments, for example, could develop regulations that require advertising to become more responsible. Years ago, governments banned the advertising of cigarettes on television, for reasons of public health. Governments could similarly ban the advertising of passenger cars and trucks that get less than 40 miles per gallon, for reasons of public health. Governments could also support types of transit projects other than roads and highways. Public roads and highways are by far the most inefficient way to provide mobility. Think of it: We use millions of vehicles weighing thousands of pounds each to transport single individuals from one side of town to another. There has got to be a better way.

We know much of what needs to be done. We just need the political will and civic leadership to do it. Creating a sustainable transportation system is possible, but it needs help from a sustainable housing system, which is the last of the three systems for this chapter.

THE SYSTEM OF PROVIDING HOUSING

What should the housing system provide? In Chapter 5, we outlined three aspects of a dwelling: a home, a house, and real estate or property. We will consider all three here. The housing system should first of all provide a home. What a home should provide will differ from culture to culture. I believe it should ensure the necessary privacy and security for individual and familial autonomy, and have access to the provisions necessary for a good life for all its members. While it promotes autonomy, the home should not be outside of the civic sphere because all family members have the right to protection from harm and abuse. We do not advocate a moral police squad inspecting our neighborhoods, but I think most of us would want children and adults protected from domestic violence and child endangerment.

To move the home from an economics of property to an economics of provision poses one of the most challenging aspects of civilizing the economy. From our emphasis on protecting the real providers of wealth, to the replacement of the individual with the family as a basic economic image, we have tried to bring into our economic framework the status of women and children in our global community. Alongside the struggles of women for equality, fathers and husbands need to struggle with the legacy of viewing the home as their property. One can own a house, but not a home.

A house, as a building, exists as part of the natural and urban environment. Whether it is a single-family house or a rental apartment, the building is connected to the water, energy, waste disposal,

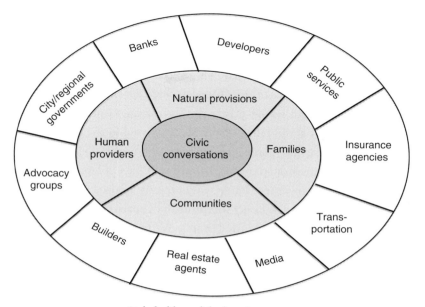

FIGURE 15.4 Stakeholders of the housing system

and other systems of provision. As a part of a community, it is also connected to all the systems that provide goods and services to these communities. When considering the systematic provision of housing, the picture of primary and secondary stakeholders shown in Figure 15.4 seems plausible.

Although providing housing for communities presents a number of challenges, one that could be addressed easily, at least in the future, is where one chooses to build houses in the first place. One of the most questionable developments in the United States is the expanding population in the southwestern area of Nevada, Arizona, New Mexico, and Southern California. This region depends on the Colorado River for most of its water, and the continuing drought in Colorado has significantly decreased the snow pack in the Rocky Mountains, the source for the Colorado River.

Outside of Las Vegas is Lake Mead, which supplies water to more than 20 million people in the region, including the people of Henderson, a city that sprang up in 1953, but now tops a quarter of a million in population. Henderson gets 90 percent of its water from Lake Mead. Because of increased demand and drought, the possibility of Lake Mead going dry is very real. In fact, a study in 2008 by the University of California-San Diego's Scripps Institute of Oceanography reported that the chances of Lake Mead drying up by 2021 were 50–50.[9] Some say not enough water; others say that rampant development of the Nevada desert should never have been allowed in the first place.

Every house has some "footprint," or impact on the planet. Houses built in areas of sprawling suburb will have a larger footprint than houses built in cities. Large single-family houses, other things being equal, have a much larger footprint than apartments. In a recent study on house size in the United States, Wilson and Boehland found that since 1950 the average size of new single-family houses has more than doubled.[10] That means twice the resources to build the house, and twice the energy to heat and cool it. Should one's financial capability be the sole factor in determining what size house one builds, or should we have zoning regulations that encourage house sizes that are in line with the availability of national resources? There are sustainable limits in the system of providing housing, just as there are in food production.

In the United States, owning a home is the "American Dream." Like our romance with cars, this dream needs a reality check. As we have already said, a good home does not require a property title to a house. To the degree that a home means autonomy and privacy, these provisions should be available to all homes, including rental units and cooperatives. In terms of the house as property, owning property, as we argued earlier, depends on belonging to a civic community that then provides title to you. This granting of title is best understood as a concession by the civic community as a means of caring for the

---

[9] Henry Brean, "Study Gives 50–50 Odds Lake Mead Will Dry Up by 2021," www.lvrj. com/news/15581197.html (retrieved on February 13, 2008).

[10] Alex Wilson and Jessica Boehland, "Small Is Beautiful: U.S. House Size, Resource Use, and the Environment," *Journal of Industrial Ecology*, Vol. 9, Nos. 1–2 (Winter–Spring, 2005), p. 277.

property and the neighborhood. The urban house, of course, never was an absolute possession. There are zoning laws, building codes, and property taxes, all of which make the house part of a community and a natural environment as well as something that can be passed on to future generations.

Owning a house, in fact, has little to do with the benefits of a home, or being at home in the world. These are elements of life that money cannot buy. We need to look at various models of ownership that already exist, such as cooperative ownership, secure rental agreements, and public housing. As we think about how to create sustainable cities, we will do better if being at home is not equated with possessing a title to a house. They are actually quite different.

The American Dream is not an empty fantasy. It is rooted, I believe, in the aspiration for security, stability, and self-development. It has taken the form of owning one's own place. Owning a place is important. If others own all the things of my life – the condition of millions of people today – there is no place for my self-development. The fact is that this need for human space – a place – is a basic human need. A just society must provide it. If we are to move toward a sustainable economy, we must rethink how we can create the conditions for the development of such places on our one planet. Such rethinking should be on the agenda of the civic conversations that will direct our housing systems in the right direction. How to facilitate such conversations is the topic of the final part of this book: a civic agenda.

These three systems of provision – food, transportation, and housing – are all interconnected because they all belong to the living planet and they are also constructed in particular ways by the stories and images that give them meaning. Some of the interventions we have suggested – different uses of incentives, threats, and persuasions – can be used with all of these systems as well as other systems of provision. It is important to remember that changing social and economic systems is not done overnight, but rather over a longer time as we shift the direction of the trends that are moving us further away from the world we desire, back toward the world we want. Our dilemma is that we do not have a lot of time. Much of what we needed to do was already known in the 1970s, well articulated and documented by that generation of environmentalists. After 30 years of denial by the United States government, we are trying to make the necessary changes. As long as these efforts stay in the legacy of an economics of property, it is doubtful if these efforts will suffice. This makes the civic agenda of the next chapters particularly relevant.

Part V A civic agenda

16 The civic obligations of corporations

Our civic agenda is quite simple to imagine: We want to organize systems of provision so all communities and families have access to what they need and value. Some of these needs are universal, such as a viable natural and social environment. Some are basic, such as food, shelter, security, and meaning. Others are necessary to participate in the current economy, such as work, credit, and transportation. And others are more contingent, such as entertainment or luxuries. In most cases, making these provisions available will include the services of multinational corporations.

At first glance, one may wonder if there is a place in a civic economics of provision for corporations, as we know them today. Here we need to make a distinction between theory and reality. In reality, a civic economics of provision does not eliminate free enterprise. It just puts it on a civic platform and places it within larger systems of provision. So what remains "free" or "private" once these changes are made? Actually, not that much has changed, at least for most businesses. Citizens will still own businesses, as before. Businesses will still need a license to operate and will have to abide by city ordinances as before. Owners will still be enterprising in improving their standard of living, as before. Entrepreneurs will still develop new products and services in response to consumer preferences as before. The actual practice of running a business, in other words, will not really be all that different. The fact is that a civic economics of provision comes closer to most business people's experiences than does the theory of free enterprise.

As we have seen, most businesses do rely on civic norms of trust and fairness. They do belong to larger systems of supply chains and government regulations. Most businesses are responsive to public opinion and do seek to maintain the good will of the communities in which they serve. Their practices reflect the attitudes and aspirations of their owners, and business people are just as likely to fulfill their civic obligations as any other group of citizens.

When we turn to major corporations, things become more confusing, because we have a habit of treating corporations as though they were individuals with the same rights as living persons. Corporations are not living, breathing beings. They do not suffer or get depressed. They may have been given the legal rights of persons, but they do not have the moral status of real living persons. Still, the standards we established in the ethics of systems can also be applied to corporations. They have a civic obligation to promote fairness in the distribution of provisions. They have a civic obligation to protect the dignity of labor and the land, and to protect money from becoming a commodity. And they have a civic obligation to fulfill their purpose in the systems of provision to which they belong. These civic obligations belong to them not because they are citizens but because they belong to a civic economics of provision.

Some people do speak of corporate citizenship, but this seems quite confusing to me, especially in a time when many only have a faint idea of the meaning of citizenship. It would help if people would clarify the differences between corporate and human citizens instead of assuming that everyone knows the difference. Andrew Crane and Dirk Matten's recent textbook on business ethics is a welcome exception. They sort out three views of corporate citizenship (CC).

- A limited view of CC – this equates CC with corporate philanthropy
- An equivalent view of CC – this equates CC with CSR [corporate social responsibility]
- An extended view of CC – this acknowledges the extended political role of the corporation in society.[1]

---

[1] Andrew Crane and Dirk Matten, *Business Ethics: Managing Corporate Citizenship and Sustainability in the Age of Globalization*, second edition (New York: Oxford University Press, 2007), p. 71. See also the January 2008 issue of *Business Ethics Quarterly*, Vol. 18, No. 1, for a further discussion of the notion of corporate citizen.

As Crane and Matten point out, we do not gain much by calling either philanthropy or corporate social responsibility acts of corporate citizens, especially when the notion of citizen is not further clarified. Crane and Matten do see some value in what they call the extended view. This view "sees the corporation as a political actor governing the citizenship of individual stakeholders."[2] The notion of the corporation as a "political actor" supports our view that corporations are part of systems of provision and should be involved in civic conversations about the direction of these systems. The question is whether corporations should be seen as "governing the citizenship of individual stakeholders." Crane and Matten argue that they should, especially when governments fail to do so. If the employees were involved in corporate governing, their argument would even be stronger. Still, in the long run, does not this represent a privatization of citizenship? If we expect corporations to govern citizen rights, are we also agreeing with the statement of the former Federal Reserve Governor we quoted earlier: "the financial system [or the corporation] is the brain of the economy"?[3] If international corporations are operating in failed states, one might first ask what they are doing there. But who will ask this question if corporations are seen as governing themselves as well as their stakeholders? Human citizens are self-governing through their participation in politics and representative governments. To understand the governing of corporations, we need to take a step back and reflect on their function in civic systems of provision.

Remember our earlier discussion of the different aspects of a dwelling? We observed that it was a home, a house, and a piece of real estate. Corporations also have multiple aspects, and for us to understand their function in any system of provision, it will be important to examine the corporation as a piece of property, a community, an agent, and a provider.

[2] *Ibid.*, p. 79.   [3] See p. 163.

THE CORPORATION AS PROPERTY

Imagine a corporation as a large hotel. The owner of the hotel hires a property manager to keep the rooms clean and attractive, to make the premises safe, and to foster a good relationship with neighbors, so that he or she can make a profit. The task of the property manager is quite clear: to carry out the owner's wishes. Milton Friedman, in a famous 1971 article on corporate social responsibility, takes this very view of the corporation. He writes:

> In a free-enterprise, private property system, a corporate executive is an employee of the owners of the business. He has direct responsibility to his employers. That responsibility is to conduct the business in accordance with their desires, which generally will be to make as much money as possible while conforming to the basic rules of the society, both those embodied in law and those embodied in ethical custom.[4]

Friedman is not wrong here if one sees a business only as a piece of private property. And most business law in the United States does support this view. The manager is an agent of the owner (the principal), and an agent has a legal obligation to carry out the principal's wishes. If I owned a hotel, and my manager decided to offer rooms to the homeless without my approval, I would feel that he or she had violated our contractual relationship just as much as Friedman seems to believe that corporate managers who promote social programs at the expense of the owner have violated their contract.

In a sense, one can see Friedman's argument as an attempt to return the control of business back to the owners, something that the modern corporate form had more or less taken away from them. As Berle and Means pointed out in their 1932 book on corporations, the modern stockholder corporation has dispersed ownership into the hands of many different shareholders, effectively leaving control of

---

[4] Milton Friedman, "The Social Responsibility of Business Is to Increase Its Profits," in *Ethical Theory and Business*, eighth edition, ed. Tom Beauchamp, Norman Bowie, and Denis Arnold (Upper Saddle River, NJ: Prentice Hall, 2009), p. 51.

the property to corporate managers.[5] This debate about the right relationship between ownership and control has not been settled, but for
the most part it remains a debate that focuses on the corporation as
property.

In our earlier explorations about the meaning of property, we
acknowledged that property is, in fact, a political institution. It is a
legal title that gives someone property rights. Given this view, it
seemed that we could usefully treat property as a concession given to
persons in situations where "private" ownership was the best means
for the economic goal of making provisions. Similarly, we can apply
this civic understanding of property to a corporation. Its existence as
property depends on its charter, which is a government license to exist.
In the United States, corporate charters are issued at the state rather
than the federal level, although one could argue that corporations that
operate nationally should have national charters. In any case, the
corporation as property is not totally under the control of its owners.
As Friedman recognizes, it must obey the laws and the norms embedded in ethical customs. It this sense, it mirrors a dwelling as real estate
and as a house, but it ignores the notion of a home. To include this
more human element, we need to recognize the corporation as a
human community.

THE CORPORATION AS A COMMUNITY

If one views the corporation only as property, the people working there
become invisible. One sees only their productivity, which has been
purchased. But who can deny that a corporation is a collection of
persons who work together to provide some product or service? The
very presence of workers in corporations requires that managers shift
from the simple task of property management to the more complex
task of community organizing. We might even say they have to move
to the task of community leadership. If managers take on the role of

---

[5] Adolf A. Berle and Gardiner C. Means, *The Modern Corporation and Private Property*
(New Brunswick, NJ: Transaction, 1991).

community leaders, they can recognize without much trouble that they should treat workers as they would expect to be treated – with reciprocity.

Part of the legacy of the economics of property is that workers have been seen not as citizens who deserve respect, but as a resource whose worth is determined by the bottom line (as human resources). An economics of property sees workplaces, not workers; workplaces that can be moved, refilled, rebuilt, or eliminated, as one would change office furniture. Labor unions were successful in some cases in protecting workers from this type of treatment, and in the 1980s and 1990s many corporations developed much more admirable policies toward the work community.

Robert Levering and Milton Moskowitz have been documenting the performance of companies in regard to their treatment of employees since the 1980s. They first published their findings in the book *The 100 Best Companies to Work for in America* in 1984.[6] In 1998, they founded the Great Place to Work Institute, which publishes annual reports of the best companies to work for. Their work recognizes those companies that do create "great places to work," and prompts other companies to do the same. The most important aspect of work relationships for the institute is trust, which they see expressed in daily work as credibility, respect, fairness, pride, and camaraderie.[7] Although these are not referred to as civic norms or relationships, one can easily see them as such.

We would only add that relationships at work should be guided by the civic norms of moral equality and reciprocity, an effort that some companies certainly make. This community definition of the corporation tends to focus on its internal character rather than on its role in economic systems, which is the focus of the third and fourth aspects of the corporation: as an agent and a provider.

---

[6] Robert Levering and Milton Moskowitz, *The 100 Best Companies to Work for in America* (New York: Addison-Wesley, 1984).

[7] www.greatplacetowork.com/great/index.php

THE CORPORATION AS AN AGENT

Defining a corporation as an agent highlights that it acts through a decision-making process. Corporations can be considered decision makers because their decisions emerge from a process that typically uses knowledge and expertise to explore the merits of different options and then selects the option that fits best with the corporation's purpose, policies, and values. Since it has choices and criteria for selecting among them, a corporation can be held responsible for its decisions as a moral agent, even though it does not have a human dignity.

A key to the effectiveness of a corporation as an agent is the design of its decision-making process. The likelihood of a corporation making good decisions will depend on its answers to such questions as: "Who is involved in the process?" "Are the participants in the process there for the good of the business?" "What considerations really count?" "What values (explicit or implicit) drive the decision?" and, finally, "Are the incentives in line with just actions?" The advantage of the corporation over the individual person as an agent is that there is no concern about weakness of will. The disadvantage is that any individual can easily sabotage the process for individual gain. Strong leadership is necessary to maintain an inclusive and constructive process of making decisions.

It is important to note that corporations always act in relationship with others. The other party may be a human agent or institution, such as a competitor, a government agency or a nonprofit. These relationships can be hostile or collaborative. In an economics of property relations, the best that one could expect would be win/win arrangements between them. In a civic economics of provision, the expectation is higher. Only by all agencies in any system of provision sharing the same overall goal can the system achieve its purpose. This is not a question of individual will, but rather a question of organizational design. All agents in a system of provision should be designed to make collaborative decisions.

Like human agents, corporations are responsible for the consequences of their decisions. In fact, it is only by looking at the actual results or consequences of their actions that we can finally know what corporations are doing. If extensive advertising contributes to a consumer culture, for example, advertising companies can be held responsible for such a culture – to the degree that one can show actual causal links. This notion of responsibility is usually refered to as corporate social responsibility (CSR). Although CSR has various interpretations, it generally refers to corporate efforts to respond to social and ecological issues. Many multinational corporations, for example, today engage in what is called triple-line reporting, which entails a yearly report of their financial, social, and environmental performance. By reviewing and comparing reports from year to year, one can get a sense of the progress a company is making in these areas. As I observed in my book *Corporate Integrity*, corporations have never before done so many good works as they have since the advent of CSR programs.[8] What is particularly striking is that they have done this, for the most part, on a voluntary basis. In fact, as William Frederick reminds us, CSR has been a business initiative from its beginning.

> CSR was not born in opposition to the business order but was encapsulated within the capitalist system and became an integral part of the free-enterprise market economy – and was subordinated to that system's central values. Until one understands the original provenance of CSR, all attempts to "curb" excessive business behavior in the name of social responsibility or ethics can be seen as historically naïve and socially futile.[9]

I think Frederick is right here, and one actually finds this limitation in the CSR mantra of "Doing well by doing good." Being responsible, in other words, will have a positive impact on the bottom line.

The assumptions behind the CSR movement, it seems fair to say, are those of an economics of property. The corporation is the property

---

[8] Marvin Brown, *Corporate Integrity: Rethinking Organizational Ethics and Leadership* (New York: Cambridge University Press, 2005), p. 20.

[9] William C. Frederick, *Corporation Be Good: The Story of Corporate Social Responsibility* (Indianapolis, IN: Dog Ear Publishing, 2006), p. 7.

of the owners, and if CSR programs enhance the value of the property – such as its brand image – then it makes sense to have them. If there is a market for virtue, to use David Vogel's phrase, then corporations will engage in CSR.[10] If we turn from the perspective of property owners to that of citizens, we face an interesting question: "Who should decide what good a corporation should do?" Or, to employ another popular notion, "Who should decide what a corporation gives back to the community?"

From a civic perspective, one finds a rather strange irony in the recent history of corporate giving. On the one hand, corporations have certainly given more through philanthropy than ever before. On the other hand, they pay fewer taxes than ever before. As recently as 1943, US corporations provided nearly 40 percent of the US tax revenues. At the beginning of the twenty-first century, they paid a lot less.[11] Why? Largely because of offshore tax shelters. The US government's recent report on the corporate use of tax shelters noted the following:

- The effective U.S. tax rate on U.S. multinational corporations as of 2004, the most recent year for data, was 2.3 percent [instead of the 35 percent official rate].
- Eighty-three of the 100 largest U.S. corporations had subsidiaries in tax havens, according to the Government Accountability Office.
- Bermuda, the Netherlands and Ireland – all small, low-tax countries – claimed nearly a third of all foreign profits reported in 2003 by U.S. corporations.[12]

What is happening here? On the one hand, corporations are deviously finding ways to not pay their fair share of taxes. On the other hand, they are deciding what they will give back to the community through

---

[10] David Vogel, *The Market for Virtue: The Potential and Limits of Corporate Social Responsibility* (Washington, DC: Brookings Institution Press, 2005), p. 26.

[11] Lucy Komisar, "Tax Activists: Big Business Must Pay Its Fair Share," http://thekomisarscoop.com/category/offshore/tax-evasion (retrieved on April 12, 2005).

[12] news.yahoo.com/s/mcclatchy/20090504/pl_mcclatchy/3226240

corporate social responsibility projects. Is this anything other than a privatization of taxes?

Taxes and CSR are both ways to give back to the community, but the key difference between them is that CSR programs are voluntary and taxes are obligatory. To understand the option here, consider this question: "Should corporations decide what taxes they pay, or should citizens?" If taxes were a civic obligation, then it would make sense for citizens to determine the taxes that corporations pay. That is, of course, if we believe corporations should pay taxes at all.

Whether corporations should pay taxes depends on what aspect of their identity we emphasize. Does it make sense to tax them if they are only property? Perhaps a property tax, but not an income tax. What about taxing them as a human community? Or what about their character as a moral agent? To understand a corporation's civic obligation to pay a fair tax, we need to move to the fourth facet of corporations: corporations as providers.

CORPORATIONS AS PROVIDERS

From the perspective of an economics of provision, corporations exist in the space between the ecological household and the family household. They transform natural resources into goods and services, and they facilitate that process. As facilitators of the making of provisions, they can be considered providers themselves. They are also the recipients of provisions. Land, labor, credit, and knowledge, as well as ingenuity, are provided to corporations.

The corporate business of making provisions involves first of all the gathering of the traditional providers – land, labor, and money – as well as the more modern providers of technological innovation and human ingenuity. Land and labor have a legitimate claim on the corporation to develop policies that respect them as living providers. The non-living providers – money and knowledge – also can make legitimate claims to be treated as valuable entities and not wasted or carelessly managed. The goods and services that the corporation provides should fit in with the system of provision it belongs to and promote the effective distribution of the specific provisions to consumers and citizens. These processes of production and distribution should not violate the ethical guidelines that belong to any system of provision.

Corporations not only provide goods and services; they also engage in a systematic provision of wealth. A wealthy community can be defined as one in which people are well provided for. The economist Amartya Sen believed that a community is well provided for when all the community members have the capability to "lead the kind of lives they value – and have reason to value."[13] The opposite, of course, would be a community in which people had no such capacities to get the things they have reasons to want. As Sen writes:

> There are good reasons for seeing poverty as a deprivation of basic capabilities, rather than merely as low income. Deprivation of elementary capabilities can be reflected in premature mortality, significant undernourishment (especially of children), persistent morbidity, widespread illiteracy and other failures.[14]

For an economics of provision, poverty is the lack of provisions – provisions that all human communities need to live a full human life. A wealthy community not only has provisions but also is active in the process of making provisions for this and future generations. The activity of wealth creation, in other words, is one of enhancing the well-being of the community through innovative and sustainable practices. Individual persons, in positions of control, can always exploit this process to their own advantage, of course, and take the wealth as their own. In order to recognize this when it occurs, it may help to make a distinction between wealth and profit.

Wealth belongs to the whole system of provision, and is created by that system. Profit, on the other hand, is what a corporation has when its income exceeds its expenses. One could imagine a situation in

---

[13] Amartya Sen, *Development as Freedom* (New York: Alfred A. Knopf, 1999), p. 18.
[14] *Ibid.*, p. 20.

which a community increases its wealth while corporations earn very low profits, or where a community is impoverished while corporations rake in huge profits. As Georges Enderle has said, "'Making money' can be destroying wealth while creating wealth can be losing money."[15] The point is that how well we provide for one another (wealth) may have little to do with profit margins. The beginning of capitalism in the eighteenth century brought great wealth to many in Europe while it impoverished the peoples of Africa and America, a situation we are still living with today. So wealth and business profit can be quite different.

What they have in common is that they are both creations of systems rather than particular organizations. Corporate profit, in other words, is a result of the whole system in which corporations exist, not the corporation itself as an isolated entity. From the perspective of an economics of property, it makes sense to see profit as belonging to the owners of property. From that of an economics of provision, it would belong to all who contributed to its development. In other words, most stakeholders in a stakeholder economy would have made some contribution to a system that placed profit in the hands of the corporation. If this profit comes at others' expense, then a corporation would have a civic obligation to change its procedures so that people are not exploited. If the profit results in a net gain for everyone, then the only civic obligation is that of paying a fair tax that redistributes the profit to the system in a manner that renews or even improves the system for future generations. So what would be a fair tax rate? The real question is who should decide. This question must be answered in the conversations that maintain the civic foundation of an economics of provision. The next chapter will explore how to create the circumstances so these conversations could be successful.

Corporations may not have an obligation to engage in philanthropy, but they do have an obligation to pay their fair share of taxes. As part of systems of provision, they also have an obligation to align

---

[15] Georges Enderle, "Business Ethics and Wealth Creation: Is There a Catholic Deficit?" *Erasmus Institute: Occasional Papers* (2004 Series Number 1), p. 4.

1. The purpose of the corporation is to harness private interests to serve the public interest.
2. Corporations shall accrue fair returns for shareholders, but not at the expense of the legitimate interests of other stakeholders.
3. Corporations shall operate sustainably, meeting the needs of the present generation without compromising the ability of future generations to meet their needs.
4. Corporations shall distribute their wealth equitably among those who contribute to its creation.
5. Corporations shall be governed in a manner that is participatory, transparent, ethical, and accountable.
6. Corporations shall not infringe on the right of natural persons to govern themselves, nor infringe on other universal human rights.

FIGURE 16.1 Principles of corporate design

themselves with the system's purpose and to play their role in providing those things families and communities need and value. These requirements are not that unusual. Various groups have been working hard to reformulate the purpose and function of corporations in our society. One of the more interesting is the group called Corporation 20/20. They have developed the corporate design principles shown in Figure 16.1.

These principles conform to the picture developed here of a corporation's civic obligations. Even though the principles do not speak of taxes directly, the fourth principle does refer to the distribution of wealth based on contribution rather than ownership. If we place this view of the corporation in a stakeholder economy grounded in civic relations, then these principles can give us further guidance for the type of civic conversations we need to have.

Corporations, however, should not be expected to make the necessary changes by themselves. As we have said before, systems of provision include business, government, and nonprofit agencies. It is only by all agents working together that we have a chance to make the changes that are necessary for a just and sustainable world. This requires that all these groups engage each other in civic conversations. How this could happen is the topic of the next chapter.

17 Creating circumstances for civic conversations

At the core of the economics of provision – the practice of providing, protecting, and creating purpose for our families and communities – is the engagement in civic conversations. So far, we have assumed that such conversations are possible. In a sense, we know they are because we have participated in them. Still, in some places they would be out of place because the context would not be appropriate. In some circumstances, civic conversations might be easy but without much consequence. In other circumstances, they may be very difficult to start, but could effect great change. This chapter examines how we might alter difficult circumstances so that civic conversations not only happen but also make a difference.

Back in the 1990s, a small group of people on our street organized a block party. We did the usual preparation: obtained a permit from the city, borrowed the city's barriers for the afternoon, put flyers in mailboxes and so on. More than sixty people came to the afternoon event. Not only has the event continued on a yearly basis, it has also spurred us to hold irregular soup nights, establish a list serve, raise money for earthquake preparations, and have a monthly coffee hour on Saturday mornings at the local café. Our conversations include topics such as how people are doing on the street and how safe people feel living here, as well as local, national, and international events. I mention this because the creation of circumstances for good conversations can begin on the streets where we live.

We need to rebuild a civic foundation for our lives together, beginning with our relationships with our neighbors and extending through various levels to our global community. We live in our homes, but we also live in houses that face our street and therefore face a space that we share with each other. On too many streets, this

Civic conversations:

- are based on mutual recognition as global citizens;

- are guided by such civic norms as reciprocity and moral equality;

- serve to bridge social differences;

- promote deliberation by weighing merits of alternative courses of action.

FIGURE 17.1 Civic conversations

common space is empty – if not scary – because the people in the houses have not created a civic space that binds them together. In this chapter, we talk about creating circumstances – not only on the street where we live, but also in the multitude of organizations in which we work – that foster conversations that will make a difference. Throughout the book, we have pinpointed key characteristics of such conversations, which are summarized in Figure 17.1.

Civic conversations occur among people who recognize each other as global citizens, as being members of a global civil society. The conversations are guided by such norms as reciprocity, which means that people treat others as they wish to be treated and expect that their contributions will be recognized. Civic conversations also transcend social differences and conflicts not by ignoring them, but by recognizing these differences as relative and not absolute, which allows people to see beyond them. And finally, at their center, these civic conversations use the process of deliberation, guided by civic and ethical norms, to weigh different courses of action and to choose that which best aligns with our aspirations for a just and sustainable economy.

These characteristics refer to relationships and processes, but not to content. On any particular topic, people come with their own resources to propose what should be done. Some people may be experts and others novices. Some topics may include scientific data that participants need to know, and sometimes even the scientists will disagree about what the data means. Mark Brown's book on the role of science in democracy demonstrates that we should not place scientific

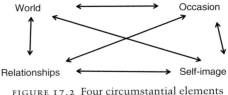

FIGURE 17.2 Four circumstantial elements

knowledge beyond politics, but rather see science as part of political deliberation.[1] Some people may assume that they did not have the expertise to engage in particular conversations. How many of us know the scientific details of global warming? Instead of remaining silent, however, we can educate ourselves about issues, develop criteria for understanding, and learn how to assess our assumptions about facts and values.

What topics people will explore depends largely on the interpretation of their circumstances. Circumstances refer to the conditions of any situation that define it in a particular way. They are what surround (circum) us. In this chapter, we will explore different types of circumstances and imagine how we might make them more conducive to civic conversations. The basic model for our exploration is from W. Barnett Pearce's book *Interpersonal Communication: Making Social Worlds*.[2] The model proposes that our circumstances are constituted by four different elements: the world in which the conversation occurs, the particular occasion that elicits the conversation, the kinds of relationships among those involved, and the participants' self-image. All of these are interrelated as Figure 17.2 demonstrates.

Perhaps the most accessible element is the occasion. For example, let's say that a group of people attend a meeting where there is a need to take some action. Although this may not be recognized as a public occasion, the participants do know that what they decide will affect others. This occasion, of course, takes place in a world, the

---

[1] Mark B. Brown, *Science in Democracy: Expertise, Institutions, and Representation* (Cambridge, MA: MIT Press, 2009).
[2] W. Barnett Pearce, *Interpersonal Communication: Making Social Worlds* (New York: HarperCollins College Publishers, 1994).

second element. The term "world" refers to the material context in which we live, such as the world of technology or of work. Once the people encounter each other, the two other conditions become more relevant: relationships that unite and separate the participants and each participant's self-image.

Given these brief descriptions of these four elements, consider the following scenario. A joint committee of public and private agencies meets to discuss the problem of continuing traffic snarls during commute time. The committee is supposed to give recommendations to city and state governments. Most of the participants are familiar with this kind of occasion. Depending on their past experiences, they may see the meeting as a way of preventing action or as a way of preparing for action. The world in which the meeting occurs may be characterized by bureaucratic infighting, by public-private cooperation, or by some other dynamic. The understanding of the world could determine if a group relies on experts or depends on citizen deliberations to determine the course of action. One can imagine that people may have both official and unofficial roles – as experts, neighborhood spokespersons, business representatives, and citizens. People's understanding of these relationships could be just as forceful in setting expectations and limitations as either the occasion or the understanding of the world. Finally, each person brings a self-image of who she or he is, especially at this type of meeting. Individuals may use some sort of psychological typing or even gender distinctions to gain this self-understanding. In any case, any person's self-image could either increase or decrease the range of possibilities for good conversations.

Any one of these four elements could play a dominant role in setting the framework for the conversation's deliberation. Furthermore, any one of them could provide a different angle from which to view the other three. Participating in relationships of trust, for example, could provide a different view of one's own self-image than participating in relationships of utility. Or, an informal occasion might foster relationships different from that of a formal occasion. What local circumstances give us, in other words, depends on how we interpret the character of the four circumstantial elements and how we perceive their interaction. To increase our capacity to interpret and influence these elements, we will examine them more closely. We begin with a few reflections about occasions, since the occasion is the most visible, if not always the most influential.

Occasions

Each different kind of meeting you attend during a normal week constitutes a very different occasion. Each of these occasions will have different expectations about what to say and not say, and probably different expectations about appropriate relationships. You may even see yourself as a somewhat different person in different meetings. An occasion may begin with one agenda and move over time to another. A team meeting to discuss production schedules may become an occasion to examine work relationships. A participant in the meeting may decide that this is the right occasion for sharing her experiences of working with this team, or perhaps that it would not be the right time to talk about such things.

Have we not all waited for the right occasion to say something to someone, or to bring up something that has been bothering us? In a typical meeting, we may wait until we feel that our voice will be heard, or that others will have a chance to respond. These chances will largely depend on the members' perceptions of how the other circumstantial elements provide constraints and possibilities for interpreting the situation. In many cases, the most important element is the relationships among the team members.

Relationships

Every occasion brings people together, but how they connect with each other depends on much more than the occasion. If there is a history in an organization of people shutting down others or not respecting others' experiences, then relationships of mistrust may create circumstances that block the possibility of engaging in disagreements. Without disagreements, of course, people have little to deliberate about, because the different options never appear on the table. In such cases, the dominant person usually gets his or her way. On the other hand, an organization that has a history of practicing mutual respect may support disagreement so that they can actually consider different options.

Relationships are often multidimensional. At one level are the formal or institutional relationships, such as employer-employee, administrator-teacher, or co-workers. At another level are the informal relationships that arise from experiences of interaction. These relationships may be based on similarities as well as differences. There are also relationships among persons from different social groups. How people see themselves defined in terms of such groups can have an enabling or limiting effect on a group's process. Relationships will also have an impact on each person's self-image.

Self-image

Whether self-image or the relationships are the most forceful circumstantial element is always difficult to say; one's self-image arises largely out of relational experiences, but the character of current relationships depends largely on people's self-image. Some people tend to ignore the relational dimension of the self-image and focus more on what one makes of one's self. Actually, we are both unique individuals and social beings, and whether one gives more weight to one factor or the other has a lot to do with our self-image. The balances we find usually depend on the world in which we live.

World

Whatever the occasion, it occurs in a particular world. We are using the term "world" here to refer to the domain of things that are made – our stuff. The world is not, of course, simply a pile of things, but rather a network or system of things that create a place in which to live and work. In the workplace, the world includes all the things we use to make other things, including social structures and technical instruments. In short, "world" refers to our material conditions.

Actually, it refers to more than the stuff that surrounds us. It also includes the meanings of the stuff and, perhaps more importantly, how the different aspects of the world are related. There are different worlds, of course, such as the world of cooking, the world of commerce, or the world of sports. For example, if you don't play golf – or at least talk as though you did play golf – you probably cannot really understand this world. Every world has its own "piety," by which we mean a sense of how things fit together. One way to say that someone does not understand your world is to say that they don't "get it." What they don't "get" is how this particular world functions. There is no one world, of course. In this book we have investigated the eighteenth-century world of Atlantic commerce, which was dominated by the slave trade. We live in a very different world today. How we construct this world will largely determine what kinds of conversations make sense.

If we agree on these general notions of the four elements of circumstances, then we can begin to think about how to create circumstances that will promote civic conversations. We can start with the ideal circumstances, so we have some notion of where we would like to move those that are less than ideal.

IDEAL CIRCUMSTANCES FOR CIVIC CONVERSATIONS
Ideal circumstances, as one might imagine, will more or less mirror the key characteristics of civic conversation – respect others, apply civic norms, bridge social differences, and engage in deliberation. If we imagine what circumstances would actually encourage such conversations, we might come up with the picture in Figure 17.3.

World	Occasion
Civic pluralism	Deliberation
Relationship	Self-image
Mutual respect	Global citizen

FIGURE 17.3 Circumstances that promote civic conversations

Such circumstances would be ideal, of course, which means that they provide a goal we can strive for. They also represent some of the key aspects of a civic economics of provision.

Civic pluralism

We have described civil society as a realm that holds together social differences, such as differences of class, gender, race, and so on. Civic pluralism acknowledges that we are all embedded in various social contexts defined by cultural and social norms. That is the pluralism part. Civic pluralism also promotes the honoring of civic rights and moral equality of all persons. That is the civic part. Civic pluralism, in other words, has a descriptive aspect (we are different) and a normative aspect (we all should be treated with respect). In too many situations, civic pluralism is waiting to happen.

Deliberation

At the center of civic conversations is the practice of deliberation. We have already presented civic deliberation as the practice that creates and maintains the civic sphere and civil society. Without deliberation, the civic world would simply collapse. At the same time, deliberation can only really flourish in a world where people reach beyond their group identities and identify with each other as global citizens. In this sense, one's self-image cannot be ignored.

Global citizen

To engage in civic conversations, we need to see ourselves as part of a global community of citizens. This is obviously a rather thin notion of community, since our knowledge of many other people's lives would at best be superficial. Still, what happens today in any part of the world may affect our chances – as well as the chances for our children and grandchildren – to live in a just and sustainable world. We all belong to the same natural world. That is the descriptive part of the notion of global citizen. The normative part – we are all citizens of the world – is a moral challenge. Or, is it a moral obligation? Our answer depends on how we choose to understand our relationship with others.

Mutual respect

People from different social groups will not be ready to engage in civic conversations if they believe that the conversation is set up to the advantage of some and the disadvantage of others. It is true that, in most circumstances, some people will have more resources, more influence, and even more persuasive arguments than others. If these differences create circumstances of domination then the conversations will never facilitate real deliberation among equals. Mutual respect requires that circumstances be defined by what people have in common, such as a common humanity and a common future. In a sense, the failure to recognize the other as one-of-us has been the failure of the dissociative economics that has shaped the circumstances of Western thinking. The other, as we learned in the Enlightenment view of history, was seen as "savage" or "primitive," but not like us. Only if we can move beyond our identity as owners of properties to become members of communities will we be able to forge relationships of mutual respect. If we are successful in developing such relationships, which can occur through actual encounters with others, then we can change our self-image, and even our interpretation of the world in which we live. Most civic conversations, of course, will not happen in such ideal circumstances, and, to be realistic, we need to consider circumstances where civic conversations might be almost impossible.

CIRCUMSTANCES THAT BLOCK CIVIC CONVERSATIONS

For people with a strong belief in individualism, the idea that circumstances could block civic conversations may seem naïve. If individuals have the courage and talent, they can do what they want regardless of circumstances. This view, however, ignores that only in circumstances that were produced by the European Enlightenment and its legacy would one have such a view. This self-image, in other words, is only possible in circumstances created by particular views of the world, relationships, and occasions. In fact, radical individualism is naïve because it fails to recognize that it belongs to some circumstances

World	Occasion
Civic disorder	Games of intrigue
Relationship	Self-image
Instrumental	Winner/loser

FIGURE 17.4 Circumstances that block civic conversations

and not to others. Some circumstances encourage human flourishing; some do not. Look at the chart of circumstantial elements that could block civic conversations given in Figure 17.4.

This world of civil disorder could be dominated by corruption and betrayal of trust. In such circumstances, people will usually take what they can instead of engaging in trade. If they do trade, it will be guided by self-interest, not mutual advantage or reciprocity. Relationships are used as a means for survival. They may look like relationships of respect, but an agenda of pursuing one's agenda lies behind the façade of respect, not an authentic good will toward others. In such circumstances, people see themselves as either winners or losers. If "winning is all that counts," all occasions are dealt with as games of intrigue. In such circumstances, it may be impossible to engage in civic conversations. Individuals or small groups may struggle to change these circumstances. But until the circumstances do change, any so-called civic conversation would be a sham.

Whoever controls the interpretation of circumstances more or less controls the conversations that occur in these circumstances. This control, of course, is largely invisible and finds expression in such typical statements as: "This is what we do in this type of situation," or "That is not appropriate here," or "We have a free market economy." Whenever what *is* can be used to determine what *should be*, it is impossible to engage in effective deliberation.

Remember the cycle of civic conversations explained in Chapter 12 that had the interpretation of situations as a result of images and stories and as a condition for reflection and deliberation? It showed how deliberation depends on our interpretation of situations,

World	Occasion
Competitive markets	Networking
Relationship	Self-image
Exchanges	Dealmaker

FIGURE 17.5 Current economic circumstances

and the interpretation of situations depends on stories and images. Our situation (circumstance), in other words, is not engraved in stone, but in our stories. A new story or a new image can change our circumstances, which can change the subjects of our reflections and deliberations. The potential for such a change today is the gap between the theory (story) of our current economy, and its reality.

As we have already learned, economic transactions among strangers have always relied on a civic sphere that provided a foundation for their transactions. This civic sphere also offered opportunities for civic deliberation. The eighteenth-century *theory* of economics replaced the civic sphere with the notion of the "invisible hand," which has led others to speak of the market's self-organizing capacity, when, in fact, property owners largely organized it. The theory of a self-organizing market economy, in other words, was quite different from reality. We can now use this insight to explore the possibility of civilizing the economic circumstances of our economy. If we civilize these circumstances, then we can civilize the economy itself. The opening to accomplish this is the underlying civic basis of modern economic life. We begin with the illustration in Figure 17.5 of the theory of current economic circumstances.

In this picture, people perceive the world as one of competitive markets. In such a world, relationships are assumed to be relationships of exchange. The exchanges are based largely on supply and demand, with price functioning as an indicator of value. In this particular set of elements, the relational element is mostly determined by the element of the world – competitive markets. In such a world, many different occasions are seen as chances to make new contacts or for networking. In

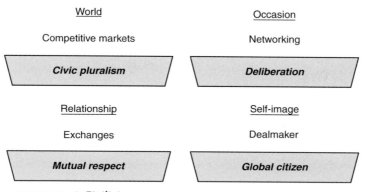

FIGURE 17.6 Civilizing economic circumstances

spite of the faith in the impersonal market, people assume, as they say, "it's not what you know but who you know" that counts. In this kind of world, one wants to be known as a dealmaker or entrepreneur. Many business people, and most of my business students, will recognize this as a familiar set of circumstances. It differs considerably from the earlier picture of circumstances that would prevent civic conversations, but it is not the ideal picture either. Still, if we look below the surface, there are seeds for moving toward the ideal set of circumstances. To expose these possibilities, we have placed the elements of the ideal circumstances directly under our current circumstances in Figure 17.6.

Remember that when strangers meet, they can withdraw, give, take, or trade. Trading required an extension of trust, which over time became mutual, creating a civic sphere. The civic sphere, in other words, already undergirded competitive markets. Does this support civic pluralism? Not necessarily. Still, it gives us an alternative to the property relations that have dominated economic narratives since the Enlightenment. It allows conversations to go beyond the meaning of goods to the meaning of the good. It gives us a basis to explore how we might move the other three elements closer to circumstances necessary for civic conversations.

Once we have exposed the civic sphere as the foundation for markets, human relationships gain a civic dimension. People can see themselves as members of civil society. The image of the individual entrepreneur or the isolated individual might pull them away from recognizing their civic membership, but the pull to enjoy the attachments of family and community, as well as the possibility of living in relationships of reciprocity, could be an even stronger pull. These shifts are not like the changing of the seasons, but rather depend on choices. Relationships of mutual respect are not determined by fate, but by choice.

The opportunity to make such choices depends on how we view the occasions when we meet with each other. For the sake of tolerance and politeness, we often overlook differences and avoid disagreements. Let the market, or fate, or luck decide. Right now, the market, fate, and luck are moving us toward the destruction of the planet's life. It is now time to organize how we will live together. We must turn the various systems of provision – from food to entertainment – toward just and sustainable practices. Justice requires that we all do it together. Sustainability requires that we do it now rather than later.

If I can engage in such deliberations with others, then I can see myself as a global citizen. This is not so much an identity that I give myself, as one that I recognize as I participate in civic conversations.

If we civilize the economic circumstances of our life together, we can engage much more effectively and meaningfully in the three basic activities of human communities – provisioning, protecting, and creating a worthwhile purpose. Our task is not to make our generation different from all others, but rather to make it the same – a generation that lives as a part of nature, making provisions, giving protection, and creating a worthwhile purpose for our families and communities.

Civilizing the economy requires, above all else, a strong notion of citizenship – of membership in a global civil society. With this common identity, we can allow civic relationships rather than property relationships to define our bonds with each other – at work, in our neighborhoods, in our cities and in global communities. If we can civilize the economy, then we can ensure that making provisions, not accumulating property, will be at the core of our economic thinking.

Appendix: Free enterprise and the economics of slavery

Of the many contradictions we witness between fact and fiction, one that would rank among the most significant is the contradiction between the small-town image commonly used to represent the essence of free enterprise and the real context of early capitalism – the Atlantic trade among the peoples of Europe, Africa, and the Americas. Here is the fiction:

> It is not from the benevolence of the butcher, the brewer, or the baker, that we expect our dinner, but from their regard to their own self-interest. We address ourselves, not to their humanity but to their self-love, and never talk to them of our own necessities but of their advantages.[1]

Such a context is not so difficult to imagine. Small shop owners provide different goods to each other, and the best way of doing this is for each to be guided by one's self-interest, since in this intimate setting it is certainly in their self-interest to provide a good product at a good price. How nice that we so easily do what is best for us and it turns out best for our neighbors.

The reality of commerce when Adam Smith was composing *The Wealth of Nations* was something else. The center of this trade was not the town square, but the Atlantic Ocean, which was used for the trafficking of millions of captive Africans to the Americas and the trafficking of American-grown sugar and tobacco to the Europeans, as well as the Europeans sending other products and services – such as credit and weapons – that went along with the development of any

---

[1] Smith, *The Wealth of Nations*, p. 15.

empire. The "success" of early British economics, in other words, was not so much the result of small-town exchanges as the result of the economic connections among Europe, Africa, and America.

Robin Blackburn estimates that of the 21 million Africans enslaved between 1700 and 1850, 9 million slaves were delivered to the Americas, 5 million were lost during the passage, and another 11 million were enslaved in Africa.[2] The numbers are astonishing. In fact, more Africans than Europeans settled in the Americas during the seventeenth and early eighteenth centuries.

> Indeed, in every year from about the mid-sixteenth century to 1831, more Africans than Europeans quite likely came to the Americas, and not until the second wave of mass migration began in the 1880s did the sum of net European immigration start to match and then excel the cumulative influx from Africa ... In terms of immigration alone, then, America was an extension of Africa rather than Europe until late in the nineteenth century.[3]

True, one finds slavery in earlier historical periods, but the Atlantic-based slavery was unique. For the first time, slavery was an integral part of the global economy. Yes, the Romans had many slaves, but they became slaves mostly due to conquest. As Blackburn writes: "One might say that many Roman slaves were sold because they had been captured, while many African slaves entering the Atlantic trade had been captured so that they might be sold." [4]

In the commercial world of the Atlantic, slavery was an economic institution. This conclusion has been carefully documented in Eric Williams' book, *Capitalism & Slavery*.[5] He traces the history of

---

[2] Robin Blackburn, *The Making of New World Slavery: From the Baroque to the Modern, 1492–1800* (London and New York: Verso, 1998), p. 388.

[3] Ronald Bailey, "The Slave(ry) Trade and the Development of Capitalism in the United States: The Textile Industry in New England," *Social Science History*, Vol. 14, No. 3 (Autumn, 1990), pp. 373–414, p. 377.

[4] Blackburn, *The Making of New World Slavery*, p. 11.

[5] Eric Williams, *Capitalism & Slavery*, with a new introduction by Colin A. Palmer (Chapel Hill and London: The University of North Carolina Press, 1994).

the plantations in the British West Indies from first using indigenous slaves and then indentured servants brought from Europe. As the plantations grew and needed more labor, and as indentured servants heard of the hard times on the plantations and refused to volunteer to move there, there rose the need for another source of labor, and African slaves were chosen. The origin of Negro slavery, Williams writes, "was economic, not racial; it had to do not with the color of the laborer, but the cheapness of the labor."[6] Only later, as whites became afraid of slave rebellions, did they begin to see Africans as racially inferior. As Williams says, "Slavery was not born of racism; rather, racism was the consequence of slavery."[7]

Although Williams' work has not been included in the canon of contemporary Anglo-American economics, recent scholarship has confirmed what has become known as the Williams thesis; namely, that slavery was essentially economic. Blackburn, for example, supports this thesis by describing how the sugar plantations in the West Indies were not just institutions of agriculture, but also commercial institutions:

> The plantation evidently belonged to the world of manufacture as much as to that of commercial agriculture. The plantation crops, especially sugar and indigo, required elaborate processing, and both permitted and required the intensive exploitation of labour ... On the productive side, the plantation required the coordinated and meticulously timed activities of between 10 and 300 workers. Specialist slaves, working long hours but receiving some small privileges, came to work in the responsible positions in the sugar works, as planters discovered that this was cheaper than hiring specialized employees.[8]

Plantations, in other words, were part and parcel of the economic system that created the wealth that Adam Smith enjoyed when he

---

[6] *Ibid.*, p. 19.　[7] *Ibid.*, p. 7.
[8] Blackburn, *The Making of New World Slavery*, pp. 333–334.

was collecting material for his book *The Wealth of Nations*. Instead of telling us this history, which he knew not only because he would have witnessed it as a resident of Glasgow, but also because he met for years with the Glasgow merchants of tobacco, he tells us the story of the butcher, the brewer, and the baker.

This image of economics, and others like it, such as the invisible hand or the "natural" dynamics of markets, has dominated the past decades of Anglo-American economics. The combination of Smith not telling us how wealth was actually created in his city, and of supplying images of commerce that left no room for such stories, created a legacy of market optimism that continues to shield us from seeing how the economy really functions today.

It is truly amazing that in the many current books on Adam Smith's political philosophy, his ethics, and even his economics, one finds a total absence of reference to the Glasgow tobacco lords, or to the slave-based tobacco trade.[9] After all, one of the first principles of understanding a text is to understand the context in which it was written. It is as if Smith's context was as invisible as his "invisible hand" of the market. Still, one must admit that if one only studied the written text, one would not know that the "opulence" Smith enjoyed in Glasgow came largely from the exploitation of the kidnapped Africans who labored on tobacco plantations in Virginia and Maryland. As a consequence of not knowing this story, or at least not admitting it, Smith's economics have been used as the basis for believing that an unfettered market economy promotes human freedom.

Two writers who played leading roles in the recent popularizing of Smith were Milton Friedman and Michael Novak. Friedman proposed, in his book with the apt title *Capitalism and Freedom*, that

---

[9] Recent examples of such studies on Smith are Jerry Evensky, *Adam Smith's Moral Philosophy: A Historical and Contemporary Perspective on Markets, Law, Ethics, and Culture* (New York: Cambridge University Press, 2005), Samuel Fleischacker, *On Adam Smith's* Wealth of Nations: *A Philosophical Companion* (Princeton, NJ and Oxford: Princeton University Press, 2004), and Deirdre N. McCloskey, *The Bourgeois Virtues: Ethics for an Age of Commerce* (Chicago, IL and London: The University of Chicago Press, 2006).

Smith's "invisible hand" of the market system had been more "potent for progress" than the visible hand of government.[10] Michael Novak gave expression to Smith's influence in his thinking with the following formulation of Smith's vision:

> Adam Smith's hope was that the self-love of human beings might be transformed into a social system which benefited all as no other system had ever done. Thus his purpose in granting human self-interest its due was to transform it into a system of order, imagination, initiative, and progress for all ... Each individual would then participate in a good society, in such a way that his self-love would come to include the whole.[11]

In Friedman and Novak, one finds an optimistic economics that proposes that if we would just mind our own business, so to speak, market forces will provide us with the prosperity we desire. This message found its political voice in Ronald Reagan's 1980 campaign for the presidency, where he contrasted his message of optimism and promised prosperity to Jimmy Carter's message of difficult challenges and the need for sacrifices. He won. "Reaganomics," and in Great Britain "Thatcherism," became the basic economic framework for the policies of the final decades of the twentieth century, providing the ideology for such influential organizations as the World Bank, the International Monetary Fund, and the World Trade Organization. The recent chair of the Federal Reserve, Alan Greenspan, continues this praise of Smith. Just before the advent of the financial disaster that continues to threaten our global community, he wrote in his autobiography:

> It is striking to me that our ideas about the efficacy of market competition have remained essentially unchanged since the eighteenth-century Enlightenment, when they first emerged, to a

---

[10] Milton Friedman, *Capitalism and Freedom* (Chicago, IL and London: The University of Chicago Press, 1982).

[11] Michael Novak, *The Spirit of Democratic Capitalism* (New York: Simon & Schuster, 1982), p. 149.

remarkable extent, largely from the mind of one man, Adam Smith.[12]

Now we know that Greenspan's comment was more germane than he probably intended. Smith's ideas did emerge largely from his mind, rather than from the data that was available to him in the city of Glasgow. This is also somewhat true of Benjamin Friedman's use of Smith in his arguments for a positive relationship between economic growth and morality. In his book, *The Moral Consequences of Economic Growth*, Friedman writes of Smith's *The Wealth of Nations*:

> For the first time people saw the possibility of acquiring wealth in a way that need not be inherently exploitive. At the individual level, the idea of voluntary exchange was that in any transaction both parties expected to come out ahead. But the same point applied even more strikingly at the level of the entire society. The route to national wealth was commerce, not conquest.[13]

Was the enslavement of millions of Africans not conquest? Was the occupation of and the extermination of native peoples merely commerce? What a mind-twisting game. It is time to repair this disconnect between the image of commerce we have inherited from *The Wealth of Nations* and the reality of the context in which this book was written, which was the world of the Atlantic slave trade. Part of the repair requires that we fully understand the economic aspects of slavery.

Today, of course, one is more likely to focus on the role of slavery in the development of racism in the United States than on its role in our economic development. My intention is certainly not to minimize the reality of racism, or to obscure the structures of white privilege.

---

[12] Alan Greenspan, *The Age of Turbulence: Adventures in a New World* (New York: The Penguin Press, 2007), p. 260.

[13] Benjamin M. Friedman, *The Moral Consequences of Economic Growth* (New York: Vintage Books, 2007), p. 39.

Still, if we are to understand the economy that continues to drive us toward an unsustainable future, we must recognize the role of slavery at the very beginning of its development. Part of the difficulty in seeing this clearly is the shifts in the seventeenth and eighteenth centuries between a political and an economic view of slavery, which this appendix tries to sort out. We begin with the case of John Locke, who many consider the political philosopher behind the United States' Declaration of Independence.

THE CASE OF JOHN LOCKE

John Locke lived in the seventeenth, not the eighteenth century. British slavery was much more in the Caribbean than in North America. Still, in terms of the Atlantic slave trade, Locke was actually much more involved than Adam Smith. Although many of us learned about John Locke as a philosopher, he was an investor in the Royal Africa Company (the British slave trading business), as well as from 1673 to 1675 the Secretary of the Council of Trade and Plantations. So on the one hand he argued for, as it is stated in the Declaration of Independence, man's "inalienable rights of life, liberty, and the pursuit of happiness," and on the other hand he was deeply involved in the commerce of slavery. He actually invested his money in the business of buying and selling of slaves. How are we to understand this? I think it makes sense only if we separate the "economic" from the political or moral view of slavery. Locke never completed this separation, but he laid the groundwork for it, and that is what we need to understand.

In his *Second Treatise of Government*, Locke is clear that no man can become a slave of another except as a result of war.

> But there is another sort of servants, which by a peculiar name we call slaves, who being captives taken in a just war, are by the right of nature subjected to the absolute dominion and arbitrary power of their masters. These men having, as I say, forfeited their lives, and with it their liberties, and lost their estates; and being in the state of slavery, not

> capable of any property, cannot in that state be considered as any part of civil society; the chief end whereof is the preservation of property.[14]

If the only slavery that could be justified was the slavery that was the result of a just war, then why did Locke invest his money in the trading of slaves and serve on the Committee on Trade and Plantations, which supervised the slave trade? Surely the large-scale assaults on African communities to kidnap millions of men and women could hardly be described as a "just war." So how could Locke justify his investments in the slave trade?

One possibility is that Locke turned away from the question of how Africans became slaves and focused only on the slave trade itself. If he separated the capture of Africans and their enslavement from the buying and selling of slaves – the slave trade – then he could invest in such trade, because the captured Africans were already slaves. To explore this possibility of understanding Locke's behavior, we can review his view of the relationship between property and government.

In his introduction to John Locke's *Second Treatise of Government*, C. B. Macpherson writes that what was unique about Locke's arguments in the context of the seventeenth-century debates about the role of government was his theory of property and property rights.[15] Locke's theory of property begins with his imagined state of nature:

> Though the earth, and all inferior creatures, be common to all men, yet every man has a *property* in his own person: this no body has any right to but himself. The *labour* of his body, and the *work* of his hands, we may say, are properly his. Whatsoever then he removes out of the state that nature hath provided, and left it in, he hath mixed his *labour* with, and joined to it something that is his own, and thereby makes it his *property*. It being by him removed from the common state nature hath placed it in, it hath by this labour something

---

[14] John Locke, *Second Treatise of Government*, ed. C. B. Macpherson (Indianapolis, IN: Hackett Publishing Company, Inc., 1980), p. 46.

[15] C. B. Macpherson, "Introduction," in John Locke, *Second Treatise of Government*, ed. C. B. Macpherson (Indianapolis, IN: Hackett Publishing Company, Inc., 1980), p. xvi.

annexed to it, that excludes the common right of other men; for this labour being the unquestionable property of the labourer, no man but he can have a right to what that is once joined to, at least where there is enough, and as good, left in common for others.[16]

The question behind this statement is: How does a property owner get to own property? Locke's answer is that we gain ownership through improvement of the land. Property is something one acquires through labor, such as when one cultivates a field. European settlers certainly occupied land in the Americas in this manner, and it seems like Locke must have had such experiences in mind. There certainly was no unsettled land in England. In fact, the enclosure movements in England forced peasants off the land so the owners could treat it as their private property. Still, this idea of mixing labor with land to acquire property does not seem to help us understand Locke's view of slavery. We need to add a couple more of Locke's ideas to see the connections and the disconnections.

This acquisition of property through labor occurred in what he called the state of nature, which was prior to the formation of civil society and government. In the state of nature, property owners only collected as much as they could use or supervise, which was quite limited, until the introduction of money. Money allowed property owners to buy more land than they could cultivate themselves, and this land, through purchase, also became their property. Locke does not develop his ideas about money very much, but he does argue that it gives owners the opportunity to enlarge their possessions. Money, for Locke, also belongs to the state of nature, so there is no question here of it belonging to government. It exists prior to government.

The final piece of the small Lockean puzzle we are creating here is the piece that states his belief about the formation of civil society and government. Because owners in the state of nature cannot feel secure without protection of their property, Locke believes that they formed a "Commonwealth" wherein they gave up some of their freedoms in exchange for the protection of their property.

[16] Locke, *Second Treatise*, p. 18.

So how did slave owners acquire slaves in the Americas? Locke never tells us. He knew they were shipped on slave ships from Africa. He knew they were then sold on auction blocks in the Americas. They were bought and sold. To participate in these market transactions, of course, one needed money, which was available in Locke's version of the state of nature. So here is Locke's dissociative economics. As a political philosopher, he believes that the only justification of slavery is the choice of the victors of war to enslave rather than to kill their victims. He also believes that the most precious thing we have is our property, which he understands as "life, liberty and estate."[17] For Locke, "life, liberty, and estate" are properties. Property is not a thing for him, but really a kind of self-possession. Property, in other words, is the basis for human freedom. For Locke, slaves have lost their property. They have become the property of the property owner. And this is not the result of war, but the result of a market transaction. Slavery, in other words, perhaps for the first time, was solely an economic institution.

Or so it would seem. It actually depended on where the slaves were. On the British Isles, the buying and selling of persons was not supported by British law. In the British colonies, on the other hand, slavery was legal. This difference needs an explanation.

SLAVERY IN EIGHTEENTH-CENTURY BRITAIN

It is well known that Adam Smith was against slavery. This is actually not so unusual for a Scottish intellectual of the eighteenth century. Scotland, and even the whole of Britain, did not tolerate slavery. As Blackburn points out, by the end of the sixteenth century there were very few slaves left in Europe.[18] In fact, emerging out of the late middle ages was the so-called doctrine of "free air." Perhaps originating in some of the new towns, the idea was expressed in a 1569 court of common law: "England was too pure an air for slaves to breathe in."[19] This

---

[17] Ibid., p. 46.   [18] Blackburn, *The Making of New World Slavery*, p. 62.

[19] Charles P. M. Outwin, "Securing the Leg Irons: Restriction of Legal Rights for Slaves in Virginia and Maryland, 1625–1791," *Early American Review* (Winter, 1996), p. 14, www.earlyamerica.com/review/winter96/slavery.html (retrieved on July 10, 2008).

doctrine was also used in a 1762 court case of Shanely v. Harvey, which stated: "As soon as a man sets foot on English ground he is free: a negro man maintains an action against his master for ill usage, and may have a Habeas Corpus if restrained of his liberty."[20]

Ten years later, in the famous Somerset case, Lord Mansfield ruled that slavery was not supported by natural or common law. This case involved James Somerset, who had been brought from Jamaica to England as a slave. He escaped, and was captured by his owner and placed on a ship to be returned to Jamaica. The courts intervened and Justice Mansfield ruled that slavery was so odious that nothing but positive law could support it. In other words, slavery could not be supported by natural or any higher law, but only positive, or in this case property, law.

Another case that was quite similar to the Somerset case involved Adam Smith's mentor and colleague Lord Kames. An African-born slave, Joseph Knight, who had been bought in Jamaica by John Wedderburn, was brought to Scotland in 1769. Three years later, Knight heard about the Mansfield decision that slavery was contrary to the laws of England, and asked for back wages for the work he had done for free. His master refused, Knight ran away, and then was captured. The case passed through the lower courts and ended up at the Supreme Court of Scotland, the Court of Session in Edinburgh. This Court, with Lord Kames as one of the justices on the bench, ruled that Knight should be free. Their argument was clear: "No man is by nature the property of another."[21]

Adam Smith must have known about these cases, although there is no mention of them in *The Wealth of Nations*. There is another story that actually involved the Scottish Highlanders that is also missing from Smith's writings on slavery, which is the story of the settlement of the colony of Georgia.

In 1739, Thomas Oglethorpe was granted a trusteeship of the land between the Carolinas and Florida to create a buffer zone between

---

[20] Wright, *Slavery and American Economic Development*, pp. 35–36.
[21] Quoted in Herman, *How the Scots Invented the Modern World*, p. 105.

the British colonies and Spanish Florida. It was to be a free colony without slaves. Oglethorpe enlisted 250 Scottish Highlanders to settle in Darien, which was named after an earlier failed attempt by the Scots to have their own colony. The highlanders were selected because of their fighting capacity to guard the border between the British and the Spanish. In 1739, they signed a petition against slavery, branding it a sin and "shocking to human nature."[22] The slave-free colony did not last, however, and by 1748 slaves were being sold on Savannah streets. Oglethorpe returned to England, and wrote a letter to David Hume, a friend of Adam Smith, disagreeing with Hume's assertion that dark-skinned people were genetically inferior to Europeans. His protests did not block the slave trade, but the story of the Scottish Highlanders in Georgia does help us recognize the diversity of opinion in the period when Smith was writing about the wealth of nations. These views, however, had little impact on the growth of slavery in the eighteenth-century global economy. In the Americas, slavery was something else than it was in Britain.

SLAVERY IN THE AMERICAS

In the British colonies, the colonists did not obey the same laws as those at home. In fact, colonists justified slavery by appealing to Roman law, instead of the English common-law tradition. In other words, not the laws of nature or the common law, but only statutory law protected a person's right to his property – to his slaves.

> The slave status in the Americas was defined by two core features –
> namely that slaves were private property and that, after a while, only
> those of African descent were enslaved. The most important feature
> fixing slave identity in the Americas was the property regime and
> appropriate title deeds. The Roman *jus gentium* and its acceptance of
> private property in persons furnished elements of a model in all the slave
> colonies. But running it a close second was dark skin pigmentation; the
> terms black, *nègre* or Negro were used interchangeably with that of

---

[22] Blackburn, *The Making of New World Slavery*, p. 464.

slave. The presence of some free people of colour could still allow for the assumption that blacks were slaves, a circumstance which affected the outlook of even coloured slaveholders.[23]

The position was tragically displayed in the famous trial involving the slave ship named *Zone*. In 1781, the captain of the *Zone* ordered his crew to throw 133 slaves overboard to their deaths. Many of them were sick because of their treatment during the voyage. The owner of the ship then made an insurance claim to be compensated for his loss of property. It turns out that the reason the slaves were killed was that if they had died of natural causes, such as illness, the insurers would not pay. If they were thrown overboard to save the ship, the insurers would. So the ship's captain claimed that there was a shortage of water on board, but it was later discovered that was not true. The ensuing trial was not about murdering slaves, but about insurance fraud. The insurers won the case. From an economic point of view, slaves were nothing but property.

As time passed, slaves were not only property for the plantation owners, but also the means of creating more property. According to Allan Kulikoff:

> Once slaves achieved natural increase, masters no longer had to buy slaves to expand their labor force. Mid-eighteenth-century slave-owners, then, possessed both the means of production (land and slaves) and the means of reproduction of the means of production. The more slaves one owned, the more one would eventually possess, and the wealthier one would become.[24]

To increase one's wealth though the increased size of slave families seems odious to us today, and yet at the time the possession of slaves was a sign of financial success. At the center of this world were the privileges of ownership, which gave property owners the means to create a "civilized" world. In a slave society, Kulikoff explains:

---

[23] *Ibid.*, p. 563.

[24] Allan Kulikoff, *Tobacco and Slaves: The Development of Southern Cultures in the Chesapeake, 1680–1800* (Chapel Hill and London: University of North Carolina Press, 1986), pp. 381–382.

Only slaveholders, moreover, possessed high social standing: "The custom of the country is such" wrote a Baptist minister, "that without slaves, a man's children stand but a poor chance to marry in reputation," or even according to another commentator, "to appear in polite company."[25]

This slave-based culture was the foundation for the economic growth of the slave states in the eighteenth and nineteenth centuries. Furthermore, even industrial development of the northern states depended on the slave production in the southern states and in the West Indies. As Gavin Wright points out: "As late as 1768–1772, the British West Indies were the largest single market for northern-colony commodity exports, accounting for more than half the overall total and dominating sales of such items as wood products, fish, and meat."[26] The famous textile mills of New England, in other words, were as involved in the economics of slavery as were the various industries in Scotland that exported their products to American plantations.

Perhaps no one recognized the economic aspect of slavery more than Abraham Lincoln. In a 1860 speech in Hartford, Connecticut, Lincoln said:

The entire value of the slave population of the United States is, at a moderate estimate, not less than $2,000,000,000. This amount of property has a vast influence upon the minds of those who own it. The same amount of property owned by Northern men has the same influence on their minds ... Public opinion is formed relative to a property basis. Therefore the slaveholders battle any policy that depreciates their slaves as property . What increases the value of this property, they favor. [27]

After the Civil War, of course, slavery was abolished in the United States, but the structures of white privilege that were built on the economics of slavery remain with us. The privilege is essentially the

[25] *Ibid.*, 382. [26] Wright, *Slavery and American Economic Development*, p. 30.
[27] Quoted in *ibid.*, p. 72.

same as when slaves were the providers of wealth for the tobacco plantation owners and the tobacco lords in Glasgow – the privilege of ignoring the plight of others who continually work to make our clothes, clean our offices, and provide us with the necessities of life.

This is not to suggest that slavery was instituted to meet basic human needs. In fact, the opposite was the case. It should not escape our attention that the reason for the enslavement of millions in the Atlantic globalization was for the production of such "luxury" products as tobacco and sugar. Especially tobacco – the product that enriched Adam Smith's friends, the tobacco lords of Glasgow – was a controversial product even then, as well as today. As Blackburn points out, the use of tobacco was disapproved of in Europe in the sixteenth century.[28] Through shrewd marketing, it became, in Blackburn's words, "the first exotic luxury to become an article of mass consumption." [29]

Would it have made a difference if slaves had been used for national defense or to supply primary goods such as food or housing? Not really. Here is another truth at the very core of capitalism: It does not matter what the product is or what harm it does, the only question is whether there is a profit in producing it. This is part of the freedom of free enterprise. In a property-based economy, all property is gray, whether it rests in the misery of slaves or the deadly risks of smoking tobacco. Any regulation of property is seen as an attack on free enterprise. This is also an economic view that continually uses Adam Smith's *The Wealth of Nations* to buttress its position. Smith, of course, did not create this world, but his work does aptly illustrate it.

ADAM SMITH'S ECONOMICS OF PROPERTY

Adam Smith never visited the Americas. It is hard to know how much he knew about the plight of slaves on the tobacco or sugar plantations, or how much his readers wanted to know. We do know that he knew a lot more than he told about the role of slaves in the creation of the wealth of

---

[28] Blackburn, *The Making of New World Slavery*, p. 149.
[29] *Ibid.*, p. 19.

Glasgow, and especially the wealth of the Glasgow tobacco lords. In a sense, his views about slavery repeat those of John Locke. Slaves in the Americas were not the result of war, but of purchase. They belonged not in the realm of politics, but in that of economics. In this sense, the slave trade was unique in terms of its justification. As we have already noticed, John Locke did not have a theory that justified slavery in the colonies. Adam Smith does. At least it seems that he does. It is the Enlightenment's theory of human evolution – the four stages of history.

The four stages – stages of human communities from hunting, to shepherding, to farming, and finally to trading or commercial society – had been widely used in various forms before Smith employed them in his writings. The Scottish historian Arthur Herman believes that the legal scholar and judge Lord Kames presented the four stages in the form in which Smith used them. One finds them in Kames' *Historical Law Tracts*, which were published in 1758, so perhaps Smith borrowed the four stages from Kames.[30] Other historians believe that Smith developed the stages himself. In Smith's early book *A Theory of Moral Sentiments*, published in 1759, he did not use this four-stage model, although he did use it in his lectures of jurisprudence a few years later. His biographer Ian Ross says that he "adopted" the model for his lectures on law.[31] If so, then he could have used Kames' four-stage theory. In any case, he appears to have repeated Kames' intention, which was to use the different stages as a story of the progressive accumulation of property and, with this increase of property, the increased role of government to protect property. As Herman suggests, for Adam Smith, the theme was "with the accumulation of property, the development of civilization."[32] To understand the importance of these stages for Smith, read the following passage from his *Lectures on Jurisprudence*:

> It is easy to see that in these several ages of society, the laws and regulations with regard to property must be very different. – | In

[30] Herman, *How the Scots Invented the Modern World*, p. 94.
[31] Ian Simpson Ross, *The Life of Adam Smith* (Oxford: Clarendon Press, 1995), p. 83.
[32] Herman, *How the Scots Invented the Modern World*, p. 100.

Tartary [Asia Minor], where as we said the support of the inhabitants consist(s) in herds and flocks, *theft* is punished with immediate death; in North America; again, where the age of hunters subsists, theft is not much regarded. As there is almost no property amongst them, the only injury that can be done them is depriving them of their game. Few laws or regulations will (be) requisite in such an age of society, and these will not extend to any length, or be very rigorous in the punishments annexed to any infringements of property … In the age of agriculture, they are not so much exposed to theft and open robbery [as are herds and flocks], but then there are many ways added in which property may be interrupted as the subjects of it are considerably extended. The laws therefore tho perhaps not so rigorous will be of a far greater number than amongst a nation of shepherds. In the age of commerce, as the subjects of property are greatly increased the laws must be proportionately multiplied. The more improved any society is and the greater length the several means of supporting the inhabitants are carried, the greater will be the number of their laws and regulations necessary to maintain justice, and prevent infringement of the right to property.[33]

As a careful reading of this passage indicates, the four stages are as much a story of property and property relations as a story of the evolution of the means of production. As we know, Smith never mentions the role of slavery in the commercial society he enjoyed, but here we do see how important it was that there were laws to protect an owner's property, or in the case of slavery, to protect the slave owner. For Smith, the economics of property always overrides the rights of humans, and especially the rights of those who did not belong to "commercial society." At the same time, it is always possible that Smith did not tell us about the role of slavery in the creation of wealth because he could not totally separate the political or moral dimension

[33] Adam Smith, *Lectures on Jurisprudence*, ed. R. L. Meek, D. D. Raphael, and P. G. Stein (Indianapolis, IN: Liberty Classics, 1978), p. 16.

of slavery from the economic. At one point in *The Wealth of Nations*, Smith writes the following:

> The pride of man makes him love to domineer, and nothing mortifies him so much as to be obliged to condescend to persuade his inferiors. Wherever the law allows it, and the nature of the work can afford it, therefore, he will generally prefer the service of slaves to that of freemen.[34]

How are we to understand this explanation? When Smith speaks of "the pride of man," does he have the tobacco lords in mind? Are these "men" members of the political economics club he attended in Glasgow? We don't know. We do know that Smith lived in a world where it was common to see Americans, Africans, and Asians as inferior to Europeans. Still, the terminology of superior and inferior places both groups in the same species, instead of different types of things: humans and property. Perhaps the key here is the law.

Since the purpose of the law is to protect property, and slaves were property, the law, at least in the colonies, not only allowed, but actually enforced slavery. If all of human history had been aiming for the stage of society Smith enjoyed, how could slavery be a mistake? At the same time, if the commercial stage of society required slavery, then how could Smith be right? Smith's decision in the face of this quandary was to omit the story of slavery in his account of wealth creation. The result: a dissociative economics that splits off the misery of the actual providers of wealth from the experiences of enjoying it. This is the legacy of the Scottish Enlightenment, and Smith is its best illustration.

The truth is that Africans were the providers of much of the wealth for the Atlantic trading nations. Until we recognize this truth at the very beginning and heart of capitalism, I wonder if we can ever really find adequate solutions to the challenges we face today. Furthermore, the economics of property, which still dominates Anglo-American economics, continually hides from us the living

---

[34] Smith, *The Wealth of Nations*, p. 419.

source of land and labor by treating them as property. To move forward, we need to recognize that the land (in fact the whole biosphere) is a living system and human labor, whether in the shop, the hospital, the home, or the classroom should be understood as a provider of prosperity instead of a form of property.

The blind optimism of Smithian economics depends on ignoring the desperation and powerlessness of those who are used to produce goods and services, whether they are slaves, workers, women, children in sweatshops, or illegal immigrants. It depends on closing our eyes to the real consequences of economic growth, such as global warming, depletion of resources, and the destruction of the biosphere. Finally, it depends on maintaining the military capacity we need to protect our exclusive right to property against those who have none or not enough. We need a new economics: an economics that grounds human freedom in human dignity and civil society instead of in property. This does not require the elimination of free enterprise. If we are to be free to acquire what we have reason to value, freedom must become grounded in civic membership not property ownership.[35] We must see ourselves as members of this generation where the freedom of one depends on the freedom of all.

---

[35] Sen, *Development as Freedom*, p. 18.

Bibliography

Alexander, Jeffery C., *The Civic Sphere*, New York: Oxford University Press, 2006.

The American Heritage Dictionary of the English Language, third edition, Boston: Houghton Mifflin Company, 1962.

Ames, Roger T. and Rosemont, Henry, Jr., trans., *The Analects of Confucius: A Philosophical Translation*, New York: Ballantine Books, 1998.

Anderson, Ray C., "A Spear in the Chest," lecture at North Carolina State University, February 26, 1998, No. 1.

Aristotle, *Nicomachean Ethics*, trans. Martin Ostwald, Englewood Cliffs, NJ: Prentice Hall, 1962.

  The Politics of Aristotle, ed. and trans. Ernest Barker, London, Oxford, and New York: Oxford University Press, 1946.

Bailey, Ronald, "The Slave(ry) Trade and the Development of Capitalism in the United States: The Textile Industry in New England," *Social Science History*, Vol. 14, No. 3 (Autumn, 1990), pp. 373–414.

Banner, Stuart, *How the Indians Lost Their Land: Law and Power on the Frontier*, Cambridge, MA: The Belknap Press of Harvard University Press, 2005.

Baumol, William J. and Blinder, Alan S., *Economics: Principles and Policy*, third edition, New York: Harcourt Brace Jovanovich, 1986.

Becker, Lawrence C., *Reciprocity*, Chicago, IL and London: The University of Chicago Press, 1986.

Berle, Adolf A. and Means, Gardiner C., *The Modern Corporation and Private Property*, New Brunswick, NJ: Transaction, 1991.

Bicchieri, Cristina, *The Grammar of Society: The Nature and Dynamics of Social Norms*, New York: Cambridge University Press, 2006.

Blackburn, Robin, *The Making of New World Slavery: From the Baroque to the Modern, 1492–1800*, London and New York: Verso, 1998.

Blaney, David L. and Inayatullah, Naeem, "The Savage Smith and the Temporal Walls of Capitalism," retrieved as PDF file, December 1, 2007. Also available in *Classical Theory in International Relations*, ed. Jahn Beate, Cambridge: Cambridge University Press, 2006.

Boulding, Kenneth E., *Three Faces of Power*, Newbury Park, CA: Sage, 1989.

Boyd, Richard, *Uncivil Society: The Perils of Pluralism and the Making of Modern Liberalism*, Lanham, MD: Lexington Books, 2004.

Brean, Henry, "Study Gives 50–50 Odds Lake Mead Will Dry Up by 2021," www.lvrj.com/news/15581197.html (retrieved on February 13, 2008).

Bright, Chris, "A History of Our Future," in *State of the World 2003*, New York: Norton, 2003.

Bromley, Daniel W., *Sufficient Reason: Volitional Pragmatism and the Meaning of Economic Institutions*, Princeton, NJ and Oxford: Princeton University Press, 2006.

Brown, Lester R., *Plan B 2.0: Rescuing a Planet under Stress and a Civilization in Trouble*, New York: Norton, 2006.

Brown, Mark B., *Science in Democracy: Expertise, Institutions, and Representation*, Cambridge, MA: MIT Press, 2009.

Brown, Marvin T., *Corporate Integrity: Rethinking Organizational Ethics and Leadership*, Cambridge: Cambridge University Press, 2005.

  The Ethical Process: An Approach to Disagreements and Controversial Issues, third edition, Upper Saddle River, NJ: Prentice Hall, 2003.

  Working Ethics: Strategies for Decision Making and Organizational Responsibility, Berkeley, CA: Basic Resources, 2000.

Bruyn, Severyn T., *A Civil Economy: Transforming the Market in the Twenty-First Century*, Ann Arbor: The University of Michigan Press, 2000.

Capra, Fritjof, *The Web of Life: A New Scientific Understanding of Living Systems*, New York: Anchor Books, 1997.

Connolly, William E., *Capitalism and Christianity, American Style*, Durham, NC and London: Duke University Press, 2008.

Cooperrider, David and Whitney, Diana, *Appreciative Inquiry: A Positive Revolution in Change*, San Francisco, CA: Berrett-Koehler, 2005.

Crane, Andrew and Matten, Dirk, *Business Ethics: Managing Corporate Citizenship and Sustainability in the Age of Globalization*, second edition, New York: Oxford University Press, 2007.

Davey, Mike, "The European Tobacco Trade from the 15th to the 17th Centuries," the James Ford Bell Library, University of Minnesota, http://bell.lib.umn.edu/Products/tob1.html (retrieved on November 4, 2009).

Davidson, Daniel V., Knowles, Brenda E., Forsythe, Lynn M., and Jespersen, Robert R., *Comprehensive Business Law: Principles and Cases*, Boston, MA: Kent Publishing Company, 1987.

DeSoto, Hernando, *The Mystery of Capital: Why Capitalism Triumphs in the West and Fails Everywhere Else*, New York: Basic Books, 2000.

Devine, T. M., *Scotland's Empire & the Shaping of the Americas 1600–1815*, Washington, DC: Smithsonian Books, 2003.

Dolan, Paul, *True to our Roots: Fermenting a Business Revolution*, Princeton, NJ: Bloomberg Press, 2003.

Enderle, Georges, "Business Ethics and Wealth Creation: Is There a Catholic Deficit?" *Erasmus Institute: Occasional Papers* (2004 Series Number 1), p. 4.

Evensky, Jerry, *Adam Smith's Moral Philosophy: A Historical and Contemporary Perspective on Markets, Law, Ethics, and Culture*, New York: Cambridge University Press, 2005.

Faux, Jeff, *The Global Class War: How American's Bipartisan Elite Lost Our Future and What It Will Take to Win It Back*, New York: John Wiley & Sons, Inc., 2006.

Ferguson, Adam, *An Essay on the History of Civil Society*, ed. Fania Oz-Salzberger, Cambridge: Cambridge University Press, 2006.

Ferguson, Niall, *The Ascent of Money: A Financial History of the World*, New York: The Penguin Press, 2008.

Fisher, Roger and Ury, William, *Getting to Yes: Negotiating Agreement Without Giving In*, New York: Penguin Books: 1983.

Fleischacker, Samuel, *On Adam Smith's* Wealth of Nations*: A Philosophical Companion*, Princeton, NJ and Oxford: Princeton University Press, 2004.

Folbre, Nancy, *The Invisible Heart: Economics and Family Values*, New York: The New Press, 2001.

Frederick, William C., *Corporation Be Good: The Story of Corporate Social Responsibility*, Indianapolis, IN: Dog Ear Publishing, 2006.

Freeman, R. Edward, "Managing for Stakeholders," in *Ethical Theory and Business*, eighth edition, ed. Tom Beauchamp, Norman Bowie, and Dennis Arnold, Upper Saddle River, NJ: Prentice Hall, 2009.

Freeman, R. Edward, Harrison, Jeffrey, Wicks, Andrew, Parmar, Bidhan, and de Colle, Simone, *Stakeholder Theory: The State of the Art*, Cambridge: Cambridge University Press, 2009.

Friedman, Benjamin, *The Moral Consequences of Economic Growth*, New York: Vintage Books, 2007.

Friedman, Milton, *Capitalism and Freedom*, Chicago, IL and London: The University of Chicago Press, 1982.

"The Social Responsibility of Business Is to Increase Its Profits," in *Ethical Theory and Business*, eighth edition, ed. Tom Beauchamp, Norman Bowie, and Dennis Arnold, Upper Saddle River, NJ: Prentice Hall, 2009.

Gasper, Des, *The Ethics of Development: From Economism to Human Development*, Edinburgh: Edinburgh University Press, 2004.

Goldberg, Michelle, *The Means of Reproduction: Sex, Power, and The Future of the World*, New York: The Penguin Press, 2009.

Gould, Carol C., *Rethinking Democracy: Freedom and Social Cooperation in Politics, Economy, and Society*, Cambridge: Cambridge University Press, 1988.

Greenspan, Alan, *The Age of Turbulence: Adventures in a New World*, New York: The Penguin Press, 2007.

Grinde, Donald A. and Johansen, Bruce E., *Exemplar of Liberty: Native America and the Evolution of Democracy*, Los Angeles: University of California, 1995.

Guasch, J. Luis, *Granting and Renegotiating Infrastructure Concessions: Doing it Right*, Washington, DC: The World Bank, 2004.

Guyatt, Nicholas, *Providence and the Invention of the United States, 1607–1876*, New York: Cambridge University Press, 2007.

Handy, Charles, "What's a Business For?" *Harvard Business Review*, December 2002.

Hart, Donna and Sussman, Robert W., *Man the Hunted: Primates, Predators, and Human Evolution*, New York: Westview Press, 2005.

Hawken, Paul, *Blessed Unrest: How the Largest Movement in the World Came into Being, and Why No One Saw It Coming*, New York: Viking, 2007.

Held, Virginia, *Feminist Morality: Transforming Culture, Society, and Politics*, Chicago, IL and London: The University of Chicago Press, 1993.

Herbert, Bob, "Sweatshop U in Dominican Republic," *New York Times*, April 12, 1998.

Herman, Arthur, *How the Scots Invented the Modern World*, New York: Three Rivers Press, 2001.

Ingham, Geoffrey, "'Babylonian Madness': On the Historical and Sociological Origins of Money," in *What Is Money?* ed. John Smithin, London and New York: Routledge, 2000.

   The Nature of Money, Cambridge: Polity Press, 2004.

Johnson, Allan G., *Privilege, Power, and Difference*, second edition, New York: McGraw-Hill, 2006.

Johnson, Walter, *Soul by Soul: Life Inside the Antbellum Slave Market*, Cambridge, MA: Harvard University Press, 1999.

Kant, Immanuel, *Groundwork of the Metaphysic of Morals*, trans. H. J. Paton, New York: Harper Torchbooks, 1964.

Kaptein, Muel and Wempe, John, *The Balanced Company: A Theory of Corporate Integrity*, Oxford: Oxford University Press, 2002.

Keene, John, *Global Civil Society?* Cambridge: Cambridge University Press, 2003.

Kierkegaard, Søren, *Fear and Trembling*, New York: Wilder Publications, 2008.

Knight, Frank Hyneman, *The Ethics of Competition*, New Brunswick, NJ: Transaction Publishers, 2004.

Komisar, Lucy, "Tax Activists: Big Business Must Pay Its Fair Share," http://thekomisarscoop.com/category/offshore/tax-evasion (retrieved on April 12, 2005).

Kulikoff, Allan, *Tobacco and Slaves: The Development of Southern Cultures in the Chesapeake, 1680–1800*, Chapel Hill and London: University of North Carolina Press, 1986.

Landes, David S., *The Wealth and Poverty of Nations: Why Some Are So Rich and Some So Poor*, New York: W. W. Norton & Company, 1999.

Laqueur, W. and Rubin, B., *The Human Rights Reader*, New York: New American Library, 1979.

Lehmann, Paul, *Ethics in a Christian Context*, New York: Harper and Row, 1963.

Leopold, Aldo, *A Sand County Almanac: And Sketches Here and There*, London: Oxford University Press, 1949.

Levering, Robert and Moskowitz, Mitton, *The 100 Best Companies to Work for in America* (New York: Addison-Wesley, 1984).

Locke, John, *Second Treatise of Government*, ed. C. B. Macpherson, Indianapolis, IN: Hackett Publishing Company, Inc., 1980.

Macpherson, C. B. "Introduction," in John Locke, *Second Treatise of Government*, ed. C. B. Macpherson, Indianapolis, IN: Hackett Publishing Company, Inc., 1980.

Margolin, Malcolm, *The Ohlone Way: Indian Life in the San Francisco-Monterey Bay Area*, Berkeley, CA: Heyday Books, 1978.

Marx, Karl, "Economic and Philosophic Manuscripts of 1844," in *The Marx-Engels Reader*, ed. Robert Tucker, New York: W. W. Norton & Company, 1963.

McCloskey, Deirdre N., *The Bourgeois Virtues: Ethics for an Age of Commerce*, Chicago, IL and London: The University of Chicago Press, 2006.

McConville, Ben, "Cleaning the Air on the Clearances," Scotsman.com, September 2005 (retrieved on December 10, 2007).

McDonough, William and Braungart, Michael, *Cradle to Cradle: Remaking the Way We Make Things*, New York: North Point Press, 2002.

McMahon, Christopher, *Authority and Democracy: A General Theory of Government and Management*, Princeton, NJ: Princeton University Press, 1994.

Meikle, Scott, *Aristotle's Economic Thought*, Oxford: Clarendon Press, 1997.

Miller, John H. and Page, Scott E., *Complex Adaptive Systems: An Introduction to Computational Models of Social Life*, Princeton, NJ and Oxford: Princeton University Press, 2007.

Miranda, Nicholas, "Concession Agreements: From Private Contract to Public Policy," *Yale Law Journal*, December 1, 2007.

Morgan, Kenneth, *Slavery, Atlantic Trade and the British Economy, 1600–1800*, Cambridge: Cambridge University Press, 2000.

Neeson, J. M., *Commoners: Common Right, Enclosure and Social Change in England, 1700–1820*, Cambridge: Cambridge University Press, 1993.

Nelson, Julie A., *Economics for Humans*, Chicago, IL: The University of Chicago Press, 2006.

Novak, Michael, *The Spirit of Democratic Capitalism*, New York: Simon & Schuster, 1982.

Orren, Karen, *Belated Feudalism: Labor, the Law, and Liberal Development in the United States*, Cambridge and New York: Cambridge University Press, 1991.

Outwin, Charles P. M., "Securing the Leg Irons: Restriction of Legal Rights for Slaves in Virginia and Maryland, 1625–1791," *Early American Review* (Winter, 1996), p. 14, retrieved on July 10, 2008 from www.earlyamerica.com/review/winter96/slavery.html.

Overton, Mark, *Agricultural Revolution in England: The Transformation of the Agrarian Economy 1500–1850*, Cambridge: Cambridge University Press, 1996.

Pattison, Neal and Warren, Luke, *2002 Drug Industry Profits: Hefty Pharmaceutical Company Margins Dwarf Other Industries*, Washington, DC: Public Citizen's Congress Watch, June 2003.

Pearce, W. Barnett, *Interpersonal Communication: Making Social Worlds*, New York: HarperCollins College Publishers, 1994.

Phillips, Kevin, *Bad Money: Reckless Finance, Failed Politics, and the Global Crisis of American Capitalism*, New York: Viking, 2007.

Polanyi, Karl, *The Great Transformation: The Political and Economic Origins of Our Time*, Boston, MA: Beacon Press, 1944.

Rawls, John, *A Theory of Justice*, Cambridge, MA: Harvard University Press, 1971.

Reich, Robert, *Supercapitalism: The Transformation of Business, Democracy, and Everyday Life*, New York: Alfred A. Knopf, 2007.

Rifkin, Jeremy, *Entropy: A New World View*, New York, Viking, 1980.

Ritter, Gretchen, *Goldbugs and Greenbacks: The Antimonopoly Tradition and the Politics of Finance in America, 1865–1896*, Cambridge: Cambridge University Press, 1997.

Rosen, Allen, *Kant's Theory of Justice*, Ithaca, NY and London: Cornell University Press, 1993.

Rosen, Ian Simpson, *The Life of Adam Smith*, Oxford: Clarenden Press, 1995.

Sachs, Jeffery, *The End of Poverty: Economic Possibilities for Our Time*, New York: Penguin Books, 2005.

Sen, Amartya, *Development as Freedom*, New York: Alfred A. Knopf, 1999.

Shiva, Vandana, *Staying Alive: Women, Ecology and Development*, London: Zed Books Ltd., 1989.

Simpson, Lorenzo C., *Technology, Time, and the Conversations of Modernity*, New York: Routledge, 1995.

Smith, Adam, *Lectures on Jurisprudence*, ed. R.L. Meek, D.D. Raphael, and P.G. Stein, Indianapolis, IN: Liberty Classics, 1978.

Theory of Moral Sentiments, Mineola, NY: Dover Publications, Inc., 2006.

The Wealth of Nations, ed. Edwin Cannan, New York: The Modern Library, Random House, 1994.

Smout, T.C., "Where Had the Scottish Economy Got to by 1776?" in *Wealth and Virtue: The Shaping of Political Economy in the Scottish Enlightenment*, Cambridge: Cambridge University Press, 1983.

Speth, James Gustave, *The Bridge at the Edge of the World: Capitalism, the Environment, and Crossing from Crisis to Sustainability*, New Haven, CT and London: Yale University Press, 2008.

Stiglitz, Joseph E., *Making Globalization Work*, New York: W.W. Norton & Company, 2006.

Ulrich, Peter, *Integrative Economic Ethics: Foundations of a Civilized Market Economy*, Cambridge: Cambridge University Press, 2008.

Vogel, David, *The Market for Virtue: The Potential and Limits of Corporate Social Responsibility*, Washington, DC: Brookings Institution Press, 2005.

Von Glahn, Richard, "The Origins of Paper Money in China," in *The Origins of Value: The Financial Innovations that Created Modern Capital Markets*, ed. William N. Goetzmann and K. Geert Rouwenhorst, New York: Oxford University Press, 2005.

Walzer, Michael, *Spheres of Justice: A Defense of Pluralism and Equality*, New York: Basic Books, 1983.

Warner, Michael, *The Letters of the Republic: Publication and the Public Sphere in Eighteenth-Century America*, Cambridge, MA: Harvard University Press, 1990.

Watkins, Kevin, "International Cooperation at the Crossroads: Aid, Trade, and Security in an Unequal World," *Summary Human Development Report 2005*, New York, United Nations Development Program, 2005.

Werhane, Patricia, *Adam Smith and His Legacy for Modern Capitalism*, New York and Oxford: Oxford University Press, 1991.

Werhane, Patricia H. and Radin, Tara J. with Bowie, Norman E., *Employment and Employee Rights*, Malden, MA: Blackwell Publishing, 2004.

Whiteside, Kerry, *Precautionary Politics: Principle and Practice in Confronting Environmental Risk*, Cambridge MA: MIT Press, 2006.

Williams, Eric, *Capitalism & Slavery*, with a new introduction by Colin A. Palmer, Chapel Hill and London: The University of North Carolina Press, 1994.

Williamson, Thad, "The Relationship Between Workplace Democracy and Economic Democracy: Three Views," paper given at the 2004 Annual Meeting of the American Political Science Association, September 2–5, 2004, Chicago, IL.

Williamson, Thad, Imbroscio, David, and Alperovitz, Gar, *Making a Place for Community: Local Democracy in a Global Era*, New York and London: Routledge, 2002.

Wilson, Alex and Boehland, Jessica, "Small Is Beautiful: U.S. House Size, Resource Use, and the Environment," *Journal of Industrial Ecology*, Vol. 9, Nos. 1–2 (Winter–Spring, 2005).

Wolin, Sheldon, *Politics and Vision: Continuity and Innovation in Western Political Thought*, expanded edition, Princeton, NJ and Oxford: Princeton University Press, 2006.

Wright, Gavin, *Slavery and American Economic Development*, Baton Rouge: Louisiana State University Press, 2006.

Yack, Bernard, *The Problems of a Political Animal: Community, Justice and Conflict in Aristotelian Political Thought*, Berkeley: University of California Press, 1993.

Yunus, Muhammad, *Creating a World without Poverty: Social Business and the Future of Capitalism*, New York: Public Affairs, 2007.

Index

P2